Russell Herner

CATHEDRALS

BUILT BY THE MASONS

Schiffer
Publishing Ltd

4880 Lower Valley Road • Atglen, PA 19310

Designed by Brenda McCallum
Cover by Molly Shields
Type set in Trajan/Times New Roman
All photographs by Russell A. Herner, unless otherwise noted.

Image on front cover: Salisbury Cathedral, Salisbury, England
Image on spine: St. Vitus Cathedral, Prague, Czech Republic
Image on back cover: Canterbury Cathedral, Canterbury, England

ISBN: 978-0-7643-4840-2
Printed in China

Published by Schiffer Publishing, Ltd.
4880 Lower Valley Road | Atglen, PA 19310
Phone: (610) 593-1777; Fax: (610) 593-2002
E-mail: Info@schifferbooks.com

For our complete selection of fine books on this and related subjects, please visit our website at www.schifferbooks.com. You may also write for a free catalog.

This book may be purchased from the publisher. Please try your bookstore first.

We are always looking for people to write books on new and related subjects. If you have an idea for a book, please contact us at proposals@schifferbooks.com.

Schiffer Publishing's titles are available at special discounts for bulk purchases for sales promotions or premiums. Special editions, including personalized covers, corporate imprints, and excerpts can be created in large quantities for special needs. For more information, contact the publisher.

Other Schiffer Books by the Author:

Antique Ice Skates for the Collector, 978-0-7643-1200-7

Other Schiffer Books on Related Subjects:

Stone in Traditional Architecture,
by David Campbell, 978-0-7643-3614-0

Fraternally Yours: Identify Fraternal Groups and Their Emblems,
by Peter Swift Seibert, 978-0-7643-4060-4

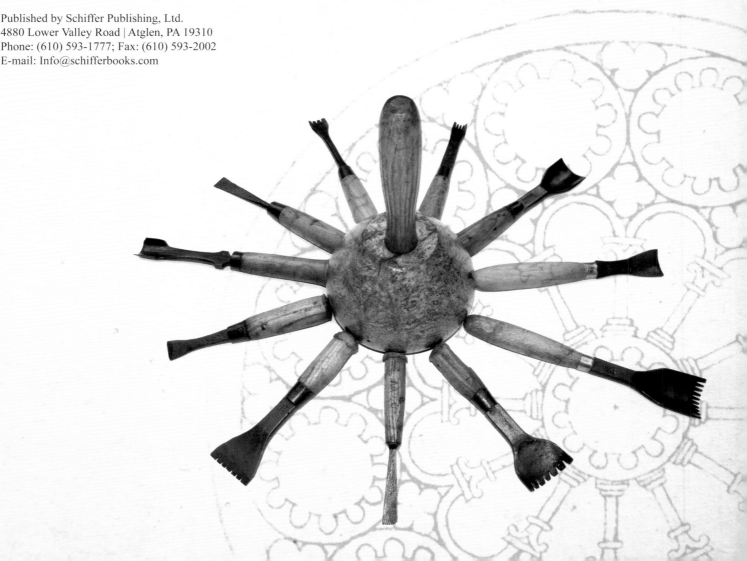

DEDICATION

This book is dedicated to my wife, Marcia; son, Mark; daughter Lori Zieber; Dr. Steve Zieber; three grandchildren Regan, Ross, and Elise; daughter Jennifer Kapadia; Jimmy Kapadia; and grandson Sam. I am very proud of you for all the things you have accomplished in your careers and for the respect, love, sensitivity, and help you have given to your family, friends, and those around you.

I also dedicate this book to my late mother and father, Art and Gay Herner, who were there for good counsel, encouragement, guidance, love, and praise. I was blessed with terrific parents.

ACKNOWLEDGMENTS

A big thank you goes to my wife, Marcia, for her help, patience, and understanding over the years during the manuscript writing process.

To my daughter Lori Zieber, I am very thankful for your invaluable help in organizing the chapters, editing the manuscript, and typing. Your thoughtful suggestions and editing improved the book immensely.

To my son Mark, thank you for your suggestions on the manuscript, help with my computer, and assistance in many other ways over the years.

To my daughter Jennifer Kapadia, I want to thank you for your help, suggestions, support, and encouragement on the book over the years.

I want to thank Jimmy Kapadia for all his invaluable help on installing, sorting, and organizing the photographs in the various computer files, formatting style codes, and help with other software issues.

A thank you also goes to my other son-in-law, Dr. Steve Zieber, for his thoughts and suggestions on the manuscript and help on computer issues.

I also appreciate the help and encouragement from my three brothers on the book: Jim, for his expert advice on the text, drawings, and photos; John for his invaluable help and suggestions in initially organizing the chapters; and Rich, for his help with computer software problems late at night!

CONTENTS

FOREWORDS

1

I have known the author for quite some time. Illustrious Brother Herner is a 33rd degree Mason, and I have heard him speak on cathedrals and the ancient operative masons on numerous occasions. I have seen his collection of the ancient operative masons' working tools. And he always impressed me as being well versed on the subject. However, it was not until he gave me the manuscript for this book and asked me to do a foreword that I really knew just how well versed he was and how he acquired his extensive knowledge. He has spent the majority of his life, forty-plus years, acquiring the information, taking the photographs, doing the illustrations, traveling to Europe on fifteen occasions, and talking to many scholars on this subject. He has assembled it all into one of the finest books of this type that I have ever seen.

Both neophyte and scholar, Mason and non-Mason will enjoy this book. If the reader has even limited interest in the cathedrals, how they were built, who built them, or architecture in general, this book is an enjoyable read. To me, what makes it so special is the knowledge of how and where all of the contents were collected and assembled. All done by the author. What an exhausting job this must have proven to be at times. You have to admire the author's dedication, tenacity, alacrity, and passion to bring all of this together in such a wonderful presentation. I know that Russ had to enjoy and derive pleasure in visiting these magnificent structures, learning how they were built, and gaining new insights into the craftsmen, the ancient operative masons and their working tools. I also feel that all who read it will experience pleasure and enjoyment not just from gaining new knowledge but also from the quality of the presentation and the beautiful photographs.

Another interesting facet of the book is that there is just the right amount of reference to the Freemasons sprinkled throughout the book to spark the reader's interest on that subject. Russ does a fine job towards the end of the book in wrapping it all up and giving the reader an incontrovertible explanation as to where the Freemasons started, how they evolved from operative Freemasons to speculative Freemasons, and where they are today.

This book is good work, square work, and I am proud to be able to call Russell Herner my friend and my brother.

Gary L. McElfresh
Master Mason
Toledo, Ohio

Gary is a 33rd degree Mason, associate grand chaplain of the Grand Lodge Free and Accepted Masons of Ohio. He is a pastor and a licensed clergyman in the state of Ohio. He is also a past executive secretary of the 32nd degree Masons Ancient Accepted Scottish Rite Valley of Toledo, a past district deputy grand master for the 11th Masonic District of Ohio, and a Past Master of Rubicon Lodge #237 F&AM.

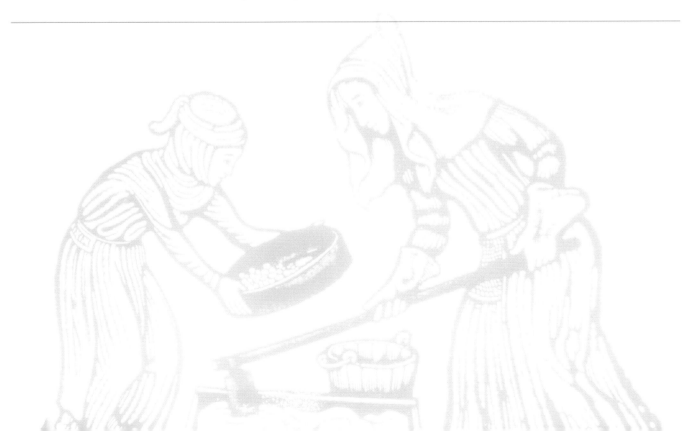

2

My familiarity with the research and writing of Russell A. Herner began decades ago after his publication of *Stonehenge: An Ancient Masonic Temple*. My curiosity about this English landmark has been strong ever since, and an image of Stonehenge is the screensaver on my laptop even today.

Cathedrals Built by the Masons will have the same impact on many readers in the years ahead.

Anyone who is involved in a current church building program, is drawn to architectural design and history, or is involved in the fraternity of Freemasonry will surely find much to read and enjoy in this book.

After my introduction to Russ Herner through the pages of *Stonehenge*, I got to know him much more closely over the years as we both were active in Freemasonry in northwest Ohio. At least twenty-five years ago, I attended an occasional lodge meeting or Masonic district educational session where Brother Herner presented a slideshow of his early research on cathedrals.

This book is a fantastic culmination of his longtime study of these huge building projects, which, as the author states in his introduction, "are still standing today after some 800 years of constant weathering and are still used for their original purpose!"

Throughout the book, author Herner focuses on the "Master Builder," and takes the reader through design concepts, the movement from Romanesque to Gothic architecture, and many interesting and educational topics that can bring new information to most any veteran Mason.

Then, in three chapters at the end of the book, he discusses the decline of the cathedral-building era (operative masonry) and the subsequent creation of speculative masonry, the fraternity that exists today. He details dozens of examples of how words and ritual commentary today exactly parallel stonemason practices of centuries earlier. Truly eye opening!

Russell Herner has spent decades researching, photographing, and writing this masterpiece, and when you start turning its pages, it will be difficult to put down.

George O. Braatz
Laurel, Maryland

George O. Braatz is a past grand master and past grand secretary of the Grand Lodge of Ohio. At the time of publication, he served as executive secretary of the Masonic Service Association of North America. Active in many Masonic organizations, he is a 33rd degree Mason, a knight of the York Grand Cross of Honour, and Past sovereign grand master of the Grand Council, Allied Masonic Degrees, of North America.

3

This is a well-illustrated book, both educational and entertaining, that had to be published. The author, Russell Herner, was a plant engineer at Dixon Ticonderoga Co. for forty-five years. He has been a Freemason since 1962 and has filled various roles. He served as Master of Roby Lodge (1969), District Deputy Grand Master (1975–1977), Master of Ohio Lodge of Research (1986), and he received the 33rd degree from the Scottish Rite Valley of Toledo in 1992. He first visited Europe in 1969, and has been conducting serious research into cathedrals ever since.

In this book, he discusses various aspects of cathedrals —their purpose, structure, evolution, and symbolism. And he talks about their connection (historical and symbolical) with Freemasonry. His work is carefully researched. He provides descriptions and pictures of thirty cathedrals in various parts of the world—fifteen in Britain, seven in France, four in Germany, and one each in the Czech Republic, Austria, Italy—and the US. He includes many photographs. And he demonstrates the connection between the cathedral builders and the Freemasons. It is all very educational and enjoyable. Enjoy it!

Wallace McLeod, PhD
Professor of Classics, Victoria College,
University of Toronto
Toronto, Ontario, Canada

Initiated 1952.
P.M., Mizpah Lodge, No 572, Toronto.
P.M., Quatuor Coronati Lodge, No 2076, London, England.
P.G.S.W., Grand Lodge of Canada in Ontario.
Past Abbot, Blue Friars.
Past President, Philalethes Society.

INTRODUCTION

Who designed and built these masterpieces of architecture called cathedrals?

The cathedrals were designed and built by a Master Builder with the help of overseers, stonemasons, and other trade craftsmen. The cathedrals were enormous soaring structures built to the heavens with lavishly decorated interiors and exteriors. They were the tallest skyscrapers of their time, built of stone to endure forever, so that future generations might admire them and their craftsmanship. Most of these cathedral masterpieces are still standing today after some 800 years of constant weathering and are still used for their original purpose!

These spectacular cathedrals have impressed and intrigued me for many years. In 1969, I made my first trip to Europe and have returned over a dozen times since to visit many of the cathedral sites in several countries. Since my first trip, I have attempted to learn more about their age, size, designs, and the Master Builders' construction techniques. After researching the cathedrals over a period of years, I came to realize the magnitude of the subject matter. They were built over a period of some eight centuries, during which hundreds of wars were fought, and major political, religious, and economic changes occurred. The language barrier also must have been problematic with the close proximity of the different countries.

The mission of this book is to tell the wonderful story of how the Master Builders designed and constructed the magnificent cathedrals of Europe during the Middle Ages, approximately 900–1700 AD, while highlighting the quality and craftsmanship displayed by the stonemasons. Although stonemason builders worked on a variety of different construction projects (cathedrals, abbeys, parish churches, castles, colleges, palaces, guild houses, bridges, mansions, private, and other public buildings), I will only be addressing the building of the cathedral and abbey structures. Building a cathedral was a very complicated business. Consider the magnitude and complexity of all the architectural designs required to construct them. This was a monumental task given to the Master Builder by the patron, cathedral chapter, or the bishop. The Master Builder had to have super intelligence, vision, concept, craftsmanship, training, talent, and a good knowledge of Christianity. Rather than crediting the kings, queens, popes, monarchs, dignitaries, and other influential citizens who may have called for the cathedral's construction, I want to give all the credit to the Master Builder, as well as to the stonemasons and craftsmen who worked by his side.

The Master Builder and his team of stonemasons were a tightly knit fraternity of men, working closely together in the craft most of their lives. They belonged to operative lodges and guilds over many centuries. They were like blood brothers who discussed work, religion, and social issues in the evenings, just as we do today. I will outline the role of the Master Builder and the craftsmen to set the stage for describing the complete building of a Gothic cathedral, from the initial design to the "finished product." This will include a detailed description of the sequential phases involved. I will also share a few parchment drawings of the designs, some 600 to 800 years old!

The amazing part of the construction of the cathedrals is that the stonemasons used only primitive hand tools. They did not have modern architectural and engineering technology. If only these tools could talk, they could tell many stories. I will explain and share photos of some of the primitive hand tools and equipment used to construct these great cathedrals.

There are hundreds of cathedrals around the world, and it is literally impossible to address all of them in this book. Therefore I have selected a few outstanding cathedrals from England, Germany, Austria, France, Italy, the Czech Republic, and the United States to share. I apologize in advance to the reader who might have a favorite cathedral that is not mentioned. All of the cathedrals around the world are wonderful, but a complete list is not feasible in this format.

For each of these select cathedrals, I will take you on a photographic walking tour and give you a brief overview. These tours will illustrate the craftsmanship of the gorgeous naves, beautiful stained-glass windows, wonderful fan vaulting, and gigantic flying buttresses. Some of the photographs will put you on top of the cathedral steeples to get a bird's-eye view of the roof and panoramic view of the surrounding town below.

The cathedrals are literally thousands of individual stonemasons' masterpieces of craftsmanship all put together in unity. No two are alike! But one will find that many of the cathedrals are similar to one another in some respects, as a natural result of the Master Builders moving their teams of traveling masons to other cathedral sites and using similar design work. These traveling masons met at conferences held at different intervals, sharing their newest inventions and design techniques with one another.

Many of the Master Builders' designs and building techniques that developed over the centuries have been lost forever. But it is my intention to capture and record some of these age-old craftsmanship techniques still known today. I will discuss some of the building secrets that our forefathers possessed in constructing these impressive houses of God, along with the "mystery of masonry" and the "secrets of masonry."

While hundreds of books have been written on cathedral building, masonry, and Freemasonry, I am going to explain how the three are related and how Freemasonry descended directly from the operative stonemasons of the Middle Ages. The transition from stonemasons working with their hands in stone to modern Freemasonry is known as the change from operative to speculative Freemasonry. I will also describe modern-day Freemasonry, the lodge structure, where it came from, what we do, who we are, our charity work, and much more.

Simply put, the cathedrals were superbly built. Cathedral building is a fusion of man's greatest accomplishments in the arts, sciences, and humanities over literally centuries. I am continually amazed by the vision, inventiveness, knowledge, ability, and success of the early stonemasons stacking thousands of tons of stone, hundreds of feet in the air, all in harmony. In this book of words, drawings, and color photography, I hope you will come to appreciate their creation and magnificence as much as I do.

Note: Throughout the text, the word "**fabric**" will be used as the traditional term for the cathedral building itself. A glossary of other cathedral-building terms is at the end of the book; when these terms are first used in the text, they will appear in bold for the reader's convenience.

PART I

CHAPTER 1

THE PURPOSE AND HISTORICAL BACKGROUND OF THE CATHEDRALS

If I were to give a definition of a cathedral in its simplest terms, I would say that it is "God's house or heaven on earth." The medieval cathedrals were built as houses of worship to God and to glorify God. They were built as physical symbols of Christianity. Prior to the reformation of the sixteenth century, Roman Catholicism was the established religion in Europe, but afterward many of the cathedrals became Anglican Church of England cathedrals.

The word cathedral got its name from the Greek and Latin word *cathedra*, meaning the bishop's chair or throne. The seat of the bishop was literally a stone chair that he sat upon, in the sanctuary of the cathedral. The cathedra chair symbolized his throne or seat of authority.

So when did a parish church officially become a cathedral? Following the above definition, a parish church could only technically be called a cathedral if a bishop were presiding over the church and diocese. The physical size of the structure had nothing to do with it. A small parish church in the countryside with a bishop in charge would officially be called a cathedral, whereas a large church in the city without a bishop in charge would only be considered a parish church.

The medieval cathedrals were the centers of activity and life for the people of the Middle Ages. In them prayers were offered, the Eucharist was distributed at Communion, the bishop's sermons could be heard, music and chants were enjoyed, and visits were made to the saints' shrines and relics. Cathedrals were frequently the destination of a large group of Christians called pilgrims, who often traveled long distances, even into other countries, to visit prominent religious sites for worship and to see saints' bones and artifacts. Coronations, baptisms, communions, marriages, and burials all took place in the cathedrals, and occasionally the cathedral also served as a place to trade goods and conduct business.

Because the cathedrals were the biggest buildings in town and funded by the people, they were also used for secular and civic affairs such as guild and town hall meetings. They really served as the cultural center or core axis of the communities and played a very important role in the lives of the people. Often after the cathedrals were built, the towns grew up around them.

Today cathedrals are quiet places where pilgrims, parishioners, and tourists can enter to meditate and reflect on life. One can step inside off the busy street to unwind from the fast lane. A cathedral is a place to say prayers and meet God face to face. It is a place to stop and smell the roses and to see the colorful rose windows glittering from the sun of God.

The majestic cathedrals standing around the world today dominate the cities and countryside with their gigantic size and lofty heights. Approaching them from several miles away, the breathtaking spires towering above the cities can easily be seen. After maneuvering through the crooked streets in town and finally arriving at the site, one is awestruck at their magnificence. One wonders how the builders could ever have raised the heavy stones to construct them. It is truly a thrilling experience to get out of a car beside one of these masterpieces, walk up to one of the intricately carved stone archway entrances, and go in for the first time.

The Master Builders designed and built the cathedrals to be viewed and admired primarily from the inside, although many of the exteriors are quite outstanding as well. Inside is where it all happens, where one is really overwhelmed by the cathedral's grandeur. The size, beauty, decoration, colors, carvings, stained-glass windows, and craftsmanship are truly impressive. It is quite an experience to witness the sun moving across the stained-glass windows, making them come alive with sparkling purples, blues, reds, greens, and yellows.

The cathedrals are permanent stone monuments preserving the skill, craftsmanship, and daring inventiveness of the Master Builders, literally over centuries. It is a wonder that man could have built such spacious and magnificent structures, much less that they were constructed 700 or 800 years ago. For those who have never visited one of these famous cathedrals, a real treat is awaiting.

CHAPTER 2

THE BRILLIANT MASTER BUILDER

"Art comprises the whole of man's works, the material outcome of his thought as expressed by his hands and through the tools of his invention" (Harvey 1971, 9).

A cathedral is a work of art, and the Master Builder, in an amazing display of talent, designed and constructed the cathedrals with a mission to replicate heaven on earth and to please God in every small detail.

The Master Builder was responsible for the entire project of designing and building the cathedral, from start to finish. He had the responsibility of creating both the functional structure, as well as an aesthetic appeal. Initially he had to have the vision, and then he needed the technical and organizational skills to carry out the execution. He was the architect, general contractor, artist, sculptor, surveyor, draftsman, teacher of the apprentices, and supervisor of the craftsmen. He was in charge of the quarries and responsible for the procurement of the materials. He also had to advise, explain, and communicate the progress of the project to the patron, chapter members, bishop, and others responsible for funding the cathedral. He wore many hats in completing this awesome task and was an extremely busy man!

The Master Builder was an influential individual in the community and enjoyed the respect and esteem of his peers. He was highly educated and thoroughly trained in the theoretical and practical phases of stonemasonry. He was generally literate in English, French, Latin, and German, which allowed him to travel from country to country to different building sites and properly communicate architectural and stonemasonry construction techniques with other Masters and craftsmen. The Master Builders became very competitive with one another in designing and building longer, wider, and higher vaults and spires on the cathedrals. And since the Master Builder was a highly skilled professional craftsman and artist himself, he commanded and was paid approximately three times the wages of the other skilled craftsmen who reported to him.

The Master Builder hired the craft employees on the site, which also put him in the personnel business. He was in charge of the stone quarrymen, the cutters, the hewers, the setters, the wall layers, the sculptures, the bricklayers, and the banker masons. Additional craftsmen who indirectly reported to the Master Builder were the carpenters, joiners, cabinetmakers, woodcarvers, plasterers, blacksmiths, glass blowers, stained-glass glaziers, painters, tilers, and plumbers. There were a variety of other common laborers working on the construction site as well, some hired and some volunteers. The Master Builder supervised all of these craftsmen, carefully communicating each detail of his cathedral design.

The designing and building of the gigantic cathedrals was a daily process of research and development, as we call it today. This process was literally a system of constant invention, experimentation, and improvement in vaulting, spanning, buttressing, and arching. The Master Builder had to contend with heights, widths, weights, side loadings, compressions, tensions, sheer, and strength of the various materials (stone, wood, glass, etc.). To this must be added the construction techniques of marrying each together into a physical building.

As B. E. Jones writes in *Freemasons' Guide and Compendium,* "Medieval building of any size consisted chiefly of masons' work. Plumbing, slating, glazing, and even carpentry were only accessory to the main structure. Every important structural problem involved in the building —the thrust of the vault, the counterpoise of the **buttresses**, the design of the **tracery**, the interpenetration of the moldings —was a masonry problem" (Jones 1975, 38).

Adding to the complexity, a variety of raw materials of nature had to be selected and brought to the construction site, such as stone, marble, plaster, mortar, lime, wood, wrought iron, tile, glass, gold, silver, and lead. All of these materials had to be quarried, hewn, squared, dressed, wrought, sawn, and cut with primitive tools and then all meticulously fitted together. The cathedral included thousands of tons of materials all assembled in harmony, well-proportioned and pleasing to the eye.

The grand new designs all took place in uncharted waters, since each new cathedral design had never been attempted or proven before. The Master Builder wrestled with architectural and engineering problems on a daily basis. If a miscalculation occurred, it could result in thousands of tons of stone collapsing, risking the lives and safety of the workers and citizens.

Once a cathedral design had been proven, it was often shared with Master Builders from other areas and countries at periodic assemblies. The Regius Poem c. 1390 (the oldest operative stonemason document) included a mandatory annual assemblage for the Masters. This is where some of the cross-pollination of designs probably occurred in the regional cathedrals.

The Master Builder was also the master of the operative construction lodge at the site. The lodge was where the Master Builder did his design work. This is also where the masons hewed the stones in bad weather, kept their tools, took their meals, received their ritual lessons, and took shelter from inclement weather. It served occasionally as a place for the craftsmen to lodge or sleep. The operative lodges were placed adjacent to and on the south side of the cathedral to take advantage of the heat and light of the sun.

The Master Builder was responsible for the apprenticeship training program as well. He was the instructor for the young apprentices, fellows of the craft, and masters in the art of geometry or masonry. He too had been brought up earlier in the apprenticeship schools, learning the various crafts himself, but as a Master Builder he now played a different role, that of teacher, architect, and engineer. He supervised all the construction phases, using his head instead of his hands, beginning with making parchment drawings on animal skins of the cathedral elevations, vaulting, and other parts of the fabric. Obviously he had many other Master craftsmen carrying out his designs and orders as part of the craftsman team on the site. This team ranged from the Master Builder to the water carrier, and they all played a vital role in building the cathedral. They worked hard from dawn to dusk to the glory of God!

It is hard to comprehend that one person, the Master Builder, could cram all of this architectural, engineering, and craftsmanship data into his brain at one time. He had all of this knowledge in his head and at his disposal in a millisecond, just like clicking the mouse on a computer today. Sadly, many times the Master Builder did not see his parchment drawing plans actually built in the flesh, since it generally took more than one generation to complete many of the cathedrals. Nevertheless, the Master Builder dedicated his life to the building of the cathedral.

What a treat it would have been to visit a cathedral construction site in 1225, to see hundreds of stonemasons and other craftsmen running around like busy bees hewing and dressing stone, lifting and swinging large timbers and stones 400 feet in the air, watching glass glaziers cutting and setting colored glass into the rose window, observing stone setters sitting on small sapling **scaffolds** placing stones into a wall, and witnessing masons on top of a tall slender spire positioning the last few stones into place. The Master Builder was an intellectual genius, and if I had to describe him in one word, I would say that he was brilliant!

CHAPTER 3

PHYSICAL PARTS OF A CATHEDRAL

The cathedrals were designed by the Master Builder to replicate symbols of Christianity. These houses of worship not only were pleasing to the eye in their symmetry and order, but also symbolically told the story of early Christianity through their carvings, sculptures, paintings, tapestries, stained-glass windows, and stone screens, and through the proportions and shapes of the physical parts.

During the Middle Ages most of the people were illiterate and relied on the church to teach them the Bible. There were few paper-bound Bibles in existence and none were available for parishioners to use in church. The Guttenberg Bible with the new movable type was not printed until 1454, and the first printed English Bible was not available until 1535. The average layman would not have owned a Bible for personal use until many years later. In the meantime monks and scholars copied Bibles, manuscripts, and other documents on parchment (animal skins) with ink pens.

In place of paper Bibles, the elaborately decorated cathedrals served as symbolic Bibles in stone, glass, wood, and marble. The Master Builder adorned the interior and exterior of the cathedrals with sculptures of saints, humans, animals, nature, and other biblical subjects, all telling the biblical story. The beautiful stained-glass window figures, along with the carved sculptures, were used by the clergy as visual props for teaching biblical lessons to the parishioners. See Figure 1. The basic overall floor plan of a Christian cathedral is in a **cruciform** shape or Latin cross, representing the crucifix cross upon which Christ gave his life. "It was St. Paul who just after the middle of the first century described the church as being the 'Body of Christ' and this cruciform way of building is itself a way of reminding worshipers and visitors of this fundamental Christian belief" (Lincoln Cathedral 2006, 13). See Figure 2.

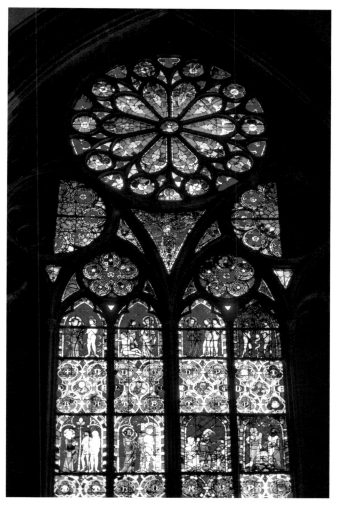

FIGURE 1. Metz Cathedral, France. Brilliant colored stained-glass rose and lancet window mounted in the cathedral wall.

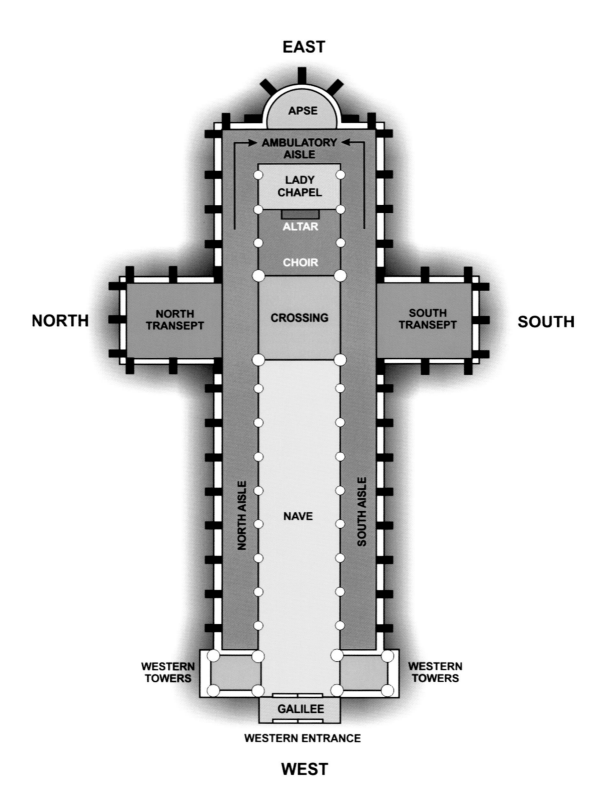

FIGURE 2. Typical Gothic Cathedral floor plan in a cruciform shape, or Latin cross.
Illustration by Robb Harst.

The cruciform also represents the shape of Christ's body suspended on the cross with his head facing east towards the rising sun (Son) or "sunlight of God." The sun (sunlight of God) shining in the stained-glass windows was a very important symbol inside the cathedral for the parishioners during the Middle Ages. The cathedral **axis** orientation was established west to east, with the entrance on the west end. Parishioners would then look east to the choir and altar during the services. For many centuries the congregation traditionally faced the east awaiting the coming of Christ. See Figure 2.

The long **nave** represents the body of Christ hanging on the vertical portion of the cross. The origin of the nave comes from both the human body (navel) and a ship nave. The nave of a **Gothic** cathedral has been described as imitating the rib structure of a large ship turned upside down. In fact, in Holland the nave is called a "ship." The ceiling of the nave represents the beautiful heavens. See Figure 2.

The north and south **transepts** are the horizontal portions of the cross, representing Christ's arms outstretched to the left and right nailed to the cross. The transepts are commonly called the arms of the church or cathedral. See Figure 2.

The **crossing** is the intersection of the cross (nave and transept), essentially the center of the cathedral. Above the crossing is generally found a central tower and steeple. What is known as the high **lantern** area is also found there containing clear windows allowing sunlight to penetrate to the center of the cathedral. See Figure 2.

The **apse** is the round eastern end of a French cathedral. Apse is an Old French word for head, representing Christ's head on top of the cross and looking east. See Figure 2.

The **choir (quire)** is east of the transepts and was one of the most important parts of the cathedral. The original spelling of "quire" was used at several cathedrals and is still used today at Wells Cathedral in England. See Figure 2.

The **sanctuary** or main part of the cathedral is east of the choir and is where the high altar is situated. See Figure 2.

The **high altar** is located east of and adjacent to the choir where the mass and services were held. See Figure 2.

The **cathedra** is on the high or elevated altar area. The cathedra was the "bishop's throne" or stone chair he sat upon and was his seat of authority.

The **ambulatory aisle** is a circular aisle going around the choir and altar area for pilgrims and parishioners to move easily about the east end of the cathedral. See Figure 2.

The **aisles** are on either side of the nave for people to move east and west through the full length of the cathedral. See Figure 2.

The **galilee** is just inside the west entrance vestibule as a gathering place to enter the nave. See Figure 2.

Prayer chapels were built around the outside parameter walls of the transepts and eastern ambulatory aisles. They varied in design and location in each of the cathedrals.

The **Lady Chapel** (Mother of Christ) is a prayer chapel generally located in the eastern end. It was always the most elaborately designed and decorated chapel in the cathedral. See Figure 2.

The **crypt** is an underground room holding tombs generally below the crossing and east end.

The large, stunning, stained-glass **rose windows** are round and fabricated out of hand-blown glass in several colors. They are framed into a giant wheel pattern of stone representing a rose and are generally mounted in the east, west, or transept ends of the upper level walls to enhance the beauty of the interior and exterior of the cathedral like the frosting on a cake. See Figure 1.

The other stained-glass windows, in a variety of shapes and sizes, are mounted all over the cathedral walls providing light to the parishioners. In the Gothic cathedrals most of the wall area is covered with colored stained glass, creating a rainbow of sparkling colors. Most of the windows are big bay areas of glass framed in vertical **lancet** shapes with pointed tops. They were made with beautifully arranged patterns of blue, red, purple, yellow, green, orange, and white glass.

Towers, steeples, and spires are the dominating features of the cathedrals, setting them apart from all the other buildings in town. They can be seen from many miles away.

FIGURE 3. St. Vitus Cathedral. Prague, Czech Republic. View of the tall spires and roof dominating the city of Prague taken from the top of the main tower.

The tall towers actually guided the pilgrims on the right path to their prayer destinations. See Figure 3. The **arcade** is a series of rounded and pointed **arch** walls on either side of the central nave extending the full length of the cathedral. These arches are supported by a variety of **piers**, single **columns**, or clustered columns taking on some of the weight of the heavy stone walls and roof. The arcade is the lower level of the traditional three level system of the nave inside the cathedral. See Figure 4.

The **triforium** level is the second level up above the arcade arches and has a walking gallery along each side. See Figure 4.

The **clerestory** is the top level of the nave, choir, and transepts. The clerestory walls have several windows cut into them allowing a great deal of light into the cathedral. See Figure 4.

The **flying buttress** was a new invention in the Gothic style that allowed the stonemasons to build much taller cathedrals. They served as the cathedral's basic structural support frame, rather than relying on heavy thick walls. They absorbed the roof and vault tonnage, transferring it outward away from the walls and down to the ground through their arches. They were also used as a counter-weight or buttress from preventing the walls from pushing outward. They were ingenious. See Figure 4.

The roof is the structural covering over the entire cathedral, keeping the rain and elements out of the fabric. See Figure 4.

The **gargoyles** were designed to take the collected roof water and transfer it out and away from the walls in a waterspout. The gargoyles are generally hollowed out grotesque-looking animals that have big round pipe mouths from which the water would gush out onto the ground. Besides transferring water, the purpose of these ugly creatures was to keep the devils away from the cathedral. They stick out of the upper flying buttresses.

Generally speaking, the English cathedrals are very long, longer than in any other country. The French cathedrals have high vaulted ceilings and are noted for their beautiful stained-glass windows. And the German cathedrals are very large and have the tallest spires in the world.

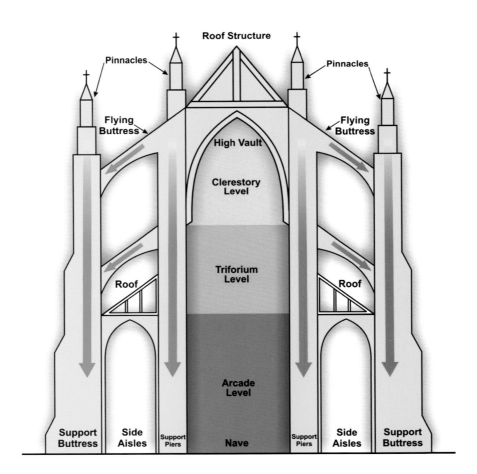

GOTHIC CATHEDRAL FLYING BUTTRESS SUPPORT STRUCTURE

FIGURE 4. This elevation of a Gothic cathedral flying buttress structure illustrates the outward and downward thrusts and weights absorbed by the buttresses in the red arrows. It also describes the various parts of the structure. *Illustration by Robb Harst.*

CHAPTER 4

COMPARISON OF ROMANESQUE AND GOTHIC CATHEDRAL STYLES

Medieval cathedrals fall into two major styles of architecture, **Romanesque** and Gothic. Romanesque cathedrals were built solid and sturdy to last forever. They had very thick supporting walls, used the round Roman arch throughout, and had few windows. The Gothic cathedrals had much thinner walls, less stone, pointed arches, vaulted ceilings, flying buttresses, elegant stained-glass windows, and were built very high to reach the heavens. See Figures 5–8.

On the continent of Europe, the early cathedrals with the round Roman arches were named Romanesque, while in England, they were called Norman. These two styles are basically one and the same, and the term Romanesque will be used for both.

The construction dates of the Romanesque and Gothic styles were overlapping and different in each of the various countries. This occurred because of old traditions, different growth rates, and the speed of cathedral style changes in each country. There were many exceptions to these dates, but they will be used as a general reference.

ROMANESQUE STYLE: AD 950–1100
GOTHIC STYLE: AD 1100–1550

While hundreds of Romanesque cathedrals were being built throughout Europe, the new Gothic architectural style came along in the twelfth century. The people liked and desired the new Gothic style with the stained-glass windows allowing the sun to shine inside.

Over the centuries, disaster struck a few of the Romanesque cathedrals, especially in the form of fires as a result of the wooden roofs. Earthquakes also occurred, damaging the cathedrals. Towers, walls, and vaulting likewise fell due to a variety of reasons. In the aftermath, the bishops, chapter members, and Master Builders had to evaluate and make the decision as to which style the cathedrals would be rebuilt. Should they completely tear down the old Romanesque cathedral and build a new Gothic one? Or should they salvage part of the old Romanesque fabric and blend the new Gothic style into the old?

Most of the administrators decided to save some of the old Romanesque structural elements and rebuild with a blend of the new Gothic style. What ensued in most cases was a smooth mix of differing degrees of both styles designed with good proportion. Consequently, many of the cathedrals today that are classified as Romanesque are actually more Gothic in appearance.

ROMANESQUE CATHEDRAL

FIGURE 5. *Illustration by Robb Harst.*

GOTHIC CATHEDRAL

FIGURE 6

ROMANESQUE STYLE ROUND ARCH THRUSTS OUT WITH WEIGHT

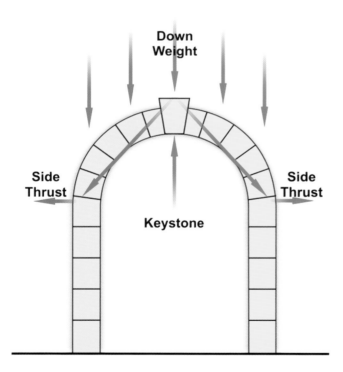

FIGURE 7.*Illustration by Robb Harst.*

GOTHIC STYLE POINTED ARCH SUPPORTS MORE WEIGHT

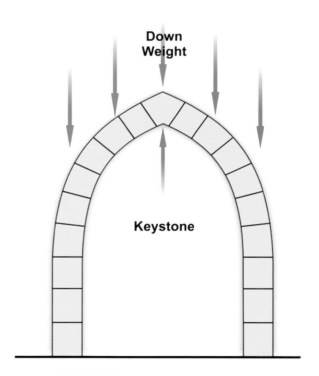

FIGURE 8. *Illustration by Robb Harst.*

CHAPTER 5

ROMANESQUE CATHEDRAL ARCHITECTURE, AD 950–1100

Romanesque architecture was a style developed during the Middle Ages near Rome, Italy, where the name was coined. The inception date of Romanesque architecture is somewhat controversial, but a general consensus confirms the span of this style between the tenth and twelfth centuries. One prominent feature identifying a Romanesque cathedral is the round or semi-circular windows and arches throughout.

Many of the early Romanesque cathedrals had an almost fortress-like appearance. From a distance, they looked like gigantic, solid, rectangular blocks of stone with two short pyramidal or square towers mounted on their front entrances. Over the years, they became more appealing with decorative embellishments added.

From the inside, Romanesque cathedrals have a massive, heavy look. The nave arcade has oversized diameter column piers, exceptionally thick walls, and only a few small windows to let in light. The Romanesque style inside is also recognized by the distinctive feature of highly carved and decorated round Roman arches and ceilings with flat roofs or **barrel vaults**. The round Roman arches can easily be seen throughout the building at the entrances, arcades, windows, and doors. The interior is also full of colorful wall paintings including plants and animals, daily life scenes, and biblical illustrations.

The huge walls usually consisted of two parallel stone shell walls with rubble stone packed inside. The Romanesque walls were thick because they had to support all of the ceiling and roof tonnage. Since the walls had to be supporting walls, very few window and door openings could be cut into them. All of the openings had round arches on top. The stone arches were highly decorated, usually with a wavy molding called a dog-tooth design.

The round Roman arch also supported the weight above. See Figure 7. When the weight pushes downward on top of the arch, it wants to spread and collapse the arch outwardly. At the deformation pressure points on either side of the arch, stone buttresses were laid up to counteract the outward thrust, propping up the arch from collapse.

Flat roofs or barrel vaults were used in covering or spanning the nave and other openings. The flat roofs were generally constructed of large wooden timbers spanning the bays. The barrel vault design was also used later on to cover the spans and was supported by the two thick sidewalls. Outside buttressing was strategically placed to help support the top of the walls from pushing or bowing outward.

Gigantic round **drum columns** were placed down either side of the nave aisles to support the heavy roof vaults. The large drum **pillars** formed the arcade walls in the lower level nave. The columns, walls, arches, and ceilings were highly decorated in the Romanesque style of the chevron zigzag, diamond, lozenge, and spiral. The Romanesque style gives the impression that the cathedrals were solidly built to last forever and most did.

PHOTOGRAPHIC WALKING TOURS OF ROMANESQUE CATHEDRALS

①* Lincoln Cathedral in England

Founded in 1072, Lincoln, is classified as a Romanesque cathedral, but was later rebuilt into the new Gothic style. Therefore it is a hybrid cathedral. Today it has the Gothic look and is a wonderful and impressive cathedral to tour.

In 1141, Lincoln had a devastating fire that destroyed the old flat wooden roof. It was later replaced by a new stone vaulted roof. In 1185, Lincoln also experienced a major earthquake that brought down the greater part of the cathedral into ruins. After the earthquake, the only thing remaining to salvage was the western **façade** entrance and the lower part of the western towers. The cathedral's west entrance carvings illustrate biblical scenes from the New Testament on the north side and Old Testament scenes on the south side. See Figure 9.

FIGURE 9. Lincoln Cathedral, England. This image, taken at night, illustrates the impressive Romanesque west façade entrance and the towering Gothic twin towers in the background.

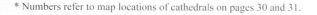

* Numbers refer to map locations of cathedrals on pages 30 and 31.

In 1192, the newly appointed Bishop St. Hugh started a major building program on the eastern end of the cathedral in the new Gothic style. The stonemasons nicely married the old Romanesque entrance with the new Gothic towers, accompanied by the flying buttresses. All three Gothic towers have spires that majestically set the cathedral off, dominating the community. Lincoln Cathedral is very long with an exterior length measuring 512 feet.

There are two rose windows, the famous Bishop's Eye with curved flowing tracery found in the south transept and the Dean's Eye in the north transept. There is a third rose window in the east end of the cathedral and it is the largest eight-pane window in England.

Lincoln has a variety of beautiful vaults found throughout the cathedral. The decorated arches of the nave arcade, triforium, and clerestory levels, along with the vaulted ceilings, are spectacular. The contrast of the dark purbeck marble clustered columns with the lighter colored stones of the arcade arches is stunning. The entire nave, looking east, is impressive with first-class craftsmanship of stone carving. The captions under the photographs describe the highly decorated carvings and richness of the interior nave of Lincoln. See Figure 10.

For centuries Lincoln Cathedral has been the custodian of one of the four remaining copies of the Magna Carta. It is displayed in the treasures of the Lincoln Castle. Lincoln is also home to the famous Lincoln Imp, a stone carving that according to legend was sent by Satan. It is sitting on top of a stone column in the Angel Choir. To see it better, one can put an English coin in a machine and a spotlight will shine on it.

Today Lincoln Cathedral has an in-house staff of skilled craftsmen including stonemasons, sculptors, stained-glass glaziers, wood carvers, plumbers, and joiners who keep up with the maintenance and needed replacement parts of the cathedral. Its a monumental challenge to keep up with the preservation of these gigantic structures after some 900 years

FIGURE 10. Lincoln Cathedral, England. This image illustrates the beauty of the Gothic nave arcade with its pointed arches and vaulted ceiling. Looking straight down the nave, the visitor sees the carved stone screen with the giant organ above it. His eyes then lift up to the vaulted ceiling toward heaven.

FIGURE 11. Lincoln Cathedral, England. This close-up shows the elaborately carved stone arches and decorated clustered columns at the triforium level with contrasting stone colors. There are dozens of these carved along the nave.

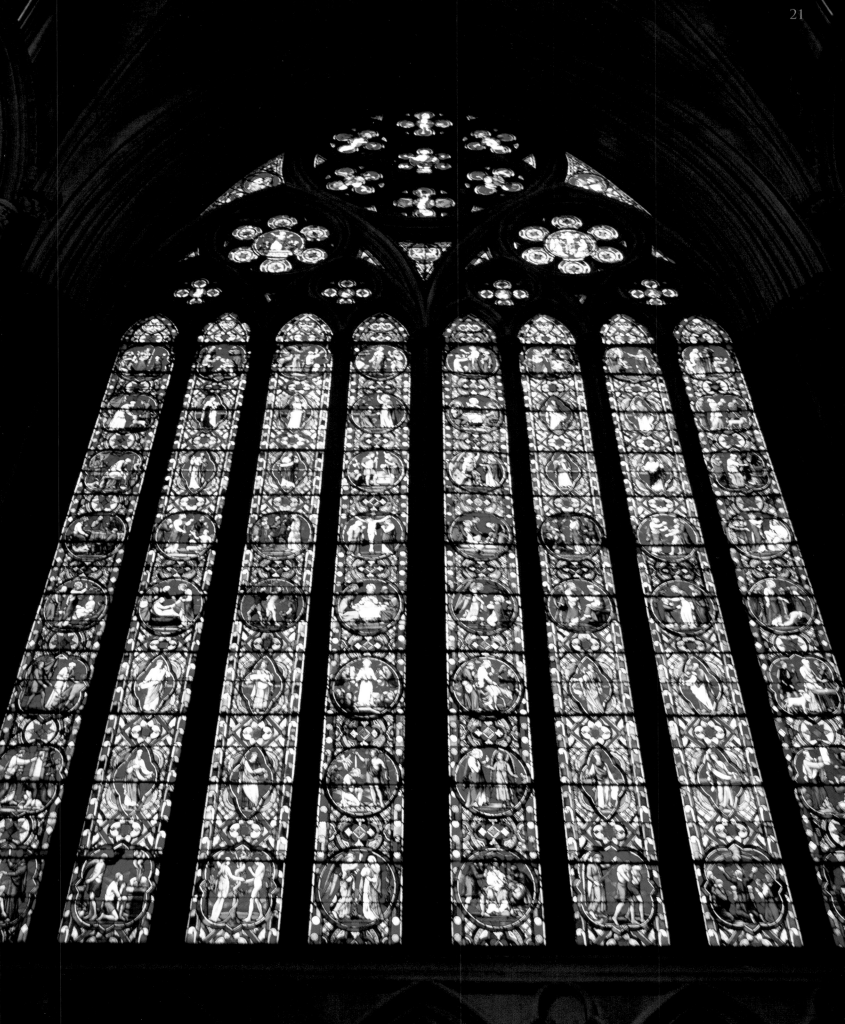

FIGURE 12. Lincoln Cathedral, England. This is the largest and earliest eight-pane stained-glass window in England. It is colorful and very impressive.

FIGURE 13. Lincoln Cathedral, England. This photo shows the large ribs of the fan-vaulted supports springing up from the clustered columns of the triforium level to the center of the vaulted ceiling.

of exposure to the elements and deterioration, But it is evident they are doing a superb job. Thousands of beautifully and intricately carved statues are mounted on the exteriors of cathedrals, especially on the west or weather side. They literally weather away with time. Visualize a newly carved human figure with detailed eyebrows, hair, and fingernails crisply carved from a cream- colored stone. Now assume for a moment it was a carving made out of a cream-colored slab of butter. It was mounted on the exterior of the cathedral, and when the afternoon sun shone on it, what happened? As the sun warmed the butter carving, it started to lose its crispy details, and eventually the facial features melted away and disappeared. The melted butter carving describes what many of the stone carvings look like today after so many years of exposure to the elements. The stonemasons at Lincoln carve new statues to replace the old weathered ones, just as craftsmen do at other cathedrals. These statues, along with many other remarkable features at Lincoln, make it a great cathedral to visit. See Figures 11-17.

FIGURE 14. Lincoln Cathedral, England. A large, detailed stained-glass window and stone tracery.

FIGURE 15. Lincoln Cathedral, England. A large colorful stained-glass window with decorated lancet panes featuring hearts and kings.

FIGURE 16. Lincoln Cathedral, England. The decorated crossing ceiling of the transept and nave with organ on the right.

FIGURE 17. Lincoln Cathedral, England. The elaborately carved stone screen separating the nave from the choir.

② Norwich Cathedral in England

Norwich Cathedral was started in 1096 and completed in 1145 with several rebuilds and additions over the years. Norwich is classified as a Romanesque cathedral with some Gothic style rebuilds. I would call it a hybrid. The Gothic additions of the spire and nave vaulting were completed in the fifteenth century. Norwich is a very long cathedral measuring 481 feet.

An outstanding feature of Norwich is the beautiful central tower spire measuring 319 feet tall. It is the second tallest spire in England only to be outdone by Salisbury at 404 feet. It is a landmark that can be seen from many miles away.

The nave and choir vaulted ceiling are quite spectacular with hundreds of carved **bosses** mounted at the top intersections of the vaulting **ribs**. Norwich is beautiful inside and out. See Figures 18–22.

FIGURE 18. Norwich Cathedral, England. Exterior view of the tall cathedral tower from across the green and through a stone arch.

FIGURE 19. Norwich Cathedral, England. The elaborate fan-vaulted ceiling is showcased with the east end and stained-glass windows.

FIGURE 20. Norwich Cathedral, England. Fan-vaulted ceiling and large stained-glass windows.

FIGURE 21. Norwich Cathedral, England. Three bays of colorful stained-glass windows.

FIGURE 22. Norwich Cathedral, England. Large stained-glass window bay with detailed scenes.

③ Durham Cathedral in England

Durham Cathedral was built in a very short period of time from 1093 to 1133, a mere forty years, with the exception of the towers built in the thirteenth century. What an unbelievable achievement! It is a very large cathedral with the following dimensions: 502 feet long, 192 feet wide, and a central tower 218 feet tall.

Durham is described by many as the largest and best example of Norman/Romanesque architecture in England and possibly anywhere. It is in the northern part of England near the Scottish border. It was magnificently sited on top of a horseshoe-shaped peninsula, high above the River Wear overlooking the city of Durham.

The cathedral displays a striking view from across the river with its twin towers dominating the hill. I suggest parking the car on the other side of the river, walking across the bridge, and then following the narrow streets up to the hilltop and onto the cathedral green. See Figure 23.

At the north entrance, a grotesque lion head sanctuary knocker is mounted on the door.

It is a bronze casting with a handle mounted in its mouth. A fleeing criminal could grasp it and claim the "right of sanctuary" inside the cathedral. Durham is a sanctuary cathedral, meaning fugitives had immunity from the law inside the fabric. See Figure 24.

FIGURE 24. Durham Cathedral, England. Grotesque lion head sanctuary door knocker on the entrance door.

FIGURE 23. Durham Cathedral, England. Exterior view illustrating the central tower and the twin towers on the west end.

FIGURE 25. Durham Cathedral, England. View looking down the nave to the east with organ pipes on either side and large support pillars on each side. The altar is in the center with the rose window above.

The nave of Durham features huge columns on both sides alternating with clustered piers to support the upper vaulted weight. The large columns are seven feet in diameter or twenty-two feet in circumference, which equals exactly twenty-two feet in height. The Master Builder purposely sized the round columns so that the circumference equaled the height. The columns are strikingly unique with decorated incised surfaces chiseled completely around them. There are four different designs, namely the lozenge, chevron, spiral, and diamond patterns that give the nave a nice balanced variety. See Figure 25.

Many of the round Roman arches in the fabric are also highly decorated with carved chevrons. I was able to take a tower tour up into the cathedral and explore the details of the fabric including the hidden flying buttresses. See Figures 26–28.

FIGURE 26. Durham Cathedral, England. The rose window with colorful lancet windows beside and below it. The photo was taken from the seldom-visited upper triforium level.

FIGURE 27. Durham Cathedral, England. Close-up of a massive support column with chevrons carved on the outside. The round Roman arches have dog-tooth decoration around them.

FIGURE 28. Durham Cathedral, England. The flying buttresses, a Gothic design element, are hidden under the roof the full length of the nave.

CHAPTER 6

CATHEDRAL LOCATIONS, ENGLAND

①	LINCOLN	⑥	YORK	⑪	LICHFIELD
②	NORWICH	⑦	WELLS	⑫	BATH
③	DURHAM	⑧	EXETER	⑬	BEVERLEY
④	SALISBURY	⑨	WORCESTER	⑭	WESTMINSTER
⑤	CANTERBURY	⑩	ELY	⑮	ST. PAUL'S

Cathedral Locations, Continental Europe

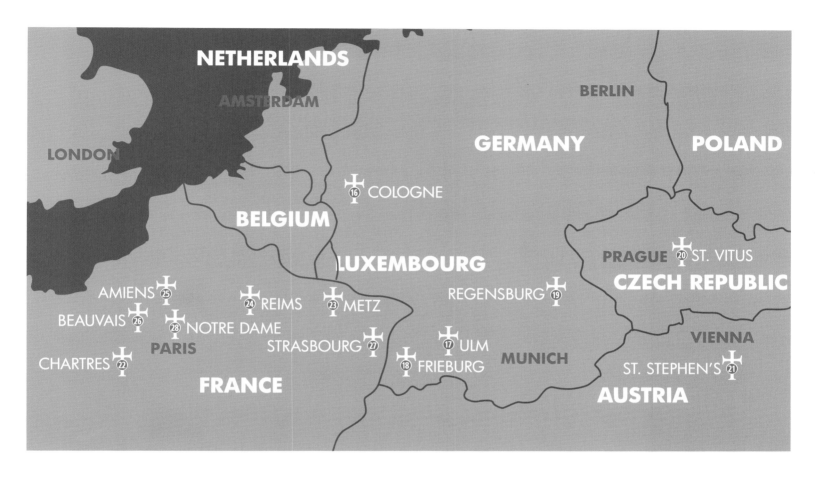

⑯	COLOGNE, GERMANY	㉑	ST. STEPHEN'S, AUSTRIA	㉖	BEAUVAIS, FRANCE
⑰	ULM, GERMANY	㉒	CHARTRES, FRANCE	㉗	STRASBOURG, FRANCE
⑱	FREIBURG, GERMANY	㉓	METZ, FRANCE	㉘	NOTRE DAME, PARIS, FRANCE
⑲	REGENSBURG, GERMANY	㉔	REIMS, FRANCE		
⑳	ST. VITUS, CZECH REPUBLIC	㉕	AMIENS, FRANCE		

Cathedral locations not shown on the maps

㉙ ST. PETERS, ROME, ITALY
㉚ WASHINGTON NATIONAL, D.C. USA

CHAPTER 7

GOTHIC CATHEDRAL ARCHITECTURE, AD 1100–1550

Gothic cathedral architecture in Europe will never again be equaled in design, grandeur, beauty, spaciousness, magnificence, or scale—nor will it ever be replicated. No one man was responsible for the development of the Gothic architectural style; it was a composite development of several highly skilled Master Builders over a period of time. This new architectural design took cathedral building to a whole new level. Literally hundreds of magnificent edifices sprang up all over Europe within a short period of a few hundred years. Louis Charpentier speaks of this dramatic movement in his book *The Mysteries of Chartres Cathedral*: "One has to bear in mind that in northern France alone, at the time Chartres was being built, nearly twenty cathedrals of the same importance were under construction" (Charpentier 1972, 15).

Bernard Jones, a noted Masonic scholar, describes Gothic architecture this way: "Gothic had those beautiful proportioned columns, with their dignified **capitals**; it had in particular the pointed arch and the ribbed vaulting of the roof; and often externally the flying buttress to give strength to the walls and carry the weight and thrust of the roof." (Jones 1975, 29).

Up to the time of the Gothic style, there were limitations of width, span, and height in the Romanesque-style buildings. The thick walls had to support the entire roof tonnage and side thrusts. There was a limit on the strength of the materials themselves to support the wide spans without collapsing and without using several additional support columns.

The new Gothic style with the flying buttress design and pointed arches made it possible to build considerably wider and higher edifices. This allowed a new era of architecture of height, breadth and spaciousness. The unnecessary stone was pared down to the skeletal bones on all the structural members leaving just a bare minimum framework to hold the fabric safely together. This permitted the erection of cathedrals with thinner walls and a minimum amount of stone, saving thousands of tons of material, labor, and costs to build each cathedral.

CHARACTERISTICS OF GOTHIC ARCHITECTURE

Flying Buttresses

The gigantic circular rib arches of stone resembling a rib cage and surrounding the cathedral body are called **Flying buttresses**. They were attached to the top of the exterior walls, serving as a skeletal framework by propping and holding up the roof tonnage while preventing the walls from spreading out. They serve the same purpose as wooden beams do inside a barn structure, but they are on the outside of the cathedral. The flying buttresses were made of thousands of cut stones fastened together with mortar. See Figure 4.

Instead of having the walls support the roof tonnage as was done in the older Romanesque cathedrals, the roof weight was transmitted down to the ground through the flying buttress arch system. All of the roof's vertical and side thrust tonnage was captured and tranferred into the graceful buttress arch supports before being delivered down to the foundation stones. The flying buttresses absorb the roof weight and transfer it down to the ground almost like water being diverted off a roof through a series of gutters and downspouts.

The flying buttress design was the Master Builder's secret in constructing thousands of tons of stone hundreds of feet in the air, all strategically and delicately balanced in strength, beauty, and symmetry.

> If it is to last, the Gothic movement requires perfect adjustment between weight and thrust; the weight that creates the thrust becomes itself its own negation. The activity in the stone is therefore in a state of constant tension which the art of the Master Builder can "tune" like a harp-string. (Charpentier 1972, 43)

No one really knows who the brilliant Master Builder was who conceived and designed the first flying buttress system. It is a very ingenious invention of structural support in the Gothic cathedrals.

Stained-Glass Windows

The large stained-glass windows installed in the cathedral walls is another Gothic feature. Because the thinner Gothic walls were not used as supports, the Master Builder was able to maximize the window area by cutting large openings and inserting colossal stained-glass windows. Large rose and lancet windows allowed the natural sunlight to brighten the interiors in a beautiful display of flickering colors.

Pointed Arches

A variety of high pointed arches were used throughout the fabric on the vaulted ceilings, nave arcade, entrances, exterior walls, and windows. The pointed arch design could support much more vertical weight than the older Roman round arch. This allowed the masons to stack stones much higher on the arcade walls and vaulting that permitted taller cathedrals to be built. See Figure 8.

Rib Vaulting

Stone rib vaulted arches were used in the cathedral ceilings to replace the older flat wooden ceilings susceptible to fire. The masons used this new invention of the cross-ribbed vaulted ceiling to span the openings across the wide naves, choirs, aisles, and Lady Chapels. Each one of the rib-vaulted ceilings is unique and fantastic.

Clustered Column Support Piers

Clustered column support piers replaced the old round Roman support columns in the nave arcade. The masons joined together several smaller column shafts into one large support pier that was capable of supporting several more tons of tower weight than a single column could. These gigantic clustered shafts or columns soared all the way to the vaulted ceilings and were unique to the Gothic style cathedrals.

Long and High Vaulted Naves

The Gothic cathedrals had very long and high naves designed to direct one's attention forward when entering the cathedral and then upward to the heavens when reaching the crossing. The English cathedrals were especially long, Canterbury and Exeter being two examples, while the French cathedrals are noted for their tall vaulted nave ceilings.

In summary, the Gothic style emphasized verticality in its design with the use of high vaulting, towers, steeples, and spires, creating the impression that the cathedrals reached the heavens. The overall appearance is of lightness and loftiness with high skeletal stone frames holding together acres of beautiful stained-glass windows.

When the Master Builders fully developed the Gothic style it became the zenith in cathedral architecture, engineering, and craftsmanship. The design enabled the builders to enclose millions of cubic feet of space under one roof using a minimum of tonnage of hewn stone. This development and refinement of the Gothic design occurred over a period of approximately 250 years, from AD 1100-1350. In later years, the Gothic designs were basically copied in other structures with few subtle enhancements.

If one can be separated from another, I believe Salisbury Cathedral, the construction of which commenced in 1220, is the purest expression of Gothic architecture in all of England. Salisbury was built as a Gothic cathedral from scratch and stands essentially the same as it did some 800 years ago. Salisbury is unique in this regard, as very few cathedrals stand as originally designed without remodeling.

THE BIRTH OF GOTHIC ARCHITECTURE

Durham Cathedral, England

Durham Cathedral is unique in that it is one of the best examples of Romanesque architecture while also possessing the first elements of Gothic architecture: flying buttresses, pointed arch vaulting, stone ribbed cross vaulting, and clustered shaft support piers. I believe Durham was the first cathedral to introduce these new features. It should also be noted that these four design elements were built into the fabric initially and not added later during a rebuild project.

Durham's Master Builder must have been a pioneer and on the cutting edge of architectural design in cathedral building. The innovative features incorporated into Durham eventually became known as Gothic style, and these design features migrated into other areas and countries, all the while being expanded and refined.

I visited Durham in 1986 for the first time and arranged a special tower tour on the triforium level. When I arrived in the upper walkway gallery of the triforium I was quite surprised to find gigantic flying buttresses concealed under the roof level over the side aisles. They were arranged the full length of the nave and strategically connected to the nave arcade walls. They were hidden under the tribune roof and not visible to the public from the outside or inside. I wondered what flying buttresses were doing in a Romanesque cathedral when they were supposed to be one of the design features of the Gothic style that came later. See Figure 28.

On a return trip to Durham in September of 2010, I took a closer look at the fabric and confirmed more Gothic features: the pointed arch in the ribbed vaulting of the nave, stone ribbed cross-vaulted ceilings, and clustered columns for support piers. I was also surprised by the early dates of these Gothic construction elements, all completed by AD 1133.

A BRIEF TIMELINE OF DURHAM'S CONSTRUCTION

1093	Durham's choir, the heart of the fabric, is started.
1096	The stone ribbed cross-vaulted ceilings of the choir side aisles are completed. (These rigid stone vaults resemble an egg carton turned upside down.)
1099 to 1104	The stone ribbed cross-vaulted high ceiling of the main choir is constructed.
c. 1110	The stone ribbed cross-vaulted ceilings in the north and south transepts are completed.
c. 1099 to 1128	The nave walls are built.
c. 1128 to 1133	The nave incorporates pointed, ribbed **transverse arch** vaults in the ceiling. (These pointed transverse arch vaults are used in the nave ceiling for the first time in Durham. They are mounted on clustered column piers across and opposite from one another in the nave arcade, and they alternate with the regular round support columns down the nave.)
1133	The stone ribbed vaulting covering the entire roof is completed. (Durham Cathedral is the earliest building in Europe to have stone ribbed vaults constructed throughout.)
c. 1128 to 1133	The flying buttresses hidden in the triforium level are built.

Durham's Master Builder initially designed and built the flying buttresses into the upper arcade walls to support and prevent the walls from spreading out. They were hidden under the aisle roofs, and I wonder if the Master Builder put them there to keep the mortar joints and buttresses dry in order to extend the life of the building. In later years, cathedrals' flying buttresses were built outside and exposed to the elements. The flying buttresses were the first of their kind used in a cathedral.

The flying buttresses, pointed arch vault, ribbed cross-vaulted ceiling, and clustered column piers were all put together for the first time in Durham Cathedral by 1133, beginning the era of Gothic architecture. Cathedral towers, however, were often built several years after the fabric was enclosed and already being used. Many times the huge project of adding towers required additional funding that usually had to wait. Durham built two large twin towers on the western end in 1226 and completed a large central tower in 1262.

St. Denis Abbey, France

For the last few centuries, art historians, architects, and other writers have stated that St. Denis Abbey, just north of Paris, France, is where Gothic architecture originated. To this day, many writers make the same statement. But there is evidence to suggest that this may not be the case.

Durham Cathedral in England's four Gothic architectural elements were built into it before any Gothic rebuilding took place at St. Denis. When comparing the construction dates of the Gothic features of both structures, Durham predates St. Denis by several years.

When the abbey needed several repairs, the officials decided to completely rebuild the fabric c. 1135. For years writers have speculated that Abbot Sugar, appointed to St. Denis in 1122, was the design architect and builder responsible for the new Gothic design and rebuilding project at St. Denis. The abbey was rebuilt in three phases:

First Phase: West Façade Entrance in Romanesque (c. 1137–1140)

St. Denis was the burial place for most of the French kings, and it became a popular pilgrimage site for visitors. Consequently, Abbot Sugar wanted to enlarge the entrance to allow more visitors in and out of the abbey with less congestion. This would increase the revenues of the abbey and help pay for the rebuilding project.

The west façade entrance was rebuilt by first adding two towers and three large doors to accommodate more visitors. The nave length was also extended to the west. It is interesting to note that this first phase was done in the old Romanesque style and not in the new Gothic style.

Second Phase: Choir and East End in Gothic (c. 1140–1144)

The second phase was completed using the new Gothic style of architecture. The sanctuary was rebuilt with a new choir and ambulatory aisle surrounding it, incorporating the ribbed vaulting, pointed arch ceilings, and flying buttresses. The east end, with **radiating chapels** built around it, had flying buttresses outside to support it. This allowed for the use of stained-glass windows in the walls to let more light into the choir.

After the new choir project was rebuilt in the Gothic style, Abbot Sugar arranged a large dedication celebration held on June 11, 1144. He invited the king of France, archbishops, bishops, clergyman, political figures, influential merchants, and all the local folks to the ceremony. Abbot Sugar wanted to show off his new choir and stained-glass windows to the world.

Third Phase: Nave, Transepts, Crossing, and Rose Window in Gothic (c. 1231–1264)

The third phase of rebuilding the nave, transepts, crossing, and rose windows in the Gothic style was delayed many years. It was not completed until 120 years after the choir was dedicated in 1144.

The chart illustrates that four Gothic design elements were used together for the first time in Durham Cathedral, some forty years before the elements were used in St. Denis Abbey. Durham is a Romanesque cathedral with the first Gothic elements built into it and was fully vaulted by AD 1133. St. Denis Abbey was originally a medieval abbey completely dismantled and rebuilt into a Gothic abbey in three phases ranging from AD 1137 to 1264. Today Durham looks like a Romanesque structure and St. Denis looks Gothic, but that is not my argument; my claim is Durham Cathedral in England was the first structure into which combined Gothic elements were introduced. It was where Gothic architecture was born.

COMPARISON DATES OF GOTHIC ELEMENTS BUILT INTO DURHAM AND ST. DENIS

DURHAM CATHEDRAL, ENGLAND	ST. DENIS ABBEY, FRANCE	COMPARISONS
1096 Ribbed cross-vaulted ceilings in choir side aisles completed.	**1140** Ribbed cross-vaulted ceilings in narthex addition completed.	Durham's vaulted ceilings were completed 44 years before St. Denis.
1104 Main choir construction completed.	**1144** Main choir construction completed.	Durham's choir predated St. Denis by 40 years.
1133 Nave, transepts, crossing, flying buttresses, and ceilings using the pointed ribbed transverse vaults and clustered support piers finished.	1264 Rebuilding of the nave, transepts, crossing, rose windows, and ceiling vaulting finished.	Durham Cathedral preceded St. Denis in completing the four Gothic building elements by 131 years.

Abbot Sugar's Role in Rebuilding St. Denis Abbey

Abbot Sugar was born in 1081 and at the age of ten was given as an oblate (offered up) to the abbey of St. Denis for religious training under the monks. He remained there in training for some thirteen years where he met the future king, Louis VI of France, with whom he became friends. He became a monk and later served as advisor to the king. He held several other positions until he was appointed abbot of St. Denis in 1122. He was a very powerful man in France both politically and religiously.

Abbot Sugar gave his entire life to St. Denis starting with his training at the abbey at age ten, working as a monk, serving as secretary to the abbot, and finally being appointed as the abbot himself from 1122 until his death in 1151. It has been reported that Abbot Sugar was the designer and builder responsible for the Gothic rebuilding project at St. Denis.

Abbot Sugar has also generally been credited for first introducing Gothic architecture in cathedral building, but there is data to the contrary. First of all, Durham's side-aisle choir's vaulted ceilings built in the Gothic style were completed in 1096 when Abbot Sugar was only fifteen years old and still in religious training school, leaving little doubt that he was not the first one to introduce Gothic features. In addition, the first phase of rebuilding at St. Denis, under Abbot Sugar's watch, was done in the Romanesque style. If Abbot Sugar was the architect of the new Gothic style, why was it not used in the first phase? I believe Abbot Sugar hired a Master Builder schooled in the old Romanesque style to oversee the first phase of rebuilding and then hired a second Master Builder c. 1140 trained in the new Gothic style of architecture to complete the second phase of rebuilding.

It is also curious that no accounts have ever surfaced that indicate Abbot Sugar attended any stonemason apprenticeship or Master Mason training schools. In all the extensive writings made about Abbot Sugar no mention was ever made of him graduating from any architectural schools. From what I have seen, all the schools Abbot Sugar attended were strictly of a religious nature. In the absence of mason training, how could he have assumed and carried out the enormous duties of a Master Builder?

Serving as the patron of St. Denis, Abbot Sugar certainly promoted the new Gothic style of architecture when it emerged during the second phase of rebuilding the choir. He wanted to make a record of the abbey's rebuilding projects, including the collections procured of precious gems, stones, paintings, gold, and silver during his administration.

Abbot Sugar wrote extensively about the history of St. Denis, the rebuilding of the fabric, and the fine decorations and treasures he put together. He gives the impression that he was responsible and instrumental in the design and rebuilding of the fabric. Here are a few examples of his writing:

I carried this task out the more gladly…
I undertook to enlarge and amplify the monastic church consecrated by the devine hand…

I, who was Sugar, having been leader while it was accomplished.

The Abbot Sugar put up these altar panels.
(Sugar c. 1144-8)

Professor Otto von Simson, a medieval art historian, had this to say about the extensive writings that Abbot Sugar made about his own administration concerning the rebuilding of St. Denis: "Sugar's intention clearly was not that of writing an edifying treatise. Whatever he wrote was directly related to the main purpose of his career" (Simpson 1974, 124).

In his writing, Abbot Sugar never mentioned the names of any Master Builders or craftsmen who may have designed and built the new Gothic choir. He never gave credit to any of the people who may have done the design work and construction. Instead, he had his name engraved on bronze doors and carved panels explaining what he had done during the rebuilding. He gave the impression that he was the man responsible for the project and he welcomed praise for it. It should also be noted that the third phase of rebuilding at St. Denis in the Gothic style was completed more than 100 years after Abbot Sugar had passed away. Many visitors and writers for the last few centuries may have mistakenly assumed that the current beautiful Gothic abbey was all completed under the watch of Abbot Sugar.

Centuries ago, when art historians started to research the origin of Gothic architecture, they probably found Abbot Sugar's writing, naming himself as the builder of St. Denis. After several generations of authors repeating what Abbot Sugar wrote, eventually he became known as the presumed design architect. In my opinion, in all probability, he was the patron and fundraiser only. Today a few architectural scholars are now questioning Abbot Sugar's role as the builder of St. Denis.

PHOTOGRAPHIC WALKING TOURS OF GOTHIC CATHEDRALS

For locations of these cathedrals, please see the maps of Cathedrals in England and Cathedrals in Continental Europe, found on pages 30 and 31. The Washington National Cathedral is not shown on these maps; it is in Washington, DC, in the United States. St. Peter's is also not on these maps; it is in Rome, Italy.

④ Salisbury Cathedral in England

Salisbury is a graceful and beautiful example of a pure Gothic cathedral. It was built on a virgin piece of property in Salisbury as a replacement for the old Romanesque cathedral located at Old Sarum, two and a half miles away. The foundation stone was laid on April 28, 1220, and the main fabric was completed in 1258, a rapid speed of only thirty-eight years. In 2008 the 750th anniversary of the consecration date was celebrated.

Salisbury is one of my all-time favorite cathedrals in England and sits majestically inside of England's largest cathedral close. The close is a stone wall enclosure of the property with manicured grass and trees surrounding the cathedral. The close walls are laid up with stones from the Old Sarum Cathedral, and they still have masons' marks engraved on them. The fabric is not obstructed with houses and buildings like those of many other cathedrals. It is a thrill walking through the gate off Exeter Street and onto the green where the immense cathedral stands. See Figure 29.

The wonderful 404-foot decorated spire, the tallest in England, seems to climb to the heavens, dominating Salisbury's landscape from many miles away. On the tower tour, I climbed up the stairs and could look up into the center of the steeple spire and see the original scaffolding timbers that were used to build the spire shell. The timbers were left in place after the tower was built, for maintenance reasons I assume. I then went up to the spire level and out a small door onto a narrow walkway. What a view! I took photographs looking down over the roof below, including a panoramic view of the houses around Salisbury. See Figure 30.

It is hard to imagine the stonemasons cutting and laying thousands of tapered stones for the spire hanging from ropes and platforms 404 feet high!

The enormous tower and spire were added to the fabric from 1320 to 1334. They added another 6,500 tons of stone weight to the crossing. It was a challenge to provide enough support for this extra weight. As a result, the large crossing pillar columns are actually bent inward a bit at the top.

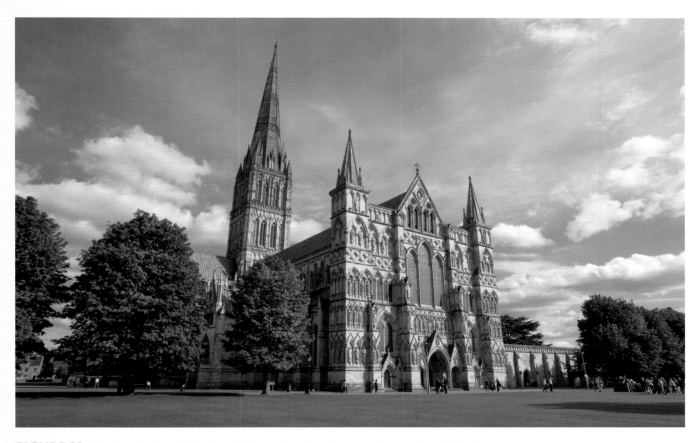

FIGURE 29. Salisbury Cathedral, England. This exterior view shows the decorated west façade entrance from across the green. The majestic 404-foot spire is the tallest in England.

FIGURE 30. Salisbury Cathedral, England. This bird's-eye view was taken from the tall central spire catwalk. Note the panoramic view of Salisbury village and the sun's shadow on the roof and green below.

The interior of Salisbury is magnificent with the impressive pointed arches in the arcade and crossing. The nave columns are made of dark polished Purbeck marble and serve as a good contrast with the other lighter colored stones around them. The three levels in the nave and vaulted ceilings are quite beautiful. See Figures 31 and 32.

There are other items in the cathedral that should be mentioned. Salisbury has the oldest working medieval clock in the world, dating to 1386. It also has a man-operated windlass wheel crane that was used to lift the heavy stones up in the building during construction. Salisbury can also boast of having one of four remaining original copies of the Magna Carta.

Visually, the cathedral is pleasing to the eye with good proportions and harmony inside and out. It is quite a large cathedral with an overall length of 473 feet. See Figures 33–35.

Salisbury has a nice size model illustrating the cathedral as it was being built with all the different stonemasons and other craftsmen working on it. It is certainly worth a visit.

FIGURE 31. Salisbury Cathedral, England. This image shows the beauty and scale of Gothic architecture in design, size, balance, and color. The dark Purbeck marble columns are a nice contrast against the lighter colored stone and painted ceiling. See the crucifix on the right.

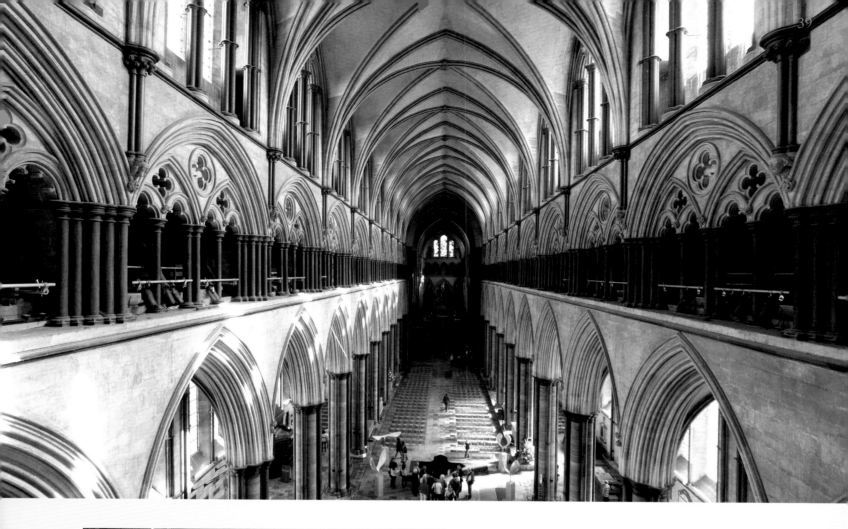

FIGURE 32. Salisbury Cathedral, England. This view shows the three levels of the nave and vaulted ceiling looking east and was taken from the triforium level. The size of the people provides a good perspective on the nave's size. This is a Gothic style nave at its best.

FIGURE 33. Salisbury Cathedral, England. Vertical view, looking up to the painted and vaulted ceiling. Note the rose and light green decorated ribs of the vaulting.

FIGURE 34. Salisbury Cathedral, England. Close-up of an elaborately decorated stone pulpit with carved statues around the top. There is a detailed carved sounding board above the pulpit to project the bishop's voice.

FIGURE 35. Salisbury Cathedral, England. This image shows the
central crossing of the nave and two transepts with netting designed ceiling.
The four clustered column supports on the corners hold up the tower.

⑤ Canterbury Cathedral in England

Canterbury is one of the most famous Gothic cathedrals in England and is the seat of the archbishop of Canterbury. In 1170, Thomas Becket, the archbishop of Canterbury at the time, was assassinated inside the cathedral and it then became one of the largest pilgrim visitation sites in all England. See Figure 36.

Canterbury is an exceptionally large cathedral with the following dimensions: 547 feet long, 171 feet wide, a tower height of 235 feet, and a nave height of 80 feet. To give a little perspective of just how long the cathedral is, one can enter the west door entrance and walk one tenth of a mile down the nave aisle toward the eastern end and still not touch the east wall. See Figures 37–44.

The site was originally founded in 597 and is one of the oldest Christian sites in England. A rebuilding of the cathedral in the Gothic style was started in 1070 and continued through 1505. A terrible fire in the eastern end of the cathedral in 1174 destroyed the choir. In 1175 a famous Master Builder, William of Sens (France), was then brought in to rebuild the choir in the Gothic style. He was finishing the choir and working on the vaulting when he fell from the high scaffolding in 1178 and was permanently injured. He managed and worked off site for a while until 1179 when he returned to France and passed away in 1180. Another famous Master Builder, William the Englishman, was hired in 1179, and he carried on the project until 1184.

The interior views of Canterbury are very impressive with the nave, arcade, vaulting, and crossing. The king's Master Mason, Henry Yevele, designed and built the beautiful nave. He was one of the most famous English Master Builders and project designers in all of England. The Bell Harry Tower was designed and built by John Wastell, including the outstanding crossing inside with the **fan vaulting.**

FIGURE 36. Canterbury Cathedral, England. This is an exterior view from the southwest at dusk with the lights starting to come on. The three Gothic towers dominate the exterior of the cathedral.

FIGURE 37. Canterbury Cathedral, England. Wide-angle view looking up into the Bell Harry Tower at the central crossing. Look closely at the ceiling in the lantern of the tower.

FIGURE 38. Canterbury Cathedral, England. A close-up of the lantern ceiling in the previous photo. The details of the design, vaulting, colors, bosses, and shapes make it the best of the best in central crossing ceilings.

FIGURE 39. Canterbury Cathedral, England. Detailed seven-pane stained-glass window.

FIGURE 40. Canterbury Cathedral, England. Close-up of the stained-glass window in Figure 39.

FIGURE 41. Canterbury Cathedral, England. Close-up of a stained-glass window illustrating the king's crown.

FIGURE 42. Canterbury Cathedral, England. Large stained-glass window with ornate stone tracery at the top.

FIGURE 43. Canterbury Cathedral, England. View of the cathedra, a stone chair or seat of the presiding bishop mounted in the east.

FIGURE 44. Canterbury Cathedral, England. Close-up view of an elaborately decorated pulpit with a carved and painted crucifix on the front. There is a large painted sounding board above the pulpit for sound projection.

⑥ York Minster in England

The site that **York Minster** sits on today goes back to the Roman days nearly 2,000 years ago. It was started in the year 1220 and building continued up until completion in 1472. York Minster is a very large house of worship with the following dimensions: 524 feet long, 244 feet wide, and a tower height of 213 feet. York is the largest Gothic church in England and one of the largest in the world. See Figure 45.

York is known for its beautiful stained-glass windows and has an enormous amount of original medieval glass. In fact, York has the largest stained-glass window in the world, the Great East Window, measuring 1,053 square feet. It was designed and built by John Thornton, Master Glazier. Another oversized stained-glass window with eight panes in width is seen on the west façade entrance. See Figure 46. Other well-known windows here include the Heart of Yorkshire, the Five Sisters, Bishop's Eye, and Dean's Eye. The rose window in the south transept is outstanding as well. See Figure 47.

York has a very impressive crossing with the lantern above painted white and gold. The view looking up into the crossing lantern is a sight to behold. See Figure 48.

Equally impressive is the stone choir screen separating the choir from the nave. It includes statues of England's kings carved in lifelike detail. See Figure 49.

In the nave, the light-colored vaulted ceilings with carved bosses and darker columns are eye catching, and the views of the arcade, triforium, and clerestory levels are truly elegant. The vaulting in the Chapter House ceiling, windows, and canopy are also impressive.

FIGURE 45. York Minster, England. West façade entrance of the largest Gothic church in England. Note the large stained-glass window above the west entrance doors.

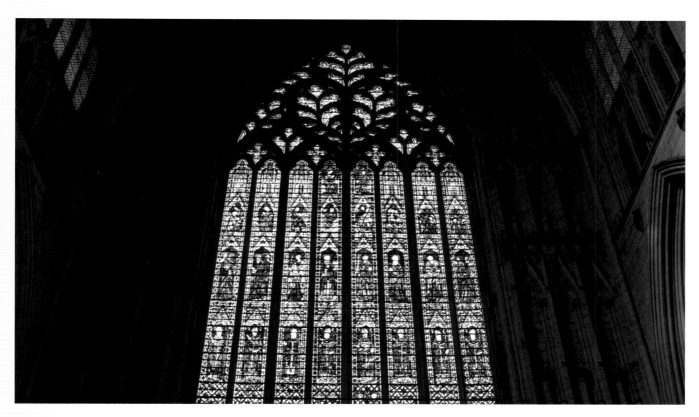

FIGURE 46. York Minster, England. This photo illustrates the same stained-glass window on the west façade entrance shown in Figure 45, but from the inside. The eight-pane window depicts archbishops and biblical scenes.

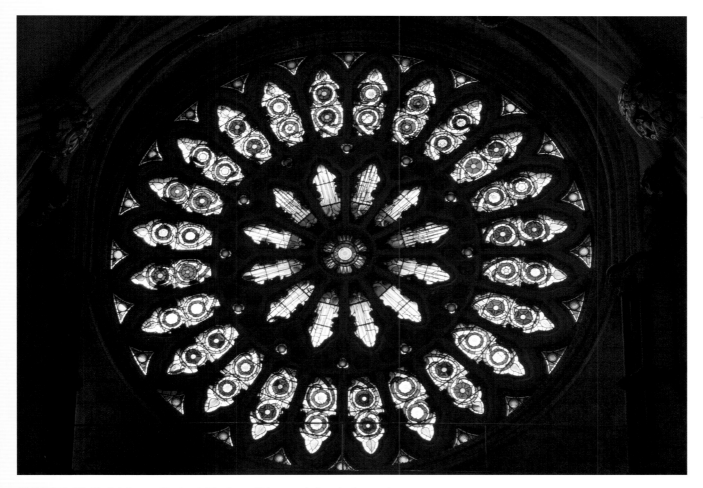

FIGURE 47. York Minster, England. The beautiful rose window in the south transept. This is an exceptionally gorgeous stained-glass window and one of my favorites.

FIGURE 48. York Minster, England. Wide-angle view of the central crossing. I turned the camera forty-five degrees to get the image. The glass in the lantern was unstained, allowing more light to enter. Note the four large column supports on the corners and the gigantic organ pipes on the left.

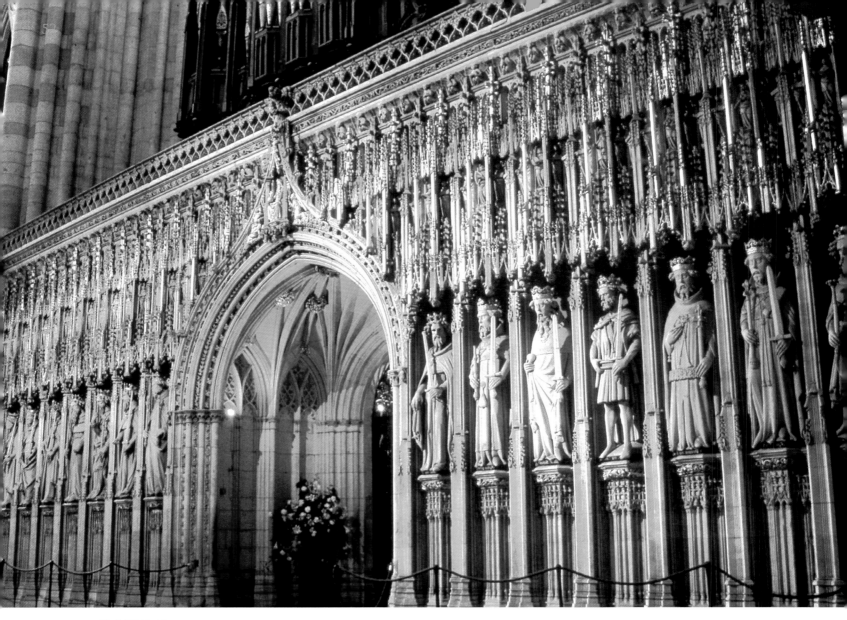

FIGURE 49. York Minster, England. The beautifully carved choir screen includes fifteen carved kings.

On one of my trips to York in the late 1970s I had the privilege of meeting and talking with the stonemasons working at the site. I watched the banker mason carve stone on his bench to match the pattern. One of the masons gave me a tour of the cathedral and showed me some of the old wooden patterns in storage. He also showed me the Trasour House with the plaster floor where the Master Builder drew his designs with the large compass. When I asked the stonemasons about mason marks in the cathedral, they gave me a list of those found on the stones inside the minster.

York Minster had a major fire occur on July 9, 1984, in the south transept destroying the roof and wooden vault below. The cathedral was completely rebuilt to its original glory after the fire. York Minster is an outstanding cathedral and visitors will be impressed with the fabric. See Figures 50–52.

FIGURE 50. York Minster, England. This view shows the arcade pointed arches, nave ceiling vaulting, and large stained-glass window to the left.

FIGURE 51. York Minster, England. Large, colorful stained-glass window.

FIGURE 52. York Minster, England. A banker mason at his bench carves a stone to the shape of the template leaning against the stone. Maul, hammer, and chisels are on the banker.

⑦ **Wells Cathedral in England**

Several cathedrals were sited on or near holy wells and springs to provide water for the traveling pilgrims and worshippers. Wells Cathedral and the town got its name from the holy wells and springs at the site. The actual starting date of the present Gothic structure is uncertain, but the choir was built c. 1175 and cathedral finished c. 1490. It measures 383 feet long, 135 feet wide, and 160 feet high at the crossing. See Figure 53.

Wells is a wonderful cathedral to visit and has several outstanding features. In the fourteenth century the four massive support piers at the crossing base started to show signs of failure from the tons of stone stacked above it. So the Master Builder designed a scissors arch support system for the four corners to brace and support the crossing. The scissor arches were constructed between 1338 and 1348, and I feel they really added elegance to the nave and crossing. A large crucifix cross with Mary and John on either side is mounted in the upper opening of the scissor. See Figures 54–57.

FIGURE 53 Wells Cathedral, England. Exterior view of the west façade with several carved statues in small recessed niches.

FIGURE 54. Wells Cathedral, England. A view looking east down the nave arcade towards the giant scissor support at the crossing. Note the large crucifix mounted on the scissor vault.

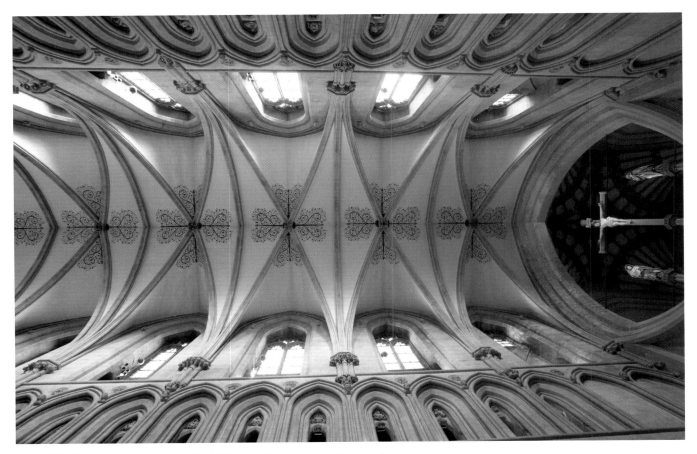

FIGURE 55. Wells Cathedral, England. View looking straight up the arcade walls to the nave ceiling with the scissor arch and crucifix to the right.

The Chapter House at Wells is incredible with a central column supporting an elegant fan-vaulted ceiling. The center fan vault is interwoven with several other vaults springing from columns around the sidewalls. The fan vaults curve upward, resembling branches of palm trees. This is the Master Mason's geometry at its best c. 1306. See Figure 58.

The Lady Chapel is a beautiful room with a geometrical vaulted ceiling and colorful stained-glass windows entirely surrounding the room. The ceiling looks like a white tent drooping down over support ribs in the shape of an eight-pointed star. Inside the center of the star is a painting of Christ. See Figures 59–61.

A famous Master Mason who worked at Wells was William Wynford, appointed in 1365. Wells also has a fourteenth-century astronomical clock that shows the phases of the sun and moon that is interesting to see. There is also a Trasour House or soft plaster floor located above the north porch. Everything about Wells is impressive.

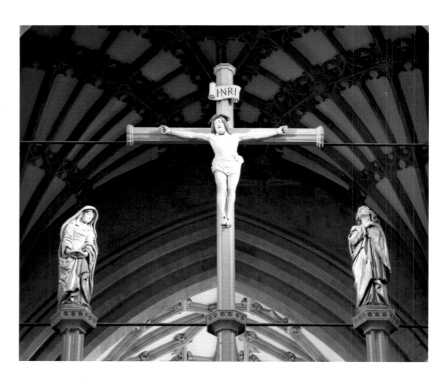

FIGURE 56. Wells Cathedral, England. Close-up image of Christ on the cross with Mary and John on either side in front of the fan vaulting.

FIGURE 57. Wells Cathedral, England. Large five-pane stained-glass window.

FIGURE 58. Wells Cathedral, England. View of the Chapter House
central stone column with vaulted ribs springing upward.

FIGURE 59. Wells Cathedral, England. The Lady Chapel with a beautiful eight-pointed
vaulted ceiling, surrounded by stained-glass windows. This is geometry at its best.

FIGURE 60. Wells Cathedral, England. Photo of some complicated geometry in the column springing and ceiling fan design.

FIGURE 61. Wells Cathedral, England. In this beautiful chapel, the columns resemble trees surrounded by stained-glass windows.

⑧ Exeter Cathedral in England

The current Gothic-style building was started in 1270 and completed in 1350. Some of the previous Romanesque elements were incorporated into the cathedral, which I call a Gothic hybrid. See Figure 62.

I believe the heart and soul of Exeter Cathedral is the fantastic tierceron vaulted ceiling that extends the full length of the nave. This is the product of the Master Builder's vision of heaven on earth at its best. This beautiful vaulted ceiling is so long one can hardly see the eastern window when entering the west door. It extends 315 feet and is the longest unbroken medieval vault in the world, fifteen feet longer than a football field!

The piers of clustered columns with different colored stones along the nave paint a wonderful picture. On top of each nave arcade column, ribs are springing upward forming the vaulted ceiling. They resemble a forest of tree branches growing together at the top. Are the bent trees that form a strong arch in a forest the origin of the pointed "Gothic arch"? I remember going through several woods in England on our last trip, and the arched trees grew right over the carriageway above looking just like the vaulted ceiling at Exeter.

Exeter has more than 400 round bosses located at the apex intersections of the ceiling rib vaults, which cover the ends like a molding. They essentially appear like a **keystone** at the top of the arches. The carved stone bosses are made larger in diameter as they progress farther away to the east so that they do not appear smaller. The Master Builders understood diminishing perspective of certain objects when viewed from different distances. There is a portable magnifying mirror that gives a close-up view of the vault and the colored bosses.

Exeter is one of the finest decorated cathedrals in England. It is worth a stop just to see the impressive nave and vaulted ceiling. It also still has a man-operated windlass wheel in the tower. See Figures 63–68.

FIGURE 62. Exeter Cathedral, England. A look at the Cathedral from the northwest. Children play in the foreground.

FIGURE 63. Exeter Cathedral, England. The nave, clustered columns, arcade arches, and impressive fan-vaulted ceiling early in the morning before the crowds arrive. Notice the uninterrupted ceiling vault the full length of the cathedral.

FIGURE 64. Exeter Cathedral, England. Note the beauty of the central crossing of the nave and transepts, as well as the gigantic organ and vaulting.

FIGURE 65. Exeter Cathedral, England. Close-up view of the fan vault springing up from the wall to the ceiling. See the painted bosses at the intersections.

FIGURE 66. Exeter Cathedral, England. Close-up of a beautiful stained-glass window showcasing Saint Peter with the keys.

FIGURE 67. Exeter Cathedral, England. Colorful seven-pane stained-glass window with fancy tracery at the top.

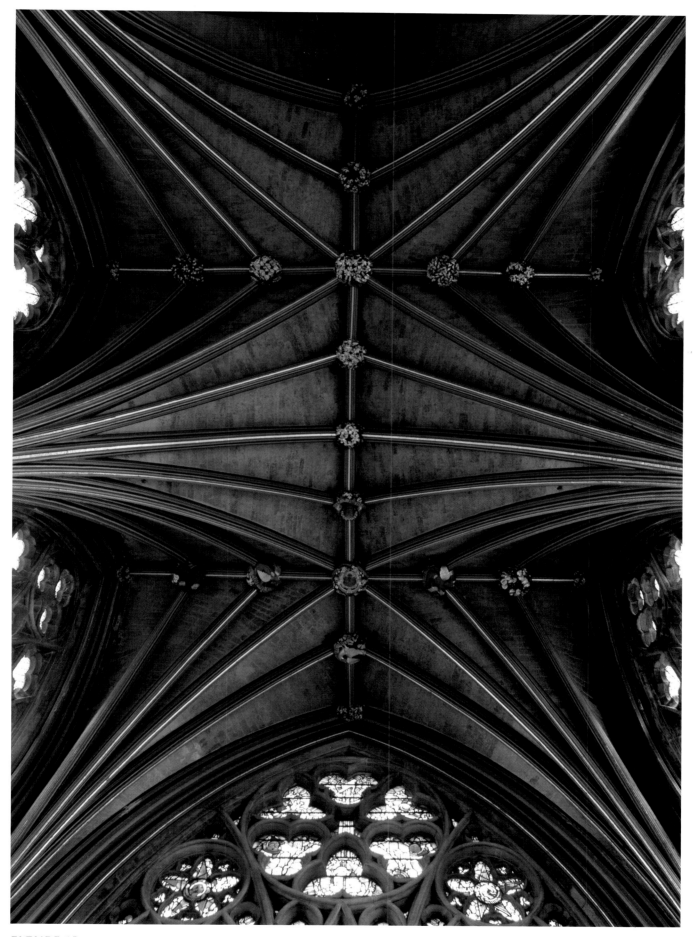

FIGURE 68. Exeter Cathedral, England. Springing vaulted ceiling with stained-glass
windows on all sides. Note the subtle pastel painted ribs and bosses.

⑨ Worcester Cathedral in England

Worcester Cathedral is sited along the Severn River and is classified as a Gothic cathedral. It was started in 1084 and had several rebuilds and additions up until 1504. It has earlier Romanesque features, but is primarily Gothic in style. The total length is 425 feet, with a width of 147 feet and tower height of 196 feet.

The choir has a wonderful painted ceiling supported by different colored columns in the arcade, triforium, and clerestory levels. See Figure 69.

It also has a spectacular and intricately carved marble pulpit in different colors. It is a masterpiece of stone carving and the best of the best. See Figure 70.

Worcester, like many others, was badly damaged during civil wars. And like all the cathedrals around the world, it is a continual battle to provide the necessary maintenance on it. As a result, most cathedrals charge a small fee to enter and others accept donations.

FIGURE 69. Worcester Cathedral, England. Wide-angle view looking up at the arcade, triforium, and clerestory levels, as well as the painted vaulted ceiling. There is a large five-pane stained-glass window on the left.

FIGURE 70. Worcester Cathedral, England. This exquisite marble pulpit shows the high level of craftsmanship of the Freemason who carved it. Eight different colored marbles were used to get the ultimate texture and color contrast. This is a masterpiece completed by a Master Carver.

⑩ **Ely Cathedral in England**

Ely Cathedral was started c. 1083 and had several additions and rebuilds up to 1536. Like many other cathedrals, Ely had a long history of continual building on the same site combining different styles. Though it is classified as a Gothic cathedral, the nave arcade is Romanesque with columns supporting a beautifully painted wooden ceiling.

Ely is a very long cathedral with a total length of 537 feet. Its width is 199 feet and the tower height is 215 feet. Ely Cathedral dominates the city of Ely, hovering above it like a vast steamship with its towers resembling smokestacks. I stopped along the roadside to get a picture of its commanding position over the city. See Figure 71.

The glory of Ely is the huge Gothic octagon-shaped tower and lantern designed and built by Alan of Walsingham. The tower and lantern mounted above the crossing is a masterpiece of medieval architecture and engineering. While the octagon tower is built of stone, the lantern constructed above the tower consists of eight sixty-foot- long wooden timbers supporting the structure. The balance of the lantern is made of glass and lead. Both the lantern and ceiling are spectacular when viewed from the nave floor. See Figures 72 and 73. Ely also has some nice stained-glass windows and a painted nave ceiling. See Figures 74–76.

FIGURE 71. Ely Cathedral, England. The cathedral resembles a large steamship docked at a pier with tall smokestacks.

FIGURE 72. Ely Cathedral, England. Wide-angled view of the octagonal-shaped tower with lantern on top. The lantern is supported by the eight sixty-foot timbers springing from the clustered columns. Massive stained-glass windows surround the lantern. It is a masterpiece of architecture.

FIGURE 73. Ely Cathedral, England. Close-up of the eight-sided lantern with stained-glass windows surrounding it. In the center of the ceiling is a painting of Christ.

FIGURE 74. Ely Cathedral, England. A four-pane stained-glass window featuring several human figure scenes.

FIGURE 75. Ely Cathedral, England. Colorful seven-pane stained-glass window.

FIGURE 76. Ely Cathedral, England. Nave painted ceiling.

⑪ Lichfield Cathedral in England

Lichfield is a Gothic cathedral started in 1195 and essentially completed in 1340. It was constructed out of local red sandstone instead of the typical limestone from which most cathedrals are built. The softer red sandstone does not withstand the elements of wind, rain, freezing, and thawing as well as the limestone does. The west façade entrance especially shows its age. Many of the sculptures on the west entrance had to be replaced.

The exterior is highly decorative and elegant with thousands of sculptures and carvings. It seems that every square foot of the entire building is covered with some kind of decorative carving. Inside, when entering the nave from the west entrance and looking east, the cathedral has a bent axis to the left starting at the intersection of the transept and choir.

The front of the cathedral boasts three towering spires. Lichfield is the only cathedral left in England that has three spires. The central spire is 258 feet tall while the two west entrance spires are 198 feet tall. The towers, known as The Ladies of the Vale, are certainly impressive. See Figures 77–79.

FIGURE 77. Lichfield Cathedral, England. Lichfield has three towering spires and a decorative west façade entrance.

FIGURE 78. Lichfield Cathedral, England. This wide-angle image captures the pointed arches of the arcade, decorated triforium level, Gothic arches of the clerestory level, and the separated bays of the vaulted ceiling. The ceiling looks like a white tent draped over the charcoal side walls.

FIGURE 79. Lichfield Cathedral, England. The beauty of the Chapter House is on display with the vaulting ribs springing from the central column support. It looks like a lily flower with the petals opening. The yellow ceiling contrasts with the brown stone ribs. The entire chapel is surrounded with stained-glass windows.

⑫ Bath Abbey in England

Bath Abbey is a smaller Anglican parish church in Bath, with a long rich history dating back to the Romans. Romanesque churches occupied the site originally and the current Gothic church was built in the early sixteenth century. Bath Abbey was classified as a cathedral at one time in the thirteenth century.

The exterior features some nice looking flying buttresses surrounding the stained-glass windows. I visited Bath to photograph the front entrance façade that has angels walking up and down the ladders to heaven on either side of the central doorway. They represent angels climbing up and down Jacob's ladder. See Figures 80 and 81.

The glory of the inside is the fantastic fan-vaulted ceiling above the nave. The nave arcade and beautiful stained-glass windows are worth a visit. See Figures 82-84.

FIGURE 80. Bath Abbey, England. West façade entrance with angels climbing up and down Jacob's ladder to heaven. There is a large stained-glass window above the door.

FIGURE 81. Bath Abbey, England. Side view of the flying buttresses supporting the upper walls.

FIGURE 82. Bath Abbey, England. Beautiful fan-vaulted side aisle ceiling. Note the American flag displayed on the left.

FIGURE 83. Bath Abbey, England. Note the wonderful fan vaulting on the ceiling of the nave and the large stained-glass window on the west entrance.

FIGURE 84. Bath Abbey, England. Five-pane stained-glass window depicting biblical scenes.

⑬ Beverley Minster in England

Beverley Minster is the largest parish church in England. It is not classified as a cathedral because a bishop is not in charge, but it has all the features of a large English cathedral. The current Gothic structure was started in 1220 and after some 200 years of building it was finally completed in 1420. It was a center of pilgrimage for visitors in the northern part of England. Beverley has an impressive nave arcade, as well as some nice stained-glass windows. See Figures 85 and 86.

Beverley also has a wonderful west entrance façade with twin towers and several decorative carved sculptures. The guide there told me the stonemason Nicholas Hawksmoor did consulting work on the west front of Beverley and was also instrumental in designing the west towers of Westminster Abbey in London. Experts have said that Beverley has one of England's best west façades.

FIGURE 85. Beverley Minster, England. A wide-angle view captures the arcade, triforium, clerestory, and vaulted ceiling bays. The huge stained-glass window is on the right.

FIGURE 86. Beverley Minster, England. This image showcases a gigantic and unusual nine-pane stained-glass window.

FIGURE 87. Beverley Minster, England. An unusually large man-operated windlass wheel crane lifted up stones to construct the cathedral. It is the largest wheel I have ever seen, some sixteen feet in diameter. Notice the man inside the crane walking and raising the large central boss cover.

In the fall of 2010 I visited Beverley Minster and the verger guide gave us an excellent tower tour above the nave ceiling just below the timber roof. There are actual full-sized tree timbers joined together supporting the vaulted ceiling. While high in the bowels of the minster, I had the pleasant surprise of seeing a giant windlass wheel crane about sixteen feet in diameter, the largest of which I had ever seen or heard about. Without any comment or warning, the verger jumped inside the wheel and started walking. The wheel crane gets its power from a man walking inside and turning the axle. As the rope wound around the axle, the large central cap (boss) covering the opening of the nave ceiling crossing was lifted. The 800 pound boss was about seven feet in diameter and the verger lifted it about six feet above the tower floor! The old windlass wheel is still used to bring up maintenance materials to a small shop in the upper tower. There are windlass wheels in several cathedrals around Europe, but in my opinion this one is the biggest and best. This manpower crane was the highlight of my visit to Beverley! See Figures 87 and 88.

A group of mason marks were found on the stones in Beverley and are displayed on a board. See Figure 89.

FIGURE 88. Beverley Minster, England. The central crossing of the nave and transepts, with a large organ on the right. There are four corner cluster column supports holding up the tower.

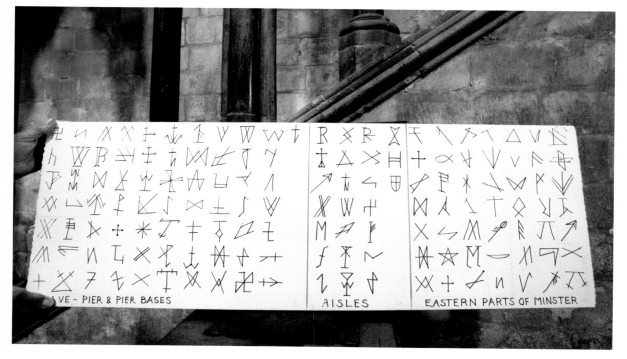

FIGURE 89. Beverley Minster, England. A board illustrates several mason marks found on the stones in the fabric and indicates their locations.

⑭ Westminster Abbey in London, England

Westminster Abbey is owned by the British royal family and is not classed as a cathedral or a parish church. It was granted cathedral status by King Henry VIII in 1540 and then lost its status as a cathedral in 1550. The current abbey structure was rebuilt in the Gothic style during a variety of building phases between 1245 and 1517. A pair of Gothic towers stands in majesty on the west entrance, constructed between 1722 and 1745.

The splendor of Westminster is certainly displayed on the inside of the abbey. An outstanding feature is the magnificent King Henry VII Lady Chapel, built and dedicated to the Blessed Virgin Mary in 1503 and consecrated in 1516. Its carved fan-vaulted ceiling with pendant vaults hanging downward is wonderful. Another feature is the Gothic nave, which has a fan-vaulted ceiling with ribs springing from the side walls up to the center bosses. It is the highest Gothic vaulted ceiling in England at just over 100 feet. Because all interior photography is strictly prohibited, I could not include photographs in this overview, but I highly recommend a visit.

FIGURE 90. Westminster Abbey, London. The west façade entrance highlighted by two Gothic towers. Westminster is the site for most of the coronation ceremonies of the English monarchs, many of the royal weddings, and most of the burials of kings and queens.

FIGURE 91. Westminster Abbey, London. A view of the abbey through a wrought-iron gate in the adjacent covered walkway highlights the graceful and colorful flying buttresses and arches supporting the sidewalls.

Most of the English monarchs have been crowned in Westminster Abbey since 1066. During the coronation ceremony they are seated in the famous St. Edward's Coronation Chair. The oak chair was made some 700 years ago and it housed the 1,000-year-old Stone of Scone under the seat. The Stone of Scone and Coronation Chair have a very long history and connection between England and Scotland. Currently the chair is on display in Westminster Abbey and the Stone of Scone has been removed and is in Scotland, where it resides in Edinburgh Castle.

Not only were most of the English monarchs crowned in Westminster, but most of the kings and queens were also buried there as well, along with royal family members and famous citizens. It has been said there are a few thousand burials in and around Westminster Abbey. See Figures 90 and 91.

⑮ St. Paul's Cathedral in London, England

St. Paul's, a Church of England cathedral, is on Ludgate Hill, the highest point in London. It was designed and built by Sir Christopher Wren from 1675 to 1710. St. Paul's is neither Romanesque nor Gothic, but instead English Baroque style. I included it because it is an internationally known cathedral.

The current St. Paul's Cathedral was rebuilt after the great fire of London in 1660. The new distinctive **dome** mounted on top of a Latin cross was patterned after St. Peter's Basilica in Rome. The dome is 365 feet high.

The highlight of St. Paul's is the magnificent interior including the decorated and painted Roman arches and ceilings, the 259 steps to the Whispering Gallery, the interior dome view, the carved woodwork choir stalls, the high altar and canopy, and various statues, sculptures, and paintings. Unfortunately, interior photography is strictly prohibited at St. Paul's; therefore no photographs will be shared in this overview.

Important royal weddings, funeral services, and celebrations have been conducted at St. Paul's for many years. Sir Christopher Wren's epitaph was inscribed on the nave floor by his son, Christopher Wren Junior. "Reader, if you seek his monument, look around you." See Figure 92.

FIGURE 92. St. Paul's Cathedral, London. West façade entrance with carved stone statues in the foreground. The large dome is hidden behind the west front towers.

⑯ Cologne Cathedral in Germany

Cologne is an outstanding Gothic cathedral started in 1248. After a long hiatus in building activity, it was finally completed in 1880. The cathedral dominates the city and very attractive from a distance, with the two Christian crosses mounted on top of the spires. It must have been a visual magnet for traveling pilgrims. The cathedral is highly decorated on the exterior with intricate carvings on the interior as well, making it an elegant building.

Cologne (Koln) Cathedral is on the Rhine River and is one of the largest cathedrals in the world. It is 474 feet long with a transept 283 feet wide. The vaulted nave ceiling is 142 feet above the floor. Birds could fly comfortably inside the nave and would not feel confined until they got hungry.

Tall rows of clustered columns that hold up the high vaulted ceiling can be seen inside the entrance. These clustered pier supports are located down through the nave on either side. The pier columns are exceptionally large at Cologne to support the heavy stone twin towers rising above them.

The mammoth twin towers soaring 515 feet on the west entrance are the most dominant feature of the cathedral. A set of the original plans for the west twin towers was discovered in the nineteenth century. These plans were followed and construction was completed in 1880. It is quite an experience to walk up the 500 steps in the tower and look over the Rhine River and city of Cologne. The twin towers were used during World War II as landmarks for the pilots. The cathedral was damaged during the war.

The area of the west façade entrance is the world's largest, measuring 75,357 square feet! Cologne also boasts the largest and heaviest free-swinging, operating cast bell in the world. It is named St. Peter's Bell. Cast in 1923, it weighs over twenty-four tons (48,000 pounds) and measures 10.56 feet in diameter! See Figures 93-100.

FIGURE 93. Cologne Cathedral, Germany. The elegant twin tower spires dominate the city.

FIGURE 94. Cologne Cathedral, Germany. Close-up of the spire showing the decorative carvings mounted on the ribs, as seen through the lacy opening of the other spire.

FIGURE 95. Cologne Cathedral, Germany. Bird's-eye-view from inside one of the twin spires looking down onto the roof, flèche spire, and flying buttresses below. It captures a view of the Rhine River and city.

FIGURE 96. Cologne Cathedral, Germany. View of the city and river from the cathedral spire.

FIGURE 97. Cologne Cathedral, Germany. Looking downward into the city from the tall cathedral tower.

FIGURE 98. Cologne Cathedral, Germany. View of the central crossing of the nave and transepts including the ceiling vaulting, nave wall, large organ, and stained-glass windows. This angle gives some perspective on the cathedral's size.

FIGURE 99. Cologne Cathedral, Germany. Upward view taken through the columns on the cathedral's eastern end. Note the painted arcade arches, triforium level, and clerestory level with stained-glass windows. The vaulted ceiling ribs rest on the capitals of the columns.

FIGURE 100. Cologne Cathedral, Germany. A large and beautiful six-pane stained-glass window with biblical scenes.

⑰ Ulm Minster in Germany

The foundation stone for Ulm Minster, a Gothic structure, was laid in 1377. The minster has the legitimate bragging rights of having the tallest spire of any church or cathedral in the world. The west façade steeple was built 530 feet tall. To put the height of the steeple into perspective, it is one tenth of a mile high! See Figures 101 and 102.

The Master Builder Matthaus Boblinger, c. 1474, made a parchment drawing of the monumental west façade steeple and spire, but it was not built at the time. Construction started in 1817 and was completed in 1890 using the original parchment drawing. I maintain that the Master Builders in the different countries competed to see who could design and build the tallest stone tower and spire in the world. The German stonemasons won the prize in my opinion with their open spire design.

FIGURE 101. Ulm Minster, Germany. View looking straight up the façade entrance of the tallest cathedral in the world: 530 feet.

FIGURE 102. Ulm Minster, Germany. Wooden scale model of Ulm illustrating the height of the front tower above the flying buttresses.

It is possible to take a tower tour at some of the cathedrals and walk up inside the steeple, around the narrow aisles, and then up on top of the ceiling below the roof. I call these tours "huff and puff tours" because they can be a physical challenge, but they are well worth the effort and time. I remember climbing the steps of Ulm in 1982 and was about a third of the way up when three young teenagers came jogging up behind me and in German told me in so many words, "Get out of the way you old codger and let us by." I obliged. Well, when I got three quarters of the way up the tower they were sitting on the steps, red faced and resting. I said to them in English "Are you young pups out of gas? Get out of my way so this old codger can get by you!"

Ulm became a German Lutheran church after the Reformation with a footprint of 405 feet long by 160 feet wide. Several famous Master Builders and Master Stonemasons worked on it over the years including Michael, Heinrich ll, Heinrich lll Parler, Ulrich of Ensingen, his son and grandson, and Matthaus Boblinger. It also has a windlass wheel housed in the tower area. Ulm Minster dominates the city and countryside around it for miles. See Figures 103–108.

FIGURE 103. Ulm Minster, Germany. Carved gargoyle sticking out from the cathedral wall, seen from the tower spire overlooking the city.

FIGURE 104. Ulm Minster, Germany. A look down on the orange tile roof and flying buttress ribs spanning from the nave walls to the buttresses.

FIGURE 105. Ulm Minster, Germany. Upward view of the colorful stained-glass windows and ribs on the fan-vaulted ceiling.

FIGURE 106. Ulm Minster, Germany. Wide-angle view of nave ceiling with rib vaulting and arcade side walls. The windows at the top allow light into the nave.

FIGURE 108. Ulm Minster, Germany. A look through the organ pipes and columns toward the colorful stained-glass window.

FIGURE 107. Ulm Minster, Germany. Beautiful star-vaulted ceiling and stained-glass windows surrounding the east end.

⑱ Freiburg Minster in Germany

Freiburg Minster was founded in 1200; several Gothic style additions commenced with the nave in 1235. The beautiful Gothic tower and spire was built between 1280 and 1330. The minster combines both the Romanesque and Gothic styles of architecture.

The outstanding feature of Freiburg is the wonderful open-air spire built by the German steinmetzen (stonemasons). Designing, carving, and constructing the steeple became a complicated and challenging project. Each of the stones had to be dressed on a taper vertically, carved inside and out on a round circular form. Then each succeeding stone layer going upward had to be carved a bit smaller, but with the same design to get the smooth lacy tapered cone. The spire is geometry and stonemasonry at its best. See Figures 109–112.

FIGURE 109. Freiburg Cathedral, Germany. This angled view of the tower and decorative spire showcases the light rose stone.

FIGURE 110. Freiburg Cathedral, Germany. View from the tower spire looking down on the orange tile roof and flying buttress ribs. Note the twin towers overlooking the city.

FIGURE 111. Freiburg Cathedral, Germany. A look up into the stone lace spire, taken from the inside.

FIGURE 112. Freiburg Cathedral, Germany. A close-up of the wooden windlass wheel crane used to hoist the stones up for construction.

⑲ Regensburg Cathedral in Germany

Regensburg is a Catholic cathedral dedicated to Saint Peter on the Danube River in southern Bavaria. After a fire, the brand new Gothic style cathedral was built adjacent to the old one. It was founded in 1273, with the choir completed in 1320. The work continued for centuries and the cathedral was finally completed in 1872, some 600 years later. The twin spires mounted above the elegant towers were not completed until 1869, many years after the founding. See Figures 113–118.

The high altar in the east is an outstanding centerpiece of craftsmanship. It is crafted out of silver and is attractive and detailed. The silversmiths created masterpieces of a crucifix, Mary, Joseph, Peter, Paul, a tabernacle, and six silver candlesticks. Regensburg also has some outstanding thirteenth- and fourteenth-century stained-glass windows in the three level fabric walls.

Mathes Roriczer served as the Master Mason architect at Regensburg from 1477 to 1495. Mathes printed the German booklets describing the design methods of building cathedral **pinnacles** and gablets in 1486. The Roriczer family of cathedral architects—Wenzel, Conrad, Mathes, and Wolfgang—worked on and off at Regensburg Cathedral from 1415 to 1502.

Two sources refer to an important meeting the masons held at the Regensburg Cathedral Lodge site in 1459. At the meeting, the masons drafted an Ordinance (Ordnung), that created a Brotherhood (Bruderschaft) of masons who agreed to uphold the Articles and Points (Artikels und Punktes) of the Ordinance. I believe these Articles and Points were no doubt patterned after the early English *Old Charges*. (See chapter 8.)

FIGURE 113. Regensburg Cathedral, Germany. Exterior view taken from the rear with the open stone spire on the upper left.

FIGURE 114. Regensburg Cathedral, Germany. Large nine-pane stained-glass window.

FIGURE 115. Regensburg Cathedral, Germany. Colorful stained-glass window framed in a Gothic pointed arch.

FIGURE 116. Regensburg Cathedral, Germany. Decorative silver set with stained-glass windows in background.

FIGURE 117. Regensburg Cathedral, Germany. Three bays of stained-glass windows at two levels.

FIGURE 118. Regensburg Cathedral, Germany. View looking up at the transept crossing ceiling.

⑳ St. Vitus Cathedral in Prague, Czech Republic

St. Vitus is a Catholic cathedral with a foundation stone date of 1344. The Gothic cathedral had several expansions added over the centuries and was completed in 1899.

A Frenchman named Matthias of Arras served as the first Master Builder of the new cathedral until his death in 1352. Peter Parler then took over as Master Builder in 1356 when he was only twenty-three years old. He was the most famous son of the Heinrich Parler family of Master Builders. Heinrich was the father and founder of the famous German family of traveling stonemasons. The Parler family designed and worked on many cathedrals scattered around Europe. Peter was responsible for designing the famous Charles Bridge and its towers, as well as some of the new city of Prague.

Peter Parler designed a new double diagonal cross rib system that spanned the entire choir ceiling vault of St. Vitus. I saw photographs of it in a booklet several years ago and for over thirty years wanted to see Brother Parler's masterpiece of stonemasonry in the flesh. The day we visited the cathedral it was closed for some special visitors program, and we were not able to get inside. We finally took a tower tour on top of the cathedral and got some super views and photographs of the roof and city below. See Figures 119–123.

FIGURE 119. St. Vitus Cathedral. Prague, Czech Republic.
A view of the south side showing the central tower and twin towers on the left.

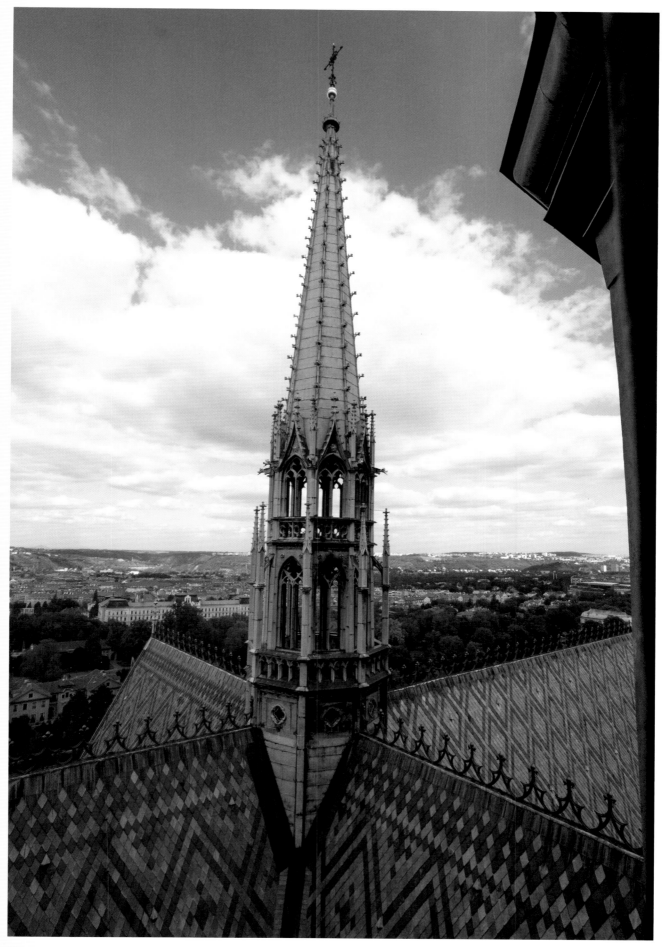

FIGURE 120. St. Vitus Cathedral. Prague, Czech Republic. Photo taken from the tower
of the flèche spire mounted on top of the central crossing overlooking the city.

FIGURE 121. St. Vitus Cathedral. Prague, Czech Republic. A view from the tower of the twin towers and roof.

FIGURE 122. St. Vitus Cathedral. Prague, Czech Republic.
Bird's-eye view of the courtyard and surrounding city from the tower.

FIGURE 123. St. Vitus Cathedral. Prague, Czech Republic.
The cathedral at night, as seen from the famous Charles Bridge.

㉑ St. Stephen's Cathedral in Vienna, Austria

St. Stephen's is primarily a Gothic cathedral with some Romanesque features remaining. The foundation stone was laid in 1359 for the first Gothic addition and construction continued until 1511 when most major building operations ceased. St. Stephen's is a Roman Catholic cathedral.

The most dominant feature of St. Stephen's is the gigantic south tower steeple that overpowers the city's landscape and can be seen for miles. It has been noted that Wenzel Parler, one of the famous Parler brothers, worked on the steeple. Hans of Prachatitz finished the steeple project in 1433. The beautiful lacy looking spire is 448 feet tall. The multicolored diamond-shaped tile roof is very attractive and an eye catcher from anywhere in the city. See Figures 124–127.

On the main entrance Christ is carved and sitting in majesty inside the Mandorla (fish-shaped) stone frame inviting pilgrims into His house. Christ is carved inside the Mandorla on several cathedral entrances around the world.

The interior of St. Stephen's is quite ornate and beautiful. There is a fabulous Gothic pulpit, exquisitely carved of sandstone. There is also a curved staircase going up to the pulpit, inside of which the bishop would have stood. Partially hidden underneath the pulpit and staircase is a wonderful self-portrait of the Master Stonemason who carved the pulpit. He is looking out of a framed window holding a compass that identifies him as a Master Builder in charge. He is also wearing a hat, vest, and gown. On top of the window frame there is a small shield with two incised marks carved on it. I believe this is his personal mason mark or signature showing that he had completed the work above, just as a painter would have signed his name on a painting. He was a skilled craftsman and proud of his work, so he left his self-portrait and mark as a permanent record of his labor. See Figure 128.

FIGURE 124. St. Stephen's Cathedral. Vienna, Austria. The tall tower and spire in front of the cathedral.

FIGURE 125. St. Stephen's Cathedral. Vienna, Austria. Close-up of the roof tiles with one of the twin spires on right.

FIGURE 126. St. Stephen's Cathedral. Vienna, Austria. View of the bright colors of the zigzag roof tile design with the tower spire beyond.

FIGURE 127. St. Stephen's Cathedral. Vienna, Austria. Stained-glass window with tracery.

FIGURE 128. St. Stephen's Cathedral. Vienna, Austria. Detailed Gothic pulpit carving including a self-portrait by Anton Pilgram holding a compass in his hand, c. 1500.

On my first visit to St. Stephen's in 1969 I was told that Anton Pilgram carved the pulpit and a (1990) dated booklet and photo from the site confirmed it: "Pulpit by Anton Pilgram, around 1500, view from the south-east" (Saliger 1990, 34). On my last visit to St. Stephen's in September of 2011, I purchased a book written by Reinhard Gruber who had a different view: "According to the latest findings, the work is probably not by Anton Pilgram after all" (Gruber 2011, 43). There was no explanation as to why he thought another stonemason might have done the carving.

Personally I believe that Anton Pilgram did carve the pulpit because he used the same self-portrait signature theme below another carving of the organ chancel in the cathedral. He completed this carving with an inscription below it dated 1513. He is again leaning out of a window holding the square and compasses and dressed like a Master Builder with a hat, vest, and gown. The carving has some pigment color added to it that makes it lifelike. I maintain the pulpit was carved when he was a younger man and the organ chancel carving was done when he was older. Both portraits look like the same man with long hair, but the latter looks older. With

some further research at the cathedral one may be able to find a drawing or stonework that has Anton Pilgram's mason mark on it. The mason mark could then be compared to the one above the portrait to see if there is a match. See Figure 129.

St. Stephen's operative mason's lodge was very influential in Europe at the time the cathedral was being built. In a lodge conference held in Regensburg in 1459, the Lodge of Vienna was recognized as the leading workshop of southeast central Europe. At this time the late Gothic building phase in St. Stephen's was probably almost completed, with the nave vaulted and the interior finished. (Saliger 1990, p. 3).

The Cathedral Lodge of Vienna at St. Stephen's has the world's largest collection of cathedral parchment drawings. "The cultural and historical significance of Vienna also have a bearing on the importance of the cathedral. Thus it is no mere chance that by far the largest collection of medieval plans in existence—a total of 298 drafts—has survived in the Cathedral Lodge of Vienna" (Saliger 1990, 45). It is my understanding that these delicate parchment drawings are not currently available to the public.

FIGURE 129. St. Stephen's Cathedral. Vienna, Austria. Self-portrait carving of Anton Pilgram, Master Mason, below the organ bracket, c. 1513.

㉒ Chartres Cathedral in France

Chartres has been a place of pilgrimage for centuries and still attracts thousands of visitors from all over the world. It is a famous Catholic cathedral with a long history of several churches that once stood on the same site. In 1194 there was a terrible fire in the old Romanesque cathedral, and all that was saved was the western end and crypt. That same year the builders started construction on a new Gothic cathedral and combined it with the earlier Romanesque remains. The current Gothic cathedral was blended into the Romanesque west tower. It was consecrated in 1260. On the **tympanum** (the carved decorated arch above the entrance door), "Christ in Majesty" is carved in stone inside the **Vesica Pices** or **Mandorla** (fish-shaped) symbol. The shape of a Vesica Pices is made by drawing two intersecting circles overlapping each other. On the right-hand doorway the "seven liberal arts and sciences" are carved in the Gothic pointed archway.

The two contrasting tower spires on the west façade entrance are the most dominant exterior feature. One is a plain pyramid-shaped spire 339 feet tall, and the other is a highly decorated Gothic spire 371 feet tall. See Figure 130.

Another prominent feature is the complex double flying buttress system surrounding and supporting the outside cathedral walls. Some of the flying buttresses are half-wheel-shaped arches with spokes giving additional support to the walls.

The inside of the cathedral is splendid with the largest collection of beautiful medieval stained-glass windows in the world. Chartres is famous for these windows, especially the three exceptionally large rose windows in the transepts and east. See Figures 131–137.

FIGURE 130. Chartres Cathedral. Chartres, France. West entrance façade with two quite different tower spires and a giant rose window wheel.

FIGURE 131. Chartres Cathedral. Chartres, France. South transept rose and lancet windows. This spectacular set of stained-glass windows is the best of the best in quality and craftsmanship.

FIGURE 132. Chartres Cathedral. Chartres, France. North transept rose and lancet windows. This set of stained-glass windows is also outstanding.

There is a large forty-foot-diameter stone labyrinth inlaid on the nave floor. One can walk around the circles or make the journey on one's knees until the sacred center is reached. The original use and symbolism has been lost for more than 500 years, though it has been said that walking this path is symbolic of walking the path to Jerusalem. In *The Rise of the Gothic*, William Anderson calls the labyrinth the Jerusalem: "The Chartres Labyrinth was also called the Jerusalem because pilgrims would carry out a figural journey to the Holy Land by following the pattern of its maze on their knees" (Anderson 1988, 156). In *Chartres Cathedral*,

Malcolm Miller refers to the labyrinth in the same way: "Christian labyrinths, however, signify that death is not the end, but the door through which the Heavenly Jerusalem may be entered" (Miller 2010, 18). This explanation seems logical to me. On the path of life, if one walks uprightly before God and man, hopefully one will reach that New Heavenly Jerusalem to enjoy life eternally. See Figure 136.

Several labyrinths were constructed on the cathedrals in France, generally in the twelfth century. Chartres, Amiens, Reims, and Sens are a few examples. Many of them were removed during the late eighteenth century.

FIGURE 133. Chartres Cathedral. Chartres, France. This image illustrates the Sun of God shining through the stained-glass windows of a Gothic cathedral wall. The edge of the giant rose window is on the left.

FIGURE 134. Chartres Cathedral. Chartres, France. Stained-glass windows showing the tools for and process of making wine.

FIGURE 135. Chartres Cathedral. Chartres, France. An angular view looking up at the crossing with the arcade, triforium, and clerestory levels shown. Note the stained-glass windows in the upper level.

FIGURE 136. Chartres Cathedral. Chartres, France. Large medieval labyrinth inlaid in the stone floor representing the path to Jerusalem.

FIGURE 137. Chartres Cathedral. Chartres, France. Very attractive chapel with stained-glass windows and wrought-iron gate and cross in foreground.

㉓ Metz Cathedral in France

The old Romanesque Metz Cathedral was started in 965 and dedicated in 1040. Like many of the other cathedrals, it had several Gothic style additions over the centuries. The current Gothic structure was started in 1220 and basically completed in 1520. Most of the Romanesque features were torn down and the resulting structure is a mixture of both styles. St. Stephen's is a Catholic cathedral in the Diocese of Metz.

The prominent feature of Metz Cathedral is the extensive number of beautiful stained-glass windows that surround the fabric. Metz boasts the largest expanse of stained-glass windows of any cathedral in the world, and the area of stained-glass walls is almost incomprehensible: 70,000 square feet of glass, or more than 1.5 acres! From inside one can see many spectacular views of the colored glass, combined with the tall vaulted ceilings and pointed Gothic arches. Metz might not be the most well-known cathedral in Europe, but it can hold its own among the best in the stained-glass window category. Metz has been nicknamed the Good Lord's Lantern. See Figures 138-142.

The nave of Metz is exceptionally high, measuring 136 feet, only to be outdone by Amiens and Beauvais in France. The stone used to construct Metz was a nice yellow, cream colored limestone. Today a great deal of the stone appears to be like new, probably from the latest cleaning process done on the stone surfaces.

FIGURE 138. Metz Cathedral. Metz, France. Exterior view of Metz showing some of the scaffolding around the tower used for rebuilding and maintenance.

FIGURE 139. Metz Cathedral. Metz, France. The large rose and lancet stained-glass windows mounted in elaborate stone tracery frames.

FIGURE 140. Metz Cathedral. Metz, France. View looking up at the arcade, triforium, clerestory, and ceiling vaulting of the eastern nave end. Note the crossing and stained-glass windows on the right.

FIGURE 141. Metz Cathedral. Metz, France. Wide-angle view of the central crossing and four support piers. The nave and eastern end walls are covered with stained-glass windows.

FIGURE 142. Metz Cathedral. Metz, France. Close-up view of the colorful stained-glass windows surrounding the eastern apse end of the cathedral.

㉔ Reims Cathedral in France

Reims is a Gothic cathedral with a foundation stone date of 1211 and a completion date of 1311. Reims Cathedral is a Catholic cathedral where the kings of France were once crowned. The outstanding west entrance façade is adorned with highly decorated statues, the King's Gallery, pointed arches and pinnacles and is topped off with the beautiful rose window above the portal entrance.

The other dominant feature of the exterior is the skeletal-looking flying buttresses surrounding the nave and apse. They are literally tons of stone arches spanning and supporting the structure. It is interesting to note that Villard de Honnecourt, Master Builder from France, made a drawing of the flying buttresses of Reims in his travel journal sketchbook c. 1225–50. See Figure 225.

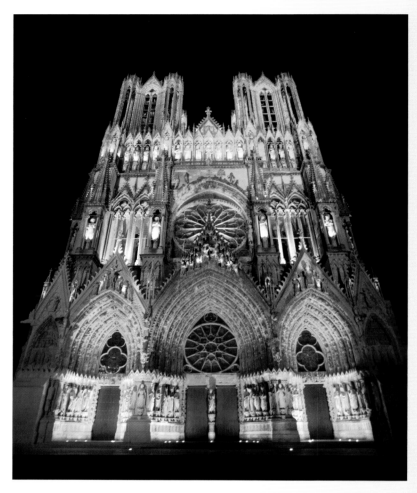

FIGURE 143. Reims Cathedral. Reims, France. The spectacular west façade entrance at night. Note the full-size statues surrounding the doors, detailed carvings inside the three pointed tympanum arches, rose windows, row of statues above the top rose, and crowning twin towers on top.

FIGURE 144. Reims Cathedral. Reims, France. Close-up view of the colorful stained-glass rose window on the inside entrance doors. Thousands of detailed pieces of colored glass make up the pictures.

FIGURE 146. Reims Cathedral. Reims, France. Close-up view of the south transept rose window illustrating the cathedral wheel design in the tracery.

FIGURE 145. Reims Cathedral. Reims, France. This image captures the beautiful colors of the rose window and stained-glass lancet windows below. See the elaborate and detailed stone tracery frames holding the glass.

FIGURE 147. Reims Cathedral. Reims, France. Lower rose window in the west façade entrance framed inside a Gothic pointed arch.

FIGURE 148. Reims Cathedral. Reims, France. Upward view of stained-glass windows in the clerestory level and vaulted ceiling.

The brilliance of the inside is the beautiful stained-glass and rose windows that encircle the interior walls. The double rose windows above the west entrance and surrounded by recessed stone statues are the focal point. Other outstanding stained-glass windows are the rose and lancet windows in the two transepts and above the choir. See Figures 143–148.

Upon entering the cathedral and looking east down the nave, there is a wonderful view of the vaulted ceiling, measuring 125 feet high. Reims is a large cathedral measuring 488 feet long by 200 feet wide. The massive Gothic towers on the west façade entrance are 265 feet tall.

In the early thirteenth century, the Master Masons at Reims had an octagonal-shaped labyrinth pathway built into the nave floor. It had the names of four Master Builders who succeeded one another at Reims, namely Jean de Orbais, Jean le Loup, Gaucher de Reims, and Bernard de Soissons. As the original purpose and meaning of the labyrinth was lost, the clergy had it removed from Reims in 1779.

FIGURE 149. Reims Cathedral. Reims, France. Mounted on a wall is the engraved tombstone cover of Master Builder Hugh Libergier. mounted on the wall.

Hugh Libergier, a Master Builder, has his engraved tombstone cover mounted on the wall in the north transept of Reims. His engraved image illustrates his important status in the church and community. He is dressed in a fine cape, robe, and cap, and he is holding a miniature model of a cathedral in one hand. The symbolic tools of his profession are also shown, namely the compasses, square, and measuring stick. On top of the tombstone there are angels mounted on a vaulted roof supported by two columns on either side. This beautifully engraved tombstone cover conveys the esteem, respect, and influence of the Master Builder in his community of peers. See Figure 149.

㉕ **Amiens Cathedral in France**

Amiens Cathedral is the largest Gothic cathedral in France and has been known as one of the purist Gothic cathedrals in the world. It is Roman Catholic with a foundation stone date of 1220. It was completed c. 1270. Amiens is 476 feet long and 230 feet wide, with a spire height of 370 feet.

The west façade entrance is outstanding with the highly decorated main portal arch containing several sculpted stone figures. One of the stone carvings on the left is a tall headless statue holding his own head in his hands. Each carving illustrates a story in the Bible. See Figures 150 and 151.

A special feature of Amiens is the 138-foot-tall beautiful stone vaulted ceiling, the tallest vault in a completed cathedral in France. Beauvais in France has the tallest vault in the world at 157 feet, but the cathedral was never completed. One wonders how a vault could be built so high with such slender columns supporting it.

FIGURE 150. Amiens Cathedral. Amiens, France. View of the west façade entrance illustrating the gigantic tympanum arch with detailed carvings.

FIGURE 151. Amiens Cathedral. Amiens, France. Upward view of the side entrance with refurbished stone and flying buttresses shown.

FIGURE 152. Amiens Cathedral. Amiens, France. Upward view of the vaulted ceiling of the south transept, with crossing on the left and stained-glass rose window on the right.

FIGURE 153. Amiens Cathedral. Amiens, France. Nave vaulted ceiling, three levels of walls, and a rose window on the western end.

FIGURE 154. Amiens Cathedral. Amiens, France. The beautiful rose window in the south transept. Note the decorative stone tracery frame holding the stained glass.

The stained-glass windows are beautiful and cover about half the height of the arcade walls to allow in more sunshine. Amiens has an outstanding collection of elaborately carved wood choir stalls and **misericord** seats, on which the monks leaned during the long services. It has been said they are the finest in Europe. There are many more detailed wooden carvings throughout the cathedral. A circular stone labyrinth path was installed in the nave floor in 1288. There is also an elaborate system of flying buttresses surrounding the entire fabric. See Figures 152–156.

FIGURE 155. Amiens Cathedral. Amiens, France. Note the intricate
designs in the north transept rose window.

FIGURE 156. Amiens Cathedral, Amiens, France. This pulpit is a masterpiece of stonemasonry. It illustrates the quality and craftsmanship of the Master Stonemason at its best. Note the detailed and delicate stone carvings on the bottom, center, and top.

㉖ Beauvais Cathedral in France

Beauvais Cathedral is a Roman Catholic cathedral in the northern part of France. This Gothic cathedral consists of an apse, choir, and transepts, but the long nave was never built onto the transepts, nor was the balance of the cathedral completed, as the tower collapsed.

The bishop's plan was to build the tallest and most beautiful Gothic cathedral in the world. Work was started on the choir and apse in 1225 and completed in 1284, with a vaulted ceiling measuring 157 feet high, the tallest in the world. Shortly after its completion, due to an inadequate flying buttress pier, a few of the flying buttresses, vaulting, and part of the ceiling collapsed. It took about forty years to rebuild the apse and choir, but further construction was interrupted due to wars. The transepts were finally started in 1500 and completed in 1548.

The bishop wanted to construct a new spire taller than the dome being built at St. Peter's in Rome. The spire, with a cross on the top, was completed in 1569 at 492 feet tall, the tallest in Europe. But in 1573, shortly after the congregation had left the cathedral, the support columns gave way and the spire came crashing down onto the choir in a pile of rubble. The choir was rebuilt one more time and services are currently conducted in the choir and transepts only.

My wife and I visited Beauvais Cathedral in 1989, and as we were walking around inside, it got very quiet. We did not see anyone around us. I remember someone earlier making an announcement in French, but we did not know what he was saying. We finally thought we better leave, but upon finding the entrance door, we found it locked! The lights went down, and we started to panic. I began to holler and look for someone to let us out. Finally a man came to our rescue and escorted us out of a small side door. He was not happy with us, gave us a few words of wisdom in French, and got on his bicycle and rode away. I believe he was late for dinner! The moral of the story is to get a translator and listen to announcements when in a cathedral! We later thought it would have been a real problem spending the night in a dark cathedral, sleeping on a hard church pew with a church mouse! See Figure 157.

FIGURE 157. Beauvais Cathedral. Beauvais, France. Exterior view of flying buttresses.

㉗ **Strasbourg Cathedral in France**

In September of 2011 I visited Strasbourg Cathedral for a second time, as it is one of my overall favorites. I spent a few hours with a museum staff member who was a gracious host, very knowledgeable, and helpful in answering questions about the cathedral.

Strasbourg Cathedral is a Roman Catholic cathedral on the river between Germany and France. It has a nice blend of French and German architectural elements and identity. As a result of several fires in an earlier cathedral, a new Romanesque cathedral was built on the site in 1176.

FIGURE 158. Strasbourg Cathedral. Strasbourg, France. This view shows the front façade entrance and single tower and spire built on the north side. A second tower on the south side was never built. Note the close proximity of the medieval buildings (upper left) to the cathedral.

But after some fifty years of building in the Romanesque style, the governing body decided to convert the building over to the new Gothic architectural style. The current Gothic cathedral therefore has some earlier Romanesque portions still remaining. Nevertheless, Strasbourg is an outstanding example of Gothic architecture with several beautiful stained-glass windows mounted in the walls.

The beautiful open lace stone spire was finally built on the north tower in 1439, essentially completing the cathedral. Though parchment drawings were made for two towers, only the north one was built. The cathedral, having only one tower, does not appear to be symmetrical in shape, but it is stunning and different. See Figures 158–160.

Strasbourg Cathedral has the second largest collection of medieval parchment drawings of cathedrals in the world. A museum staff member showed me the largest drawing in the collection, which measures approximately thirteen feet high by three feet wide. Seeing this large detailed drawing of the west façade entrance in the flesh was the highlight of my European tour. It was an ink drawing made on parchment c. 1360–1370, some 650 years ago. I was told that Hans Hammer's mason mark was placed on the drawing. The drawing is in the museum adjacent to the cathedral. The museum is an outstanding one, housing many artifacts from the old lodge along with many of the original statues and sculptures that were removed from the fabric. See Figures 161 and 162.

FIGURE 159. Strasbourg Cathedral. Strasbourg, France. Close-up view of the Gothic tympanum displaying dozens of detailed biblical stone carvings. The light pink sculptures are miniature stonemason masterpieces. See the detailed faces of the figures above the lintel.

FIGURE 160. Strasbourg Cathedral. Strasbourg, France. Upward view
of the west façade entrance with the large rose window visible above.

FIGURE 161. Strasbourg Cathedral. Strasbourg, France. Large parchment ink drawing of the west façade entrance, c. 1360–1370. This drawing was made by gluing five animal skins together to get the desired height. The details of the drawing, made some 650 years ago, are striking. *Photo courtesy of and reprinted with permission by Musée de l'OEuvre Notre-Dame, Strasbourg, France.*

FIGURE 162. Strasbourg Cathedral. Strasbourg, France. A detail of the large parchment drawing, c. 1360–1370, showing the rose window section. Note the pinprick holes in the center of the circles made by the compass needle. *Photo courtesy of and reprinted with permission by Musée de l'Oeuvre Notre-Dame, Strasbourg, France.*

The cathedral is built out of rose-colored sandstone which is a softer stone than limestone and does not stand up to weathering as well. Several of the original statues and sculptures that were on the exterior of the fabric have been replaced with copies, and the weathered originals were then placed in the adjacent museum.

The west façade entrance is an impressive view, covered with hundreds of intricately carved statues and decorations on the three portal entrances. The giant rose window tracery and carvings are finally topped off with the majestic laced spire. After Strasbourg Cathedral was built, the town literally grew up closely around it, to the point that now most of the buildings are just a short stone's throw away. The cathedral would be even more impressive if the medieval buildings were farther away. Nevertheless, it has dominated the town and landscape surrounding it since 1439.

The interior of the cathedral is very impressive with stained-glass windows, vaulted ceilings, and a large organ hanging on the wall. See Figures 163–166.

Another highlight of the cathedral is the huge west rose window when seen from the inside. The tracery is gracefully designed and has a stunning yellow-green stained-glass window mounted in it. See Figure 167.

There were a few outstanding Master Builders who contributed to the construction of Strasbourg. Erwin von Steinbach was a major player in the design of the west façade entrance c. 1277–1318. Ulrich Ensingen began the eight-sided tower, while Johannes (Jean) Hultz took over when he passed away and finished the beautiful tapered spire 461 feet high.

FIGURE 163. Strasbourg Cathedral. Strasbourg, France. This view illustrates the beautiful stained-glass windows on the arcade, triforium, and clerestory levels. The organ is mounted on the left.

FIGURE 164. Strasbourg Cathedral. Strasbourg, France. Elaborate ceiling design of the side aisle and lancet windows in the wall.

FIGURE 165. Strasbourg Cathedral. Strasbourg, France. This view looks west at the gigantic rose window and lancets below. Note the elaborately carved and painted organ hanging on the wall to the right. The detailed carved wooden case dates from 1385.

FIGURE 166. Strasbourg Cathedral. Strasbourg, France. View of one of the colorful stained-glass windows mounted in the wall.

FIGURE 167. Strasbourg Cathedral. Strasbourg, France. The gorgeous west façade rose window. The stunning color combinations and details make it one of my favorite rose windows.

㉘ Notre Dame Cathedral in Paris, France

Notre Dame in Paris is one of the most famous and recognizable Gothic cathedrals in the world. It is on a small island in the middle of the Seine River. It is a Catholic cathedral with a foundation stone date of 1163 and a completion date of 1345. Notre Dame has been a Christian site since the fourth century AD and continues to be the center of the Catholic religion in Paris to this day. It also has the distinction of being the most popular tourist attraction in Paris.

Notre Dame was one of the first major Gothic cathedrals in France and has been accepted as one of the models of Gothic architecture that other French cathedrals were patterned after. The bishop of Paris, Maurice de Sully, decided to build the new cathedral in 1163 and hired the Master Builder for the project.

The most impressive and recognizable feature of Notre Dame is the massive and graceful flying buttresses that surround the exterior nave and apse. Notre Dame was one of the first cathedrals in France to have them. Probably the best view of the cathedral is from the southeast, across the Seine, which showcases the flying buttresses. In fact, I have a beautiful watercolor painting of Notre Dame Cathedral

from that angle painted by a friend, Marius Girard, in 1988. Marius is one of the Old Master watercolor painters who painted for years in the public square in Montmartre in Paris.

Another important feature of the cathedral is the colossal west façade entrance with two immense towers reaching 223 feet high. It is interesting to note that the north tower was built somewhat wider than the south tower. I do not know the reason for this.

Notre Dame is well known and remarkable, but I have always felt that the cathedral's west façade was missing the crowning tall spires. Most likely it was a decision made by the Master Builder or a lack of funding that prevented their construction. A nice decorative spire, though, was added above the central crossing during the nineteenth century.

The transept arms of Notre Dame do not stick out past the body or nave walls of the cathedral, as most other Latin cross floor plans do. The cathedral has some very impressive stained-glass rose windows in the west and transept ends. Notre Dame Cathedral has dominated the center of Paris and surrounding landscape for over 800 years! See Figures 168–175.

FIGURE 168. Notre Dame Cathedral. Paris, France. From across the Seine, this view shows the large flying buttresses propping up and supporting the wall and roof weight above. Note that spires were never built on top of the two towers.

FIGURE 169. Notre Dame Cathedral. Paris, France. View of the front façade entrance showing the statues, rose window, and towers. *Photo courtesy of Jimmy Kapadia.*

FIGURE 170. Notre Dame Cathedral. Paris, France.
A vendor sells his wares in front of the cathedral many years ago.

FIGURE 171. Notre Dame Cathedral. Paris, France. These carved stone sculptures were designed to keep the devil out of the cathedral. *Photo courtesy of Jimmy Kapadia.*

FIGURE 172. Notre Dame Cathedral. Paris, France. A view from the tower of the flèche spire attached to the top of the crossing roof. *Photo courtesy of Jimmy Kapadia.*

FIGURE 173. Left and far left: Notre Dame Cathedral. Paris, France. A view from the tower overlooking Paris with the tall flèche spire in the foreground. *Photo courtesy of Jimmy Kapadia.*

FIGURE 174. Notre Dame Cathedral. Paris, France. Beautiful rose stained-glass window with lancets below. *Photo courtesy of Jimmy Kapadia.*

FIGURE 175. Notre Dame Cathedral. Paris, France. Detail of a stained-glass window. *Photo courtesy of Sam Kapadia.*

29 St. Peter's Basilica in Rome, Italy

St. Peter's Basilica is inside the Vatican City portion of Rome. It is neither Gothic nor Romanesque, but was built in the Renaissance architectural style. It is not classified as a cathedral either, but I wanted to include it because it is an internationally known church.

The old St. Peter's built by Constantine c. 320 AD was in bad disrepair in the fifteenth century, so a new basilica was built in its place. The foundation stone was laid on April 18, 1506, and was consecrated in 1626. It is the largest Christian church in the world, measuring 730 feet long, 500 feet wide, and 450 feet high. It has been noted that the basilica can hold 60,000 people.

The grandeur of St. Peter's is the vast 448-foot-high dome, the tallest in the world, dominating the city of Rome.

Michelangelo was responsible for redesigning the dome. The basilica is cruciform in shape and has a large decorated barrel vault nave. The entire basilica is highly decorated with stone and marble carvings, paintings, sculptures, and tiles. The thousands of square feet of colorful inlaid marble floors are amazing.

This colossal Catholic church has been a place of pilgrimage for many centuries. It is quite an experience to see St. Peter's Square full of visitors in front of the basilica. On one of my trips I had the privilege of visiting St. Peter's crypt below the altar and central dome. Many of the popes are buried in the crypts below. St. Peter's Basilica is certainly worth a visit when in Rome. See Figures 176–179.

FIGURE 176. St. Peter's Basilica. Rome, Italy. View of the front façade entrance showing the large statues on the roof and dome above.

FIGURE 177. St. Peter's Basilica. Rome, Italy. This photo was taken from the dome overlooking St. Peter's Square. Note the large statues on the roof front, Egyptian obelisk, and colonnade circling the square. Vatican Gardens is the left.

FIGURE 178. St. Peter's Basilica. Rome, Italy. This view from the Vatican Gardens shows the huge dome that dominates the area around the basilica.

FIGURE 179. St. Peter's Basilica. Rome, Italy. Taken from a catwalk inside the dome, this image illustrates the magnificent decorations inside the basilica. Notice the different colors of inlaid marble on the floor.

㉚ Washington National Cathedral in Washington, DC, United States

Washington National Cathedral is the sixth largest Gothic cathedral in the world, on Mount Saint Alban, the highest elevation in the District of Columbia. From the Pilgrim Observation Gallery on top of the west façade towers, one can see the major DC monuments several miles away. The cathedral is an Episcopal church with a foundation date of 1909 and a completion date of 1990. It was built in the Gothic architectural style, just as the medieval cathedrals of Europe were, but completed in modern times with some modern tools and equipment. See Figures 180–182.

The cathedral is built out of a cream-colored limestone purchased at an Indiana limestone company. But the marble stone for the cathedra chair was given to the Churchmen of Washington Cathedral as a gift from the Churchmen of Glastonbury Abbey. (Glastonbury Abbey is an ancient Christian site in England and currently in ruins.) The chair has since been known as the Glastonbury Cathedra Chair. The beautiful pulpit was carved out of French stone that came from Canterbury Cathedral in southern England. And the high altar was carved out of stone from Solomon's quarry near Jerusalem.

FIGURE 180. Washington National Cathedral. Washington, DC. The beautiful west façade entrance just before sunset. Note the rose window, Gothic towers, and light tan stone color.

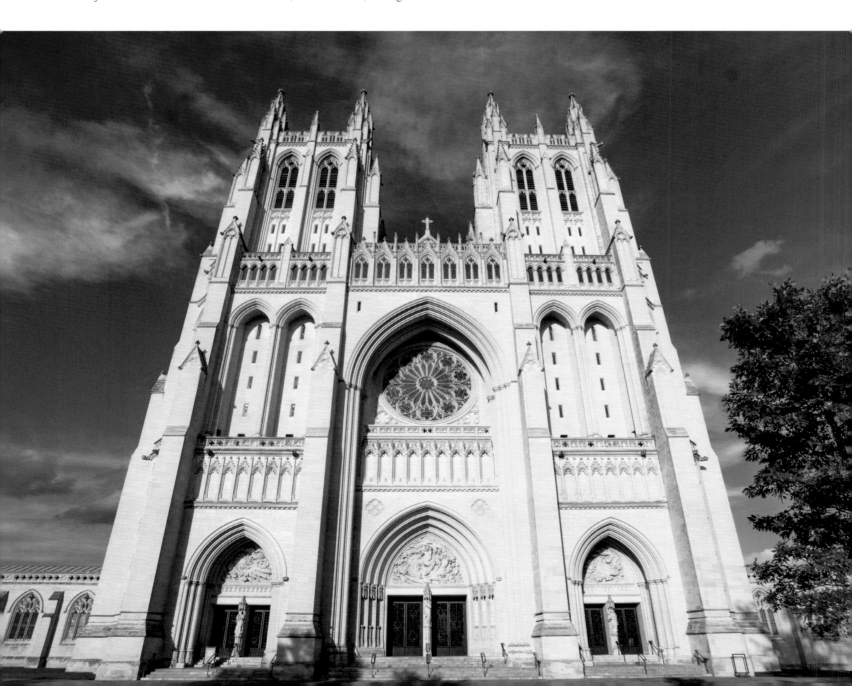

FIGURE 181. Washington National Cathedral. Washington, DC. A view from a small wrought-iron window pane in the north tower shows the nave exterior wall and showcases the flying buttresses attached to both the wall and outer buttresses.

FIGURE 182. Washington National Cathedral. Washington, DC. The exterior from the northwest, showcasing the front tower, flying buttresses, and central tower.

There are three beautiful rose windows in the cathedral, in the west façade entrance, as well as the north and south transepts. The vaulted ceiling in the cathedral nave is also quite impressive. I was unable to get photographs of the rose windows and vaulting due to black safety netting covering them for repairs. Unfortunately on August 23, 2011, a major 5.8 magnitude earthquake occurred in the Washington, DC, area and caused significant damage to the decorative stonework on the upper cathedral. See Figures 183–187.

The cathedral features several memorial bays of important people and events in American history. It also has several stained-glass windows that feature important places and events in America.

The cathedral was built on the traditional east west axis, as most of the cathedrals are in the world. But the intriguing part of Washington National is that it also followed the tradition of having a bent axis like many of the medieval cathedrals in Europe. (See chapter 9.)

FIGURE 183. Washington National Cathedral. Washington, DC. View down the nave axis looking west toward the rose window. Note the black netting above the arcade arches. It was placed there to prevent any loose stones from falling from the vaulting due to an earthquake.

FIGURE 184. Washington National Cathedral. Washington, DC. Upward view showcasing the arcade, triforium, clerestory, and vaulted ceiling. See the colored stained glass in the upper level.

FIGURE 185. Washington National Cathedral. Washington, DC. The cathedra, in the east.

FIGURE 187. Washington National Cathedral. Washington, DC.
Upward view through the side aisle piers toward the colored
stained-glass windows in the outer wall.

FIGURE 186. Washington National Cathedral. Washington, DC.
The detailed and beautifully carved pulpit.

CHAPTER 8

THE OPERATIVE MASONS
REGIUS MANUSCRIPT C. 1390: THE OLD CHARGES OF OPERATIVE MASONS

The Regius Manuscript c. 1390 is recognized as the oldest known complete operative stonemason's document, describing the history, rules, regulations, and charges governing the craft in England. The manuscript was written as a poem and has been known as the Regius Poem or Halliwell Manuscript. The Cooke Manuscript, c. 1400-1410, is the second oldest operative stonemason's document found to date. Since then, there have been some 130 different versions copied into the eighteenth century. These early manuscripts have been called *The Old Charges, Ancient Charges, Old Constitutions, York Constitutions,* and *Gothic Constitutions.* It is a miracle that all of these medieval manuscripts have survived documenting the history of the craft.

The *Old Charges* commenced with the history of masonry followed by a series of fifteen regulations, called articles, for the Master Masons and fifteen points for the apprentices. Wallace McLeod, a scholar on the *Old Charges,* described their role:

> They clearly filled the role of a Constitution, to regulate the Craft. Several of the copies actually bear the heading "Constitutions," and four of the versions were written in lodge minute books… The members of the old Scottish lodge at Sterling had a copy of the *Old Charges* and they believed that their meetings would not be legal unless the manuscript was exhibited in the lodge room… We know that they were actually used at lodge meetings… Another [version of the *Old Charges*] as written on 16 October 1646, at Warrington, expressly for the initiation of the antiquary Elias Ashmole. Yet another, written in 1693, includes a list of the members of the lodge. (McLeod 1985, 7)

These *Old Charges* were well written and have been expanded and edited to accommodate the needs and changes of the operative lodges.

Masonic scholars agree that these manuscripts were actually copies made from earlier originals, now lost. It is reasonable to assume that there were originals crafted centuries before, since the average word count of the 130 versions is 4,000 words, presumably too large of a text for a first draft. The tenth point of the Regius Poem c. 1390 even refers to an earlier version by mentioning the old days: "He must forswear the craft. Then he shall be punished according to the law which was founded in the old days" (Hunter 1975, 111).

In his detailed study of the *Old Charges* collection, Wallace McLeod believes there was an earlier document written around 1360:

> The Oldest Version was put together at some date close to 1360, quite possibly in the West Midlands of England (Gloucestershire or Oxfordshire). It was short, only about 2000 words… The history is followed by a series of Regulations called the Articles, which are intended for the Master of the Work. Then comes a further series of regulations called the Points, for the attention of the workmen. Finally there is a very brief prayer. (McLeod 1985, 9)

It would be exciting if someone would discover an older version than the c. 1390 copy now in the British Library in London, England.

In 1723, the Rev. James Anderson, a native of Aberdeen, Scotland, along with the Grand Lodge of England committee, wrote a new version of the *Old Charges* for the Masonic Lodges in England. Anderson gathered up several versions of the old operative charges and used them as patterns to write his new *Grand Lodge Book of Constitutions* (McLeod 1985, 17). Anderson published a second edition of the *Constitutions* in 1738.

Fredrick M. Hunter connects the Regius Poem c. 1390 with modern Speculative Masonry in *Regius Manuscript: The Earliest Masonic Document:*

> In the years of the transition from operative to speculative Masonry both the legend and historic fact of the Regius, the Cooke, and other related manuscripts, became the sources from which the Constitutions of 1722, 1723, and 1730 were derived under such devoted apostles and guides as Anderson and Desaguliers. (Hunter 1975, 135)

Hunter goes on to say that the fifteen articles and fifteen points are the same as what are now called the Masonic constitution and by-laws (Hunter 1975, 62).

In a later chapter, I will tie the *Old Charges* to modern Freemasonry and Masonic Lodges.

Labor, Tools, Equipment, Materials, and Mason's Clothing

The operative stonemasons were hard workers, laboring from dawn to dusk to take advantage of the available sunlight hours. Obviously more work could be done in the summer, and many stonemasons were actually laid off during the winter since the mortar could freeze and not set up properly. The term mason was the occupational name for a stonemason, one who builds with stone, brick, and other like materials. Masons have hewn, shaped, dressed, carved, and built structures with stone all over the world for centuries.

There has been some speculation regarding the word's origin. Did it come from the month of May and its association with the sun as some of the old writings refer (May-Sun or Mayson, or sons of May)? Or did it come from the name of an Egyptian chief architect named Mason? We may never know for sure.

The term freemason referred to the highest skilled operative masons. There are several plausible explanations for the origin of this term. In early cathedral building, the most complicated and highly detailed stone carvings and sculptures were carved from fine-grained sandstone and limestone commonly called **freestone**. Freestone was a softer stone with little grain so more intricate details could freely be carved from it. These very difficult and complicated carvings required the most highly trained and skilled stonemasons to execute them. In the late fourteenth century, these skilled masons, a cut above the rest, were called free stone masons, and accordingly, some believe they eventually became known as freemasons. These stonemasons had other titles over the centuries such as freestone-mason, ffre maceons, ffremason, frank mason, free-man mason, frie masons, and free-mason. "After 1396, free mason, free-mason, and freemason were used frequently and have come down to the present day" (Coil 1961, 266). The word freemason was used in the fourteenth, fifteenth, and sixteenth centuries.

A second plausible explanation for the word "free" in freemasonry comes from the ancient charges of the stonemasons that state that a mason must be free-born and descended of honest parents. Charge 4 of the 1723 Constitution states, "No Laborer shall be employ'd in the proper Work of Masonry; nor shall Free Masons work with those that are not free, without an urgent Necessity…" (Coil 1961, 143). This ancient charge originated from the 1396 Regius Poem and might have had some influence on the eventual joining of the words "free" and "mason."

A third possible explanation for the evolution of the word freemason was that an apprentice became free from his obligation to his master after he graduated from his apprenticeship school and met all the requirements of his indenture. He was no longer bound to the contract and was free to travel and take on employment himself. I believe the word freemason probably evolved from a combination of all three explanations.

Today the term "Freemason" refers to a member of the Masonic fraternity as opposed to the operative freemasons during the Middle Ages. Chapter 12 explains in detail the origin and development of Freemasonry.

Labor

There were various types of stonemasons, ranging from the most skilled to the least. While many of the masons were trained well enough to do most of the jobs on the building project, others were limited. Overall there was always a gray area among the types and skills of the masons and the work done by each at the work site.

Master Builder – Architect

The Master Builder was the most important person on the labor force at the cathedral site. He was the architect, general contractor, Master of the lodge, and was in complete charge of designing and building the cathedral. He was also in charge of the different trade craftsmen on the site.

Banker Mason – Sculptor

The banker mason was a highly trained and skilled stonemason who carved and dressed crude blocks of stone into shape. A bench called a banker held the stone steady while the mason worked, thus the mason himself became known as the banker mason. He was a Master Stone Carver and sculptor, a real artist who fully understood the anatomy of man, animals, and nature's materials. He executed life-like sculptures in great detail using a variety of chisels and mauls to dress the stones to the **template** designs.

Hewer Stonemason

The hewer mason roughly hewed or split the stones into a variety of different block sizes and shapes with heavy axes, hammers, and chisels. He prepared the **rough ashlar** stones to be dressed into perfect **ashlars** later by the higher skilled banker masons.

Setters and Layers

The setters and layers were masons who set the dressed stones into the walls by cementing them in place with trowels. They would select the proper size and shape of stones to set in the wall, making sure they were plumb, square, and level by using the proper tools (plumb, square, level, and maul).

Quarryman Masons

The quarryman masons worked at the quarry site extracting large blocks of stone. They split the blocks of stone using a series of plugs and tapered wedges driven into small holes drilled in a straight line in the quarry bed of stone. By pounding on the small wedges, large blocks of stone cracked open on the grain line and split away from the bed into smaller pieces. After the large stone blocks were cut from the quarry bed, they had to be lifted up to grade level. The stones were raised with hand-crank winches and cranes that took a lot of grunt work labor. The stones were then put onto wagons or sleds to be transported to the construction site.

The cost of delivering stone to a cathedral site was very expensive. Therefore the overseer instructed the quarrymen to rough-cut the stones at the quarry site to specific sizes, close to the required finished size. This minimized the volume, weight, and costs of delivering the stone to the cathedral site.

The quarryman's work was very arduous, and most apprentice trainees had their turn at the quarry first to learn the basic characteristics of stone. They were taught grain hardness and color variation for the various applications in the building. The quarrymen generally worked under extreme conditions including high water and humidity levels at the bottom of the quarries and amid stone dust from sawing and dressing the stones. The quarrymen usually set up an operative lodge at the quarry site to take their meals in, for rest breaks, and for sleeping quarters, similar to the operative lodges at the large cathedral sites.

Mortar Mixers, Plasterers, and Laborer Masons

The mortar mixers, plasterers, and laborers all had important jobs on the cathedral construction site. The mortar mixers had to mix the lime, sand, and water in the proper proportions for the mortar to properly set up. They prepared the mortar for the stone setters to use in placing the stones in the walls.

The plasterers had to trowel a layer of plaster over the stone vaults in the nave ceilings and walls in the cathedral. This made a smoother and more finished looking surface. The plasterers used a series of mason trowels to do their work.

The laborers had to do most of the grunt work on the site like moving the stones and timbers to the work area with wheelbarrows, handbarrows without a wheel, and cranes. The laborers hand-cranked the winch devices to raise the stones and materials up to the levels of construction. They also provided the wood to construct the scaffolding on which the masons would work.

The mortar carrier assisted the mortar mixers, plasterers, and stone setters by continuously carrying mortar, stone, brick, and all the necessary materials to keep the job moving along. They carried the mortar up ladders and along gangplanks to the stone setters on portable carriers called hods. They did many of the lesser skilled jobs, but all the jobs were necessary.

Hand Tools and Equipment

Several different trade craftsmen used special hand tools in constructing the cathedrals. A variety of hand tools were used to split, hew, cut, saw, dress, carve, plane, sculpt, grind, mold, forge, square, set, join, and then assemble all the materials together. Since the cathedrals were primarily built of stone, chiefly stonemason's hand tools were needed to construct them. The primitive hand tools illustrated in these photos are from the author's collection. See Figures 188–196.

Tools for the Master Builder Architect

The primary hand tools the Master Builder used were the plaster floor tracing slab, square, plumb, compass, proportional dividers, measuring rods, straight edge rule, templates, rope, line, scratch awl, and pen.

Tools for the Banker Masons, Hewers, and Sculptors

The banker masons, hewers, and sculptors used wooden mauls, iron hammers, wedges, pitchers, several different iron chisels, proportional dividers, bolsters, rasps and rifflers. They used the square, compasses, triangles, bow saws, spiked crandles, scalping adzes, and measuring sticks. They also used auxiliary equipment such as a variety of templates, molds, and patterns to dress and carve the stones to shape. They used a banker bench that supported the stone while they dressed it.

FIGURE 188. The wooden square and compasses were used by the Master Builders to do their design work. When combined, the square and compasses are also universally known as the Freemason's Masonic Emblem.

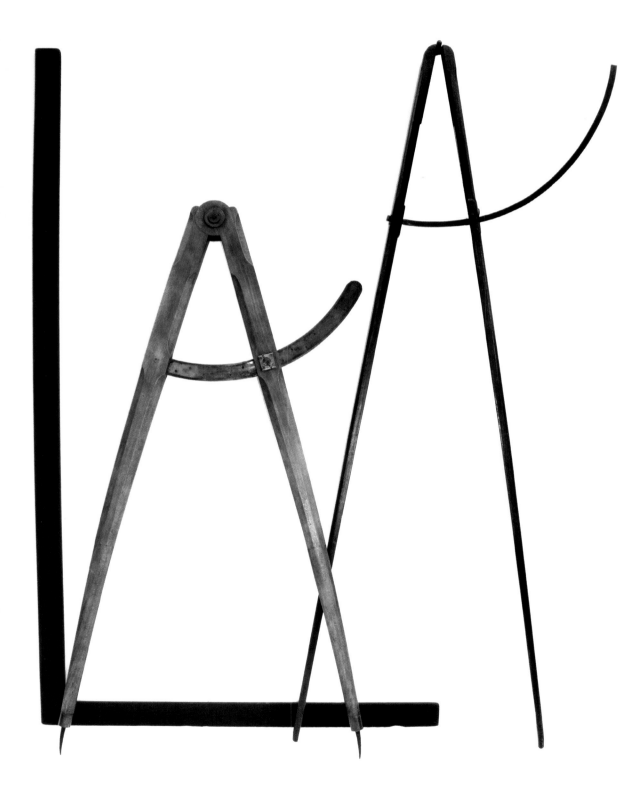

FIGURE 189. Three primitive tools used by the Master Builder for designing and checking
the work. The large wrought iron square has a 54-inch leg. The two large compasses were used
to draw arcs and circles. The larger one will draw a circle 12.8 feet in diameter.

FIGURE 190. Five stonemason hammers used to dress and shape stones to size.

FIGURE 191. Two primitive trowels used to spread the cement that binds the stones together.

Tools for the Setters and Layers

The setters and layers used the plumb, square, level, trowel, hammers, skirret, hod, mortarboard, wood and metal pry bars, and wooden buckets for water and mortar. They used auxiliary equipment such as scaffolding, ladders, wheelbarrows, handbarrows without a wheel, carts, windlass wheels, hand-operated winch cranes, iron key lewises, grapple scissor hooks, pulleys, ropes, and chalk lines.

Tools for the Quarrymen

The quarrymen used the pickaxe, scalping axe, double end picks, cross cut saw, handsaw, iron hammer, wooden maul, plugs and wedges, pry bar, and sledge hammers. They used auxiliary equipment such as sheer leg cranes, hand-operated windlass cranes, measuring rods, squares, a variety of wooden templates or molds, carts, wagons, sleds, ropes, handbarrows, and wheelbarrows.

Tools for the Mortar Mixers, Plasterers, and Laborers

The mortar mixers, plasterers, and laborers used mortar boxes, mortar pans, mortar hods, mortarboards, trowels, shovels, hoes, mortar buckets, and all the materials to make mortar.

Tools for Tree Felling, Wood Hewing, and Wood Splitting

Tree felling, hewing, and wood splitting craftsmen used the felling axes, hewing axes, hand axes, log dogs, wedges, chalk lines, wooden commander beetles, adzes, splitting froes, and froe clubs. The hewers shaped the rough logs into square beams with the hewing axes. The craftsmen prepared the wood for the carpenter, joiner, and wood carver to further reduce the wood into usable wooden products for the cathedral.

Many of these early axes were decorated with Christian symbols. Several blacksmith stamps are summarized in *Hammered Symbols* by Gustl Reinthaler (2003, 13–15), and a few in *Broad Axes* (Gamble 1986, Figures 1–12). Many decorated touch marks can be seen on the axes in the photos. See Figures 197–206.

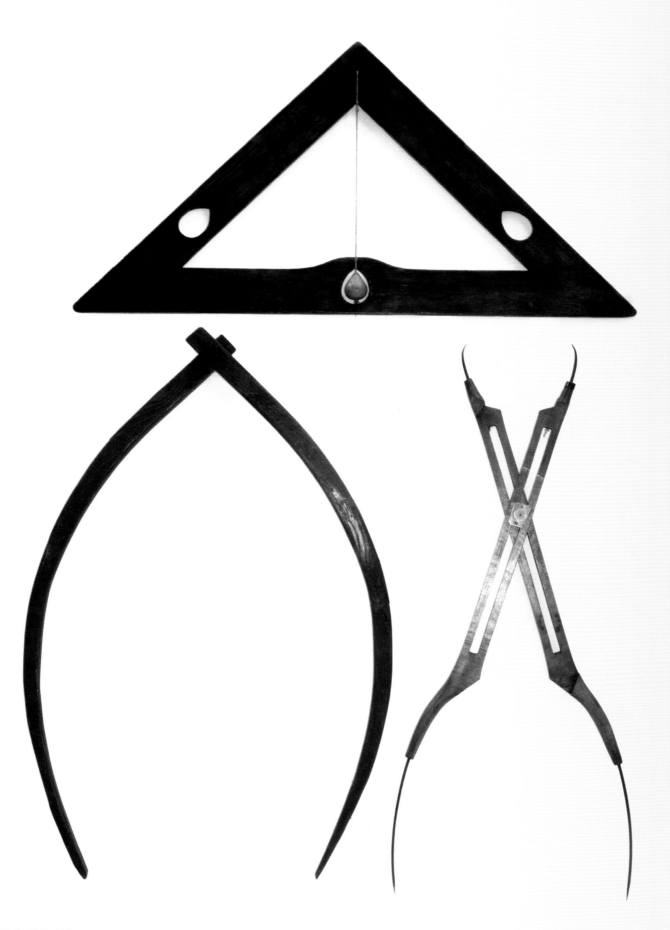

FIGURE 192. Three tools used by the setter and sculptor. The top tool is a plumb, level, and square combination. The left tool is a wooden caliper used for measurements. The right tool is a proportional caliper used to check ratio dimensions of sculptures.

FIGURE 193. This ingenious tool called a *lewis* was used to lift and guide heavy stones into place on a wall. An angular cavity was chiseled into the top center of the stone. The left and right tapered pieces were inserted first and the flat center iron piece was inserted last. A pin was put through the three slabs attaching it to the lifting ring. The stone could then be easily lifted.

FIGURE 194. This stonemason's spiked crandle was used to dress down and smooth out irregularities on top of the stones.

FIGURE 195. A variety of stonemason's chisels, gouges, clawed bolsters, and stone claws. A burl bird's-eye maul is in the center.

FIGURE 196. This is part of a French collection of stonemason smoothing planes, saws, and squares. The saws were used on the soft stone fresh from the quarry. The stone planes had different angled metal blades to dress and smooth a variety of shaped stones.

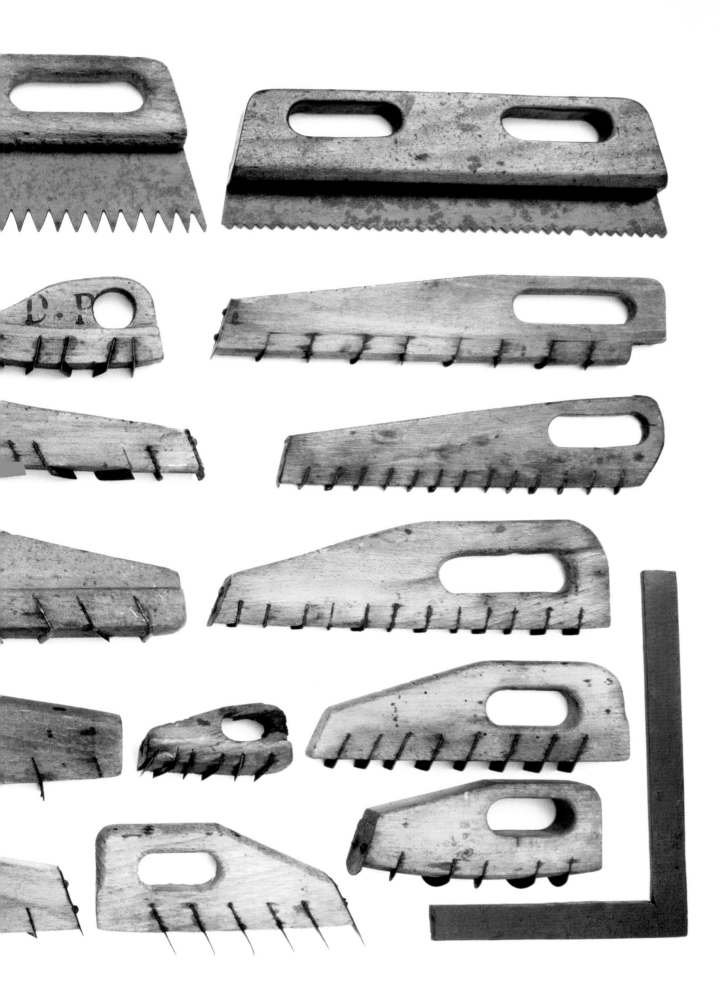

FIGURE 197. European goose wing broad axes most likely came from Austria or possibly Germany, Switzerland, and Hungary. They were used to hew and square wooden beams from logs. The two left-center axes have the shape of a goose wing, which gave them their name, and are the oldest, dating from c. the sixteenth century.

Tools for Carpenter Work, Sawing, Planing, Drilling, Joining, and Carving

The carpenter, sawyer, joiner, cabinetmaker, and wood carver used cross cut saws, pit saws, bow saws, hand saws, hand auger drills, brace and bits, pump drills, fiddle bow drills, breast spoon bit drills, wooden jack planes, horn smoothing planes, plow planes, molding planes, sledge hammers, carpenter hammers, wedges, a variety of carving chisels and gouges, wooden mauls, corner chisels, levels, compasses, proportional dividers, calipers, squares, miter squares, measuring stick rules, marking knives, race knives, scratch awls, scribes, draw knives, single-handle scorps, double handle inshaves, hand routers, files, rasps, rifflers, and mallets. They used auxiliary equipment such as workbenches, bench dogs, stools, and vices. See Figures 207–218.

Tools for Glass Blowers and Glaziers

The glass blower used the blowpipe to blow different colored molten glass for the stained-glass windows. The glass glaziers cut, fitted, and placed the stained glass into stone window frames called tracery with a variety of tools.

Tools for the Blacksmith

The blacksmith forged all the iron stonemason tools for cutting and splitting the hard stone. He also made all of the iron tools and hardware for wagons, carts, harnesses, agricultural implements, etc. He used the blacksmith anvil, a variety of anvil tools, bellows, forge, fire box with charcoal, blacksmith holding tongs, iron swedge tools, bending forks, cones, hammers, and a slack water tub.

Tools for Tilers, Plumbers, and Roofers

The tilers were craftsmen who fabricated and installed the heavy lead roofs on the cathedrals. The name plumber comes from the Latin word *plumbum* for lead, which they poured into large, thin molds. The lead sheets were cast three or four feet wide by five or six feet long. The lead solidified in the molds and the sheets were then installed over the wood framing, forming the lead roofs. The roofs were water ight and lasted for many years. Red baked tiles were also used on the roofs and were installed over wood sheeted roofs as well to keep the rain out. The tile roofs were heavy and added a great deal of tonnage to the roof structure.

FIGURE 198. Goose wing broad axe with two blacksmith maker's marks on top. A Christian Cross with three decorated blossoms surrounding it represents the Trinity. Celtic scallops with the three Trinity blossoms are stamped around the entire blade.

FIGURE 199. Goose wing broad axe with two blacksmith maker's marks on top. There are two trees of life with leaves representing rebirth and everlasting life.

Building Materials

Most of the cathedrals were built out of limestone, while a few were made of sandstone or brick. Limestone is a much harder stone than sandstone and withstood the elements of weathering much better. Sandstone is much more porous; therefore, sandstone exterior carvings and sculptures deteriorated more quickly and had to be replaced much sooner.

There were many stone quarries in England and France with good quality stone. The Master Builders would visit these quarries and arrange for the procurement of the best type of stone for their cathedral. The different stones had varying degrees of hardness and grain. The fresh stone taken from the quarries was called green stone and had moisture in it, making it softer and easier to saw, cut, and carve. After the stones were carved and dressed, they became harder as they were exposed to the air. The stones and mortar then chemically aged and became more solid over several years.

Purbeck marble was a dark gray charcoal or black-colored stone used for pillars in the arcades and for stone color contrast. It was used in several cathedral interiors for color balance. Purbeck is actually a stone that looks like marble when highly polished.

In the United States, the Indiana Limestone Co. in Bloomington, Indiana, furnished stone for the Washington National Cathedral in Washington, DC, as well as for many of the other buildings in DC. My wife and I had an interesting and enjoyable visit to the Indiana Limestone Co. many years ago. We were given an excellent tour of their facilities, sawing operations, and quarries. The manager gave us a Jeep tour of the quarries where we saw several million tons of sawn stone above ground waiting to go to Washington and around the world. He then took us to the edge of a gigantic quarry hole and asked, "Do you see that? The Empire State Building in New York City came out of that hole!" The tour was a treat for us.

Stonemason's Protective Clothing

The apron was a significant part of the working dress of the operative stonemasons. Most of the heavy labor of working with stone was done manually, which exposed the stonemason's clothing to the abrasive limestone and sandstone. The constant rubbing of stone on their clothing wore holes in their pants and shirts rather quickly, so they needed some additional protection. Because sheep were plentiful in England and Scotland, it was natural to use the lambskin as a practical solution to the problem. The lambskin leather apron was strong, thick, and long enough to protect their clothing, and it became the traditional badge of an operative mason. It was customary for the employer to provide the aprons for the stonemason workers as part of the contract between the Master and apprentice.

The leather aprons also had a flap or bib at the top that overlapped the apron itself and become an additional layer of protection. The apprentices who did most of the heavy manual labor would need this additional protection more than the overseers. The French aprons in some of the old paintings show a buttonhole at the top for the mason to button the leather flap in place.

Gloves were also part of the stonemason's clothing. They were worn when the stonemasons were working with mortar or laying stone to protect their hands from abrasion, splinters, infection, and burns from the lime in the mortar. The patrons or overseers in many cases provided gloves to the masons on the construction jobs. Both the lambskin white leather apron and the gloves became the official dress of a stonemason.

FIGURE 200. Goose wing broad axe with two blacksmith maker's marks on top. There are four stamped green leaves with three blossoms representing the Trinity. Celtic scallops with blossoms surround the entire blade.

FIGURE 201. Goose wing broad axe with two blacksmith maker's marks on top. There are two trees of life with leaves representing rebirth and everlasting life.

FIGURE 202. Goose wing axe with heart sign of love on top and a tree of life with small, pointed Christian starbursts. The six-pointed star on the left heel of the axe represents the life symbol and sun sign (Reinthaler 2003, p. 13). On the left edge of the blade is a three-branch Trinity sign with three eight-pointed starbursts.

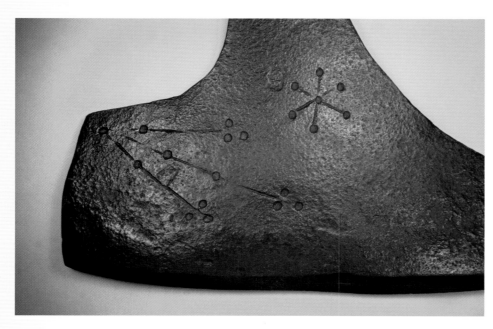

FIGURE 203. Goose wing broad axe with six-pointed star life symbol (Reinthaler 2003, p. 13). To the left is the three-branch Trinity sign with three blossoms on each sprig.

FIGURE 204. Goose wing broad axe with two small trees of life. There is a five-pointed Pentagram sign of protection against any accidents and everything evil. (Reinthaler 2003, p. 13). On the left there is the three-branch Trinity sign with three blossoms on each sprig, as well as a moon symbol on one of them.

FIGURE 205. Goose wing axe with decorative marks covering the entire blade, including chevrons, a swirling sun symbol, a Christian cross, and celtic scallops, each with three prick points for the Trinity. There is also an eight-pointed star for life.

THE STONEMASON'S LODGE

The stonemasons practiced their craft at the quarry, the cathedral site, and inside a temporary dwelling called a stonemason's lodge. The lodge was a wooden work shed usually attached to the south side of the cathedral to take advantage of the sun's light and warmth. These working lodges were shelters with roofs on them providing protection from the elements and allowing the masons to continue their work inside during the winter months and inclement weather. The lodge was used as a workshop and as a place to house tools and take meals. Occasionally it was used as a place to sleep, as some of the lodges had lofts built into them. But primarily the lodges provided a work area for the Master Builder and his craftsmen. See Figures 219–221.

Within the stonemason's lodge was a room called the trasour house, which had a plaster floor slab called the tracer floor. Using the floor as a large drawing board, the Master Builder and the craftsmen worked out their stone designs with a sharp pointer and compasses. This design room and tracing boards have been given several names over the years, such as trasour house, tracing room, tracing floor, tracing board, lodge board, and trestle board. See Figure 222.

Once the building designs were worked out on the plaster floor, the Master Builder instructed the carpenter to saw thin wooden templates or molds to replicate the shape of his completed designs. These oak templates were then given to the banker mason to hew, square, sculpt, and dress the rough ashlar stones into exact shapes of the templates. Upon completing the stone carving to the exact specifications of the template, the banker mason signed the stone with his personal mason's mark and then gave it to the stone setter. The stone setter finally mortared the stone and placed it, along with millions of other like stones, into the cathedral wall.

After construction of a particular design was complete, the Master Builder rubbed over the design on the plaster floor, erasing the images. He then gave the floor slab a new thin coat of plaster making it ready for the next new drawing. For the most important designs that he wanted to preserve, the Master Build could create parchment drawings, which were very expensive to make. The trasour house included trestle tables with wooden planks on them to hold the parchment skin drawings. Surprisingly, several of these medieval parchment drawings survived, several dating back some 800 years.

There are four major collections of these medieval parchment drawings and sketches still in existence: Villard de Honnecourts' *Sketchbook* from France, Mathes Roriczer's booklet of medieval geometry from Germany, drawings at St. Stephen's Cathedral Lodge in Vienna, Austria, and drawings at the Strasbourg Lodge in Strasbourg, France. The largest collection of medieval architectural plans in existence is found in the St. Stephen's Cathedral Lodge in Vienna, Austria, numbering 298 drafts. The Strasbourg Lodge in Strasbourg, France, has the second largest collection.

FIGURE 206. European plane with decorative carvings and touch marks. The iron blade has a tree of life symbol with nine eight-pointed Christian starbursts on the branches. The maker's mark has five eight-pointed Christian starbursts. The plane body has a carved heart-shaped throat, two carved swirling sun symbols, and a carved tulip.

FIGURE 207. Carpenter/jointer tools including a long rabbet plane, a jointer plane with dowel in front for the apprentice to pull, and a jointer plane below with a natural limb handle mortised into the body. The triangular tool is a plumb, level, and square combination. To the right are two race knives to mark the Roman numerals on wooden beams for assembly and a mortise chisel in between them.

FIGURE 208. A dozen wood carving chisels and gouges from London.

FIGURE 209. A French cabinetmaker's plow plane to cut grooves of varying widths.

FIGURE 210. Wonderful hand plane carved in the shape of a dove. It has a concave
hollowed brass sole, is around six inches long, and fits a hand perfectly for use.

FIGURE 211. Wide smoothing plane with double grips on both sides.
The dowel mounted in front is for the apprentice to pull the plane with a rope.

FIGURE 212. Small horn plane with a nicely carved throat for smoothing.

FIGURE 213. Early hand-made tongue and groove plane with hand-wrought thumb nuts.

FIGURE 214. Early adjustable plow plane for cutting grooves in a board.

FIGURE 215. Early adjustable plow plane with hand-made cut threads.

FIGURE 216. Small horn smoothing plane with carved heart-shaped throat and tulip.

FIGURE 217. Hand tools for drilling holes in wood. On top is a cage-head wrought-iron brace and below is a pump drill with a wrought-iron flywheel and leather strap. Below the pump drill is a wooden brace breast drill and a graceful hand-wrought iron brace. To the right is a breast drill. The balance of the drills are wrought-iron and wooden braces.

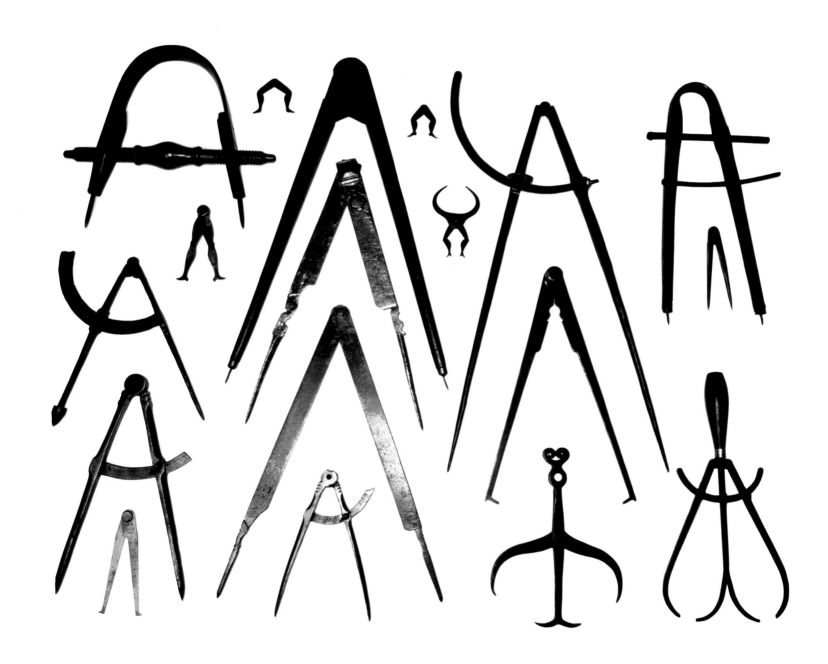

FIGURE 218. This is a collection of wooden and iron compasses,
calipers, and inside/outside calipers, with legs on a few.

FIGURE 219. *Saint Barbara* painting by Jan Van Eyck, 1437. The stonemason's lodge is right of the tower. Stones on the left are being moved about with hand barrows. Masons can be seen raising and setting stones into place on top of the tower. *Painting reprinted with permission of the Royal Museum of Fine Arts Antwerpen, Belgium.*

FIGURE 220. This is a model of Salisbury Cathedral (England) with the stonemason's lodge next to the cathedral. Note the banker masons hewing and dressing stones inside and others preparing them for construction in the building.

FIGURE 221. Salisbury Cathedral model from another view, illustrating the windlass wheel crane in the center for lifting stones. The stonemasons and carpenters are working around the fabric.

FIGURE 222. Plaster tracing floor inside Wells Cathedral in England. The photograph on the back wall illustrates the designs that still remain on the floor made by the Master Builder many years ago.

THE STONEMASON APPRENTICESHIP TRAINING PROGRAM

For centuries, the Master Masons conducted schools to teach the young apprentices the craft of stonemasonry. The apprenticeship training program was very intense and completed over several years of hard work and study. It was a combination of both practical (hands-on stonemasonry) as well as theoretical (architectural and engineering) training. The training included educating young men in the arts and sciences, especially geometry.

Geometry and masonry were synonymous terms in the stonemason's training program of the Middle Ages. Geometry and building craft secrets were passed down through the generations by word of mouth in the program. As practicing Christians, the trainees also had an in-depth knowledge of the Bible and religion. The stonemason schools were certainly the top-notch schools of the day.

Bright young men in their teens who showed potential for learning and demonstrated good manual skills were selected to enroll as apprentices in the program. The Master Mason and apprentice signed an official document called an indenture (contract) that confirmed the Master would train the apprentice in the stonemason's craft. It specified the number of years of the agreement and bound both parties to a set of disciplined work rules and conduct taken from the *Old Charges*. The *Old Charges* included a set of fifteen rules called the articles with which the Masters had to comply and a set of fifteen rules called the points with which the apprentices had to comply. There were also additional rules the apprentices had to follow that governed their conduct during work hours and off-duty hours. After both parties signed and dated the indenture, it was notch-cut into two pieces, so that both pieces corresponded exactly to each other when placed together. The Master kept one half and the apprentice the other. The notched-cut edge gave proof to both parties that the apprentice was bound to the Master under the set of rules outlined. The indenture got its name from the notched or indented edge of the cut halves.

Overall the apprenticeship program was a system of three degrees that required completion over a specified period. The Apprentice degree required one year of training, the Entered Apprentice three years of training, and the Fellow of the Craft/Master Mason seven years of training. Upon completion of the three degrees, the Master Mason typically took another three years of training to go on a Journeyman's tour to other construction sites. Not surprisingly, the graduate Master Masons from the apprenticeship schools were some of the most highly educated people in the community at the time.

Apprentice Degree

The Apprentice was selected by the Master to enroll in the apprenticeship training program. He was free born and had to have a perfect body (all of his limbs) per the requirements of the *Old Charges*. The young Apprentice had to climb around the tall cathedral some 400 feet in the air like an ant climbing around an anthill; the young men probably got accustomed to the heights or had no fear of them. They took risks working at the elevated heights where some of the older masons would not.

The Apprentice was taught the basic skills of the craft using mason's tools such as axes, hammers, picks, bars, chisels, and mauls. He learned the basic qualities of the different types of stones available in the local area, as well. He was essentially put on probation for one year to see how he progressed in the training and how he handled himself. If the Master felt he was doing a good job in accepting responsibility, taking orders and carrying them out properly and meeting the skill levels expected of him, the Master would then move him to the next level of Entered Apprentice Degree.

Entered Apprentice Degree

After one year of training, the Master *entered* the Apprentice into the lodge rolls, hence the name "Entered Apprentice." The Entered Apprentice trainee would receive additional training to widen his skill level and experience. He would be trained in the proper use of additional hand tools such as the square, level, plumb, straight edge, rule, and spiked crandle. He would also be given training in the basics of quarrying and extracting rough ashlar stones from the quarry bed. He would use the chisel and maul to dress a rough ashlar stone into a perfect ashlar stone. After three years of training, if the Master felt the Entered Apprentice had met all of the requirements, he would raise him to the highest degree level: Fellow of the Craft/Master Mason.

Fellow of the Craft/Master Mason Degree

The Fellow of the Craft/Master Mason Degree was an advanced training program for an additional period of seven years. It was an intense program including instruction in building techniques using hand tools, along with lessons in the theoretical principles of architecture and engineering design. These design principles included geometry, mathematics, proportions, material strengths, and astronomy. The Master Mason trainee would have used compasses, calipers, proportional dividers, specialized tools, and all the tools mentioned previously in the Entered Apprentice degree. He would have gotten involved in all areas of constructing a cathedral, from quarrying stone to constructing foundations, walls, vaulting, spans, roofs, and spires.

To prove his abilities and knowledge in operative stonemasonry and architecture, the Master Mason trainee would design and sculpt a piece of stonework and present it to the old Masters. This stone sculpture was known as his Masterpiece. If this piece, along with his theoretical knowledge, was approved by the old Masters, he was accepted into the exclusive group of Master Masons. This group continued their educational careers in the arts and sciences by participating in the design and building of the beautiful cathedrals. These skilled craftsmen eventually became the supervisors and overseers of the work on the large cathedral construction jobs. The Fellow of the Craft/Master Masons used both their manual skills and brains to construct the cathedrals.

The Journeyman Master Mason

After the Master Mason completed his demanding seven-year apprenticeship training program, it was customary for him to go on a Journeyman's tour for an additional three years. This tour was also called *wanderyears* or *wanderjahrs*. On this tour he would visit new cathedrals being constructed to learn the most up-to-date design techniques being used. He would visit cathedrals in his own country as well as in foreign countries to observe a variety of designs. Though he would not copy other designs exactly, he would use the basic design with some subtle decoration changes. These visits greatly broadened his knowledge base and provided him with ideas for future projects. After fourteen years of intense apprenticeship training, coupled with experience and observation from other major cathedral structures, the Master Mason was then well equipped to take on a building commission of his own. After a Master Mason received a commission to design and build his first major project, he essentially became a Master Builder.

The Master Builder

The highly skilled Master Mason was now properly trained to take on a large cathedral design. The bishop and cathedral chapter members in a community planning to build a new cathedral could hire the Master Mason to serve as their Master Builder. He was now ready to take on a commission and the monumental responsibilities that would come with it. (See chapter 2.)

Many of the Master Builders, after working on several cathedral projects, developed excellent international reputations. The Peter Parler family of stonemasons from Germany, for instance, became one of the best known families that traveled among countries in Europe working on major cathedral projects. When the patron or bishop of a cathedral project wanted to hire a builder, they would most certainly seek out the Master Builder who had the best reputation for the job.

THE MORTARBOARD HAT, A SYMBOL OF GRADUATION

There are many old customs and traditions that we participate in today without ever really knowing the original purpose for doing so. In some instances, the initial meaning of these traditions has been lost over time, and no one ever questions their beginnings. The meaning behind wearing a mortarboard hat at graduation is a case in point that I believe slipped through the cracks. But I am convinced there is credence in the idea that the tradition of wearing these hats at graduation ceremonies today originated in the medieval stonemason apprenticeship schools.

A stonemason's mortarboard is a flat piece of wood measuring about twenty-four inches square. It is usually placed on a stand on the scaffolding near the wall being built. The mortarboard held the wet mortar until the stone setter applied it to the stones with the mason's trowel. The setter then placed the mortared stone into the wall. After the mortar dried around the stone, a strong solid wall was formed.

A skullcap was a small brimless cloth cap typically worn in the ancient stonemason's day. Taken together, the mortarboard and the skullcap look remarkably similar to the modern graduation cap. Today's graduation caps are even called mortarboard hats.

What if the modern graduation cap came into being as a result of medieval Master Masons graduating from apprenticeship schools? Consider the following scenario:

Reg Eaton from Norfolk, England just graduated from apprenticeship school after many long years of intensive training, achieving the level of Master Mason. Wanting to celebrate with other masons and fellow workers, he invited them to a festive gathering with food and drink.

"Let's crown Reg 'king of the Master Masons' with a king's crown," said one of the guests.

"No, we can't do that. He's not a king."

"Well, then let's crown him with his own mason's mortarboard and use it as a crown of our craft and authority."

So the old mortarboard was washed and tacked to Reg's skullcap and placed upside down on his head. "King of the Master Masons!" they all cheered, and toasted their drinks to him in celebration.

FIGURE 223. A graduation mortarboard hat worn by millions of students today as a symbol of graduation and replicating the operative stonemason's mortarboard.

From that day on Reg Eaton and all the other graduates from the stonemason apprenticeship schools celebrated their graduation ceremonies with a mason's mortarboard hat crowned on their heads. The mortarboard hat then became the traditional symbol of graduation for schools around the world.

Over time, colleges and universities embellished the mortarboard hats with modifications and decorations such as adding tassels and a variety of colors to distinguish different branches of education and degree levels. Robes and gowns were added some years later to the mortarboard hat dress, elevating the intellectual status of the graduate. See Figure 223.

SILENCE AND SECRECY OF MASONRY

Silence and secrecy has been indelibly attached to the craft of masonry for centuries, and I maintain that it originated during the cathedral building era of the Middle Ages. The original "masonic secrets" were architectural, geometrical, astronomical, and engineering secrets developed and preserved by the Master Builders. They were essentially the building design secrets of the stonemason's trade.

The Master Builders were the select few who held this secret knowledge by which they could design and build masterpieces of architecture. They did not share these secrets with the less skilled craftsmen on the site. Instead this esoteric knowledge was held in confidence only among other Master Builders. It was passed from generation to generation by word of mouth. Because the Masters did not have a patent office to register and protect their patents, inventions, building design techniques, and tricks of the trade during the Middle Ages, they shared and preserved their building craft secrets amongst themselves. In *The Gothic World, 1100–1600,* John Harvey discusses how Masters and Journeymen shared these design secrets in meetings of several operative lodges from neighboring countries:

> The principal documents are the Lodge Ordinances which were promulgated by periodical chapters of master masons, held in various cities of the Empire at frequent intervals from 1459 until relatively modern times…The meeting of 1459 was at Regensburg, and consisted of nineteen masters and twenty-six Gesellen, journeymen. It was laid down that the Master of the Lodge at Strasbourg should always have pre-eminence, while separate spheres of influence were under the charge of the Masters at Vienna (for Austria, Hungary and the Danube lands), Berne (for Switzerland), and Cologne. Of special importance among the regulations are those which enjoin that no non-mason shall be instructed in the secrets of design, and that no one shall be taught for money. It should be noted that this German organization applied only to the Lodge-Masons who worked for the greater churches; it was entirely distinct from the guilds of local masons in the towns and cities who worked for lay patrons. (1969, 21)

Hundreds of design secrets were developed and updated over time by the Master Builders. These obscure secrets eventually became the "mysteries of masonry" in the eyes of the public. It was inconceivable to the laypeople how the Master Builders could use the sacred geometry secrets to design and build the beautiful cathedral masterpieces. Today the public is still asking the same questions. Over time sacred geometry became a synonymous term with masonry.

The earliest example of a written document that addresses the secrecy of masonry is found in the Regius Poem c. 1390,

the *Old Charges* of the masons. "His Master's council he should keep close and those of the Fellows for the same purpose. Whatever private things in lodge are done He's not to tell to anyone. Whatever you hear or see them do you tell to no one wherever." This ancient manuscript addressed the secrecy of masonry over 600 years ago and mandated that no one should discuss any lodge business or secrets of the lodge or craft with anyone anywhere.

The Melrose Manuscript, a later version of the *Old Charges,* also addresses secrecy, instructing that operative masonic secrets be kept away from the cowans. Arthur Waite writes in *A New Encyclopedia of Freemasonry* that "The Masons' Secrets were Operative Secrets and could be no otherwise in the nature of things. It has been well argued that they were practical applications of geometrical science; and we have seen that, according to the Melrose MS., the 'privilege of compass, square, level and plumb rule' was denied to 'losses' or 'cowans'" (1970, 148). Though the cowans did work as stonemasons, they were not considered legitimate masons because they did not go through the apprenticeship training program. Therefore these tools of the Master Stonemason were not shared with these untrained workers.

Albert Mackey, a noted masonic scholar, sums up silence and secrecy of masonry by pronouncing:

> These virtues constitute the very essence of all Masonic character; they are the safeguard of the institution, giving to it all its security and perpetuity, and are enforced by frequent admonitions in all the degrees, from the lowest to the highest. The Entered Apprentice begins his Masonic career by learning the duty of secrecy and silence. Hence it is appropriate that in that degree which is the consummation of initiation, in which the whole cycle of Masonic science is completed, the abstruse machinery of symbolism should be employed to impress the same important virtues on the mind of the neophyte. (1924, 675)

Around 1980, my son Mark and I visited Lon Shelby, professor of history and dean of the College of Liberal Arts at Southern Illinois University – Carbondale. I discussed the secrets of masonry, geometry, and Gothic cathedral building with Shelby, who had done extensive research on German medieval geometry and Gothic designs. He wrote the enlightening *Gothic Design Techniques,* which included, among other things, an English translation of three German Gothic design booklets written by Mathes Roriczer. Roriczer served as Master Builder of Regensburg Cathedral in Germany from 1478 to 1495 and also became an author and printer. Professor Shelby describes the booklets as genuine how-to-do-it booklets (1977, 5–6).

The first two instructional booklets are *Buchlein von der Fialen Gerechtigkeit* and *Wimpergbuchlein,* both printed in 1486. They describe in great detail the methods of designing and constructing decorative pinnacles and gablets on cathedrals, complete with drawings and text.

A third booklet, *Geometria Deutch,* printed in 1488, describes how to draw seven different geometrical figures using only a straight edge rule and compass. The most interesting description is the method of drawing a right angled square, known by the stonemasons as how to prove his square.

Shelby and others questioned whether Roriczer's printing of the booklets revealed the secrets of the stonemason's craft to the public. I believe Roriczer knowingly violated his oath of fidelity and secrecy in printing the booklets specifically to help his brother masons understand the complicated geometry in the designs. Most readers today would get lost in the geometry very quickly. Roriczer was a highly trained Master Builder, and I think he honestly wanted to assist other masons in the apprenticeship training program to better comprehend the many steps in designing and constructing the stone pieces. Up to that date, the apprenticeship training was only shared orally and through demonstrations.

Roriczer was also trained in the new technology of printing and probably thought that printing out these designs accompanied by explanations would be an innovative tool to help train the stonemasons. The printings would serve as a written formulae that the trainees could study and use as a memory jogger for future designs. In my opinion, Roriczer intended the booklets to be used for training and not for public consumption.

To be clear, geometry was the most important tool the Master Builder used in his trade. The operative stonemasons took geometry to a whole new level of architecture and engineering with the measurement and symmetry of the building parts, angles, proportions, and material strengths. Geometry played a major part in designing every inch of the cathedrals.

Through the use of geometry, the Master Builders were able to develop secret techniques for different measurements. "In the later Middle Ages there were certainly proportionate 'secrets' handed down among the masons, for determining the appropriate depth of foundations for a wall of a given height" (Harvey 1988, 61). For example, during the earlier Romanesque cathedral building era, the walls had to be built thick and substantial enough to support all the heavy roof and vaulting weight. Over time the stonemasons developed a quick "rule of thumb" engineering method of calculating how thick the walls had to be to carry the vertical weight above. The method to determine the thickness is outlined in *The Travelers Key to Medieval France* by John James (1986, 105). See Figure 224.

MASON'S RULE OF THUMB TO DETERMINE WALL THICKNESS

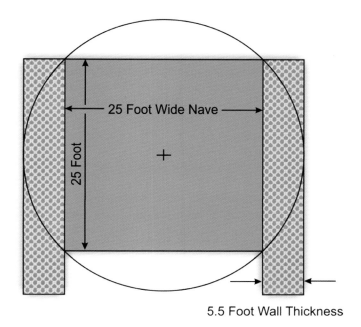

FIGURE 224. Method of determining the thickness of walls of a cathedral. *Illustration by Robb Harst.*

Figure 224 shows the Mason's Rule of Thumb in Determining Wall Thickness:

- The Master Builder first determined the width of the nave opening. In this example it was found to be twenty-five feet wide and he drew two parallel lines twenty-five feet apart.

- The Master Builder drew a twenty-five -foot square inside the two parallel lines as shown.

- The Master Builder drew a circle around the square touching the four corners of the square.

- The Master Builder drew two more parallel lines touching the outside of the big circle.

- The Master Builder measured the width of the two parallel lines that determined the required wall thickness.

- The wall would need to be five and half feet wide for a twenty-five foot wide nave.

MASTER BUILDER VILLARD DE HONNECOURT, ACTIVE FROM AD 1225 TO 1250

Villard de Honnecourt was a Master Builder from France who traveled and worked in several European countries. Villard got his last name from the small town from which he came, Honnecourt, France, south of Cambrai. He compiled an extensive book of medieval parchment architectural drawings accompanied by explanatory captions. Drawn some eight centuries ago, it includes excellent detailed ink drawings that are still legible to this day. The parchment drawings were sewn inside a pigskin cover to protect them on his travels.

Why did Villard make some 244 drawings and sketches? What was the original purpose of the book, and how was it used? There have been hundreds of opinions put forth by dozens of authors over some 150 years, all trying to answer these questions.

The drawings are better known today as *Villard de Honnecourt's Sketchbook*. When we look at Villard's own words in his preface, he clearly states that his parchment drawings were a book, and I would agree:

> Here you will find the images of the Twelve Apostles, sitting. Villard de Honnecourt greets you and begs all who will use the devices found in this book to pray for his soul and remember him. For in this book will be found sound advice on the virtues of masonry and the uses of carpentry. You will also find strong help in drawing figures according to the lessons by the art of geometry. (Bowie 1959, 7)

The book illustrates detailed construction designs of cathedral floor plans, elevations, and how-to-build sketches. Villard used two methods of making the drawings: freehand sketches and sketches made with primitive drawing instruments to achieve more detailed designs. He used the square, rule, triangles, and templates to illustrate his designs, as well as a pair of compasses to draw uniform circles; tiny holes can be seen poking through the parchment drawings where the compass points entered.

Villard used geometry throughout the book to illustrate his architectural drawings. He demonstrated the hands-on measurements of how to cut the intricately shaped stones for the building. He drew detailed drawings of the Gothic flying buttresses, towers, arcades, timber vaulting, rose windows, templates, and spires. He also included a variety of other subjects such as mechanical devices, gadgets, interior furniture, religious symbols, apostles, bishops in flowing robes, and a drawing of Christ in Majesty. In addition, he made drawings of human and animal figures based on different stick geometrical forms as though the building forms used were based on God's natural anatomy of the human body and animal figures. Villard was a professional draftsman, illustrating his architectural and engineering designs. He even used darker shadowing and a bit of color in his drawings, especially in the flowing robes and garments, to give a feeling of depth and realism.

In 1959, Theodore Bowie, professor of fine arts at Indiana University in Bloomington, Indiana, wrote *The Sketchbook of Villard de Honnecourt*, which included his translation of the French text into English. I contacted Bowie, a well-known and highly respected art historian, about his research on Villard.

The sketchbook consists of thirty-three parchment pages measuring approximately six and a quarter by ten and a half inches. Unfortunately a few sections were torn out at some point and have been forever lost. Scholars have reported that a few other Master Masons, who were custodians of the sketchbook over the years, added their sketches and captions to the book. I suspect when a Master Builder retired he would have passed the design book on to the new Master Builder. This would explain why additional drawings and text comments from others were later added to the book.

The significance of this medieval architectural document cannot be overstated. The book captured the stonemasons' cathedral designs and secrets, and it became an historical document. Today it provides us with insight into some of the detailed geometry the Master Builders used in designing and building the cathedrals using masonry and carpentry methods. It is my opinion that Villard's book of drawings and descriptive captions was used for the following purposes:

First, it was an encyclopedia of architectural designs that Villard carried around with him on his travels. He used it to make sketches of the latest, most significant inventions and unique designs that he observed on his visits to cathedral sites. Traditionally Master Builders traveled to different cathedral sites and countries to observe the latest design features being used and to share their own inventions. Many also traveled from great distances to annual assemblies of the Masters for the same reason. I believe Villard recorded what he observed at these sites and assemblies. He could have made some of the drawings during his three-year Journeyman's tour and used them as memory joggers for his new work.

Villard studied the construction of the great churches of Cambrai, Reims, Chartres, Laon of France, and others in Germany and Switzerland. He was also invited to travel to Hungary and stayed there for several years, by his own accounts. He was called a traveling mason, one who moved around to different cathedral sites securing work and giving advice to others on construction designs and building.

Second, it was used as an instructional design booklet for other craftsmen. I believe it was used to teach the upcoming Fellows and Masters of the craft the basics of the latest designs in the stonemason's apprenticeship schools. It basically served as a pictorial textbook and was used to illustrate dozens of different architectural subjects to teach the students. While Villard made sketches of several architectural designs, he only partially described their use in the text, and not in any great detail. He would later explain the details of the sacred geometry and their method of architectural use to his colleagues on the site.

Today architectural historians, engineers, and scholars still cannot explain all the meanings and symbolism of the detailed drawings in the book. This tells me loud and clear that Villard was a trained Master Builder and not just some clerk or scribe who executed the drawings and text, as some have suggested. Villard's design book is a historical document that captures and illustrates the architectural and engineering methods of medieval stonemasonry in writing and graphics.

The following are some of Villard's drawings illustrated in Bowie's book, along with my interpretations:

See Figure 225. This is Villard's drawing of the flying buttresses at Reims Cathedral in France.

See Figure 226. This is Villard's detailed drawing of the west façade rose window at Chartres Cathedral in France.

See Figure 227. The Master Builder of Laon wanted to illustrate to visitors the important role the oxen played in bringing the heavy stones to the construction site. He had several oxen heads carved in stone and placed in a prominent

place in the tower. Villard captured this scene of the oxen sticking their heads out of the tower and looking down. Villard was very much impressed with Laon tower and commented, "As you will learn from this book, I have been in many lands, but nowhere have I seen a tower like that of Laon" (Bowie 1959, 10).

Along with the oxen, on the lower right-hand side of the drawing, Villard drew a delicate feminine hand sticking out of the tower holding a flower between her thumb and middle finger. This hand was never actually built as part of the tower. Why did Villard draw it there, and what was the purpose and symbolism he was trying to portray to his viewers? I believe I have found a plausible explanation.

In the fall of 2011, I visited Reims Cathedral in France a second time and was talking to a gentleman who was demonstrating some of the construction tools. He was familiar with Villard de Honnecourt's drawing of Laon tower, so I asked his opinion of why Villard included the feminine hand and what he thought it symbolized. He told me the following: Villard and the other Master Builders wanted to convey to the reader that they were capable of designing and building gigantic towers and spires, and at the same time they could also carve very small and delicate feminine statues and flowers as decorations. He was illustrating that the Master

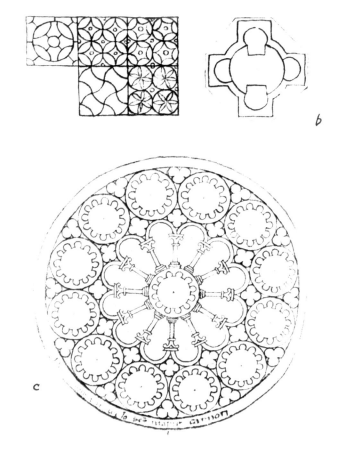

FIGURE 225. Villard de Honnecourt's flying buttress drawing of Reims Cathedral in France. *Reprinted with permission of Indiana University Press.*

FIGURE 226. Villard's west façade rose window, Chartres Cathedral, France. *Reprinted with permission of Indiana University Press.*

Builder and the artists could do it all, from constructing the massive flying buttresses and vaulting work right down to the smallest decorative stone carvings of vines, flowers, and people. There were no bounds to their craftsmanship. The Frenchman's explanation sounded reasonable to me, and I believe that is what Villard was trying to convey. I accept this explanation since I have found no others that have made any sense to me over the years.

See Figure 228. This drawing illustrates human and animal figures based on different stick geometrical forms used as the architectural geometry for building designs. Villard in his own words discusses the geometry of human and animal design features: "Here begins the method of drawing as taught by the art of geometry, to facilitate working. And in the other sheets will be the methods of Masonry" (Bowie 1959, 10).

See Figures 229 and 230. These two drawings illustrate some forty-four different sketches of geometry in architecture and masonry. Many of the sketches have brief descriptions telling the reader their purpose, but not in any detail. They seem to be pictorial formulas, used only as memory joggers for the Master Builder to use himself and to teach others the art of geometry.

See Figure 231. To my knowledge the authors, art historians, and architectural scholars refer to this drawing as two wrestlers engaged, but I have a completely different interpretation of the two young men. In my opinion, Villard used them to illustrate the structural design elevation of a Gothic flying buttress.

The young men's upper curved shoulders and backs illustrate the outer flying buttresses that hold the cathedral together. Note that Villard even added the strong rib cage ribs, representing the flying buttress rib members. Often the flying buttresses are referred to as the ribs of the cathedral structure. The men's two outer legs represent the strong buttress support legs connecting the upper flyers to the ground. The two inner legs represent the column piers that support the nave arcade walls in the cathedral. Note that Villard placed all four of their support feet on three raised foundation pads. If Villard wanted to draw two wrestlers engaged, he would have instead placed them on a flat terrain. The men's interlocking crossed upper arms form strong triangles representing the triangular **gabled** roof structure above the nave ceiling.

Villard made the drawing of the two young men in their postural support position right next to two floor plans with flying buttresses. He also made mention in the caption that further on in his book the reader would see elevations of walls and flying buttresses. Both of these details support my claim.

FIGURE 227. Villard's drawing of the carved oxen mounted in the tower of Laon Cathedral, France. *Reprinted with permission of Indiana University Press.*

FIGURE 228. Villard's drawing of human and animal figures based on geometrical forms. *Reprinted with permission of Indiana University Press.*

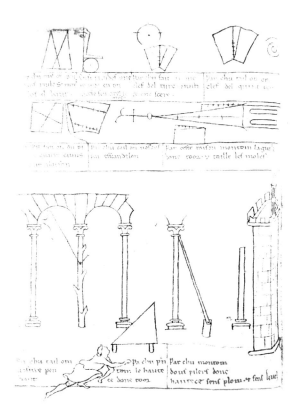

FIGURE 229. Villard's drawings illustrate the geometry the stonemasons used to design and cut stones to size. Included are drawings made for arches and for determining the height of a column by sighting a right-angled triangle. *Reprinted with permission of Indiana University Press.*

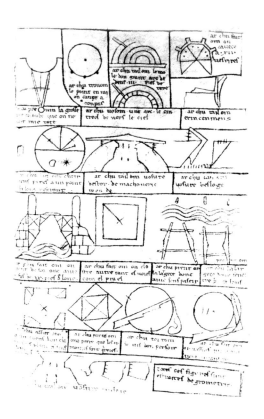

FIGURE 230. Villard's geometrical drawings illustrating the designing and cutting of a variety of stones for constructing cathedrals and other stone structures. *Reprinted with permission of Indiana University Press.*

FIGURE 231. Villard's drawing of two young men standing in a posturing support position adjacent to the cathedral floor plans with flying buttresses. *Reprinted with permission of Indiana University Press.*

CHAPTER 9

BUILDING A GOTHIC CATHEDRAL

Building a cathedral to the heavens was a dangerous job. Narrow ladders, wooden planks, and platforms just wide enough to walk on all posed a challenge. Many of the workers were hundreds of feet in the air and every step must have been a risky one to take. The young craftsmen climbing all over the cathedral had to be strong and physically fit as well. They worked hard and long hours, yet over the years of constructing cathedrals very few accidents or loss of life were recorded. See Figures 232–241.

Building a new cathedral was a monumental expense during the Middle Ages. The bishops requested gifts from the wealthy including gold, silver, coins, property, and land. Generally the bishops, archbishops, kings, and wealthy merchants all contributed to the building fund. The citizens of the community likewise contributed money, some hoping their contributions would help wash away their sins. The carrying of a box around the countryside containing the bones and relics of a saint was also an effective way of collecting additional funds.

With all the fundraisers working together, the community was sometimes able to gather enough money to construct a new house of worship. Let us turn our minds back some 800 years as I describe the basic methods of constructing a Gothic cathedral using only primitive tools. While no two cathedrals were alike, with design variations in each one, the basic construction elements were similar. The entire process was accomplished under the direction of the Master Builder.

FIGURE 232. The Master Builder is directing the apprentices. In the background, stone is being off-loaded from a boat to be transported to the cathedral.

FIGURE 233. The mortar is being mixed to cement the stones together. A well and bucket is shown, along with a water carrier.

FIGURE 234.
Stonemason setters are building a wall. Note the plumb line, square, compasses, maul, chisels, trowels, and mortar.

FIGURE 235. The banker masons are sculpting statues with a
maul and chisels. The blacksmith is in the top center.

FIGURE 236. The Master Mason is making a design layout while the banker
mason is bringing a finished stone for mounting. The banker mason on the left
is working on a stone with a pair of compasses and square.

FIGURE 237. The Master Builder is holding a large pair of compasses and square in his hands. Laborers are working on the right side.

FIGURE 238. Stonemason setters are placing and cementing the keystone on top of the Gothic arch in the wall. Other masons can be seen using a variety of tools. A mortar carrier is on the ladder at the right.

FIGURE 239. Laborers are cranking a hand-operated
crane lifting stones to a higher level.

FIGURE 240. Carpenters are framing a Gothic pointed window before setting it in a wall. Note the auger drill, square, and hammers.

FIGURE 241. A carpenter is sawing a timber with a saw, axe, hammer, and compasses. Two sawyers are cutting large timbers with a framed pit saw.

THE MASTER BUILDER DESIGNED THE CATHEDRAL

The Master Builder captured his grand new cathedral design on parchment drawings with input from the patron, cathedral chapter, and bishop. In the lodge or trasour house he would draw a floor plan, elevation views, and a full west façade entrance view. Later he would make additional parchment drawings as needed for the various phases of construction. He strove to make his design superior to the others in the area as far as length, width, height, and beauty.

Typically the Master Builder would also build a scale model to better answer any questions the patron might have about the cathedral's design and character. He would then select all of the materials, labor, and tools to construct the fabric and arrange for their delivery to the site.

Once the drawings were completed, the Master Builder would begin designing the hundreds of wooden templates or molds used as patterns to hew, carve, and dress the individual stones to their shape. The woodworker would make the wooden templates to the exact size specified on the drawings. Hundreds of thousands of stones were then hewn and dressed by the banker masons to the exact size of the templates. The process of hewing stones to the template dimensions continued for years until the cathedral was completed.

SITE SELECTION FOR ESTABLISHING A NEW CATHEDRAL

Many of the earliest Anglo-Saxon and Romanesque cathedrals were sited over prehistoric megalithic foundations (structures or monuments made of large stones). Professor Lyle Borst, an astronomer and nuclear physicist at New York University, Buffalo, did extensive research on early cathedral site selection, orientation, and architectural geometry. I visited Borst in Buffalo over a weekend in 1982. He pointed out that down through the ages the builders usually preserved the original sites and foundations when constructing new churches and cathedrals. Even today, many of the Gothic cathedral floor plans show parts of walls from the earlier Saxon or Romanesque predecessors.

Borst bridged the gap between megalithic stone circles (henge monuments) and the cathedrals of the Middle Ages built by the Master Builders. His research documented that the magnificent cathedrals of Europe were the result of Master Builders constructing edifices over prehistoric sites, thus preserving their original orientations. His book, *Megalithic Software*, addresses the subject of church orientation to the sun, moon, and stars, construction dating by the church axis alignment method, and Pythagorean triangle geometry in the megalithic foundations and pillars. He points out that cathedrals and churches were built right inside of prehistoric henge circles, circular banks, and ditches.

Knowlton Church, as Borst points out, is unmistakably connected to a prehistoric foundation since it is placed right inside of a henge ring. Sometimes called a church henge, Knowlton is about fifteen miles southwest of Salisbury, England. With evidence of round Roman arches in the masonry, Knowlton Church was built in the twelfth century and placed inside of a henge ring dating c. 2000 BC. See Figure 242.

John Michell, the noted prehistory scholar from London, called Knowlton Church "a church within a Stone Age Sanctuary." He also said, "The early Christian practice of building churches on ancient sacred sites is well illustrated at Knowlton, where the crumbling ruins of a Norman church, unused since 1647, stand in the center of a prehistoric henge or sacred enclosure" (1988, 111). Borst concurs: "The association of church with henge ring is not in doubt" (1975, 50). Both henge ring and medieval church are still standing today and stand as witness to the association between a pre-Christian sanctuary site and a Christian worship site used by the people of Britain.

Many cathedrals were also sited over fresh water springs, near rivers, over holy wells, and on elevated hills. The people needed water, so it made sense that cathedrals were built near a water source. When pilgrims traveled many miles to a cathedral site, they needed water and found it many times at a church. The water wells under many of the cathedrals became holy wells and cathedrals were named after them such as Wells Cathedral in England.

FIGURE 242. Knowlton Church, England. This ruined Norman church is inside the center of a Neolithic henge, ditch, and bank earthworks.

CATHEDRAL AXIS ORIENTATION EAST TO WEST

After the site selection process was completed, the altar location and axis orientation of the cathedral was established. Most of the cathedral axes were intentionally oriented from east to west. The masons did not just select some farmer's hay field and start building a cathedral any which way! See Figure 243.

There were several steps in orienting the cathedral axis:

Step 1: The Master Mason selected the sacred site for the altar stone and planted it. This was the most important stone and at the heart of the sanctuary. The altar was where the most significant services and ceremonies took place.

Step 2: To orient the cathedral axis alignment to the east, facing and bisecting the rising sun, two masons' surveying rods were used. (Surveying rods or deacons' rods were originally used to orient building structures to the four cardinal points: east, west, north, and south.) The first Master Mason placed one rod in line with the altar stone.

Step 3: The first Master Mason then directed the second Master Mason several yards away to move his rod back and forth until it bisected the sun's full orb tangent on the horizon at dawn. These two plumb sighting rods established the orientation of the cathedral to the east. The masons placed two stakes in the ground where the two rods were temporarily located and stretched a tight rope between them, establishing the axis of the cathedral. The masons would have made the above orientation alignment on March 21 or September 21, the spring or autumn equinox, to have the sunrise shine exactly true east and west through the cathedral rose window.

The sunrise swing on the horizon moves daily from the northeast over to the southeast and returns back to the northeast again in one year. The halfway point swing is directly east to west, so if the masons aligned the axis of the cathedral to the east on the equinoxes, it would receive the maximum sunlight shining through the windows. In my opinion this is the reason most of the cathedrals were oriented to the east, to receive the maximum amount of sun into the nave. A large rose window was placed in the east end of the cathedral for the sun to brighten the interior and for the visitor to witness a colorful reflection through the stained glass.

In his book *Circles and Standing Stones,* Evan Hadingham, a British archaeologist, speaks of Freemasonry and cathedral orientation: "It has also been suggested that authentic megalithic traditions were somehow secretly transmitted into historical times when they were incorporated into Christian sanctuaries. Among those supposed traditions was the practice of orientation, which determined the long axes of churches and cathedrals. Freemasons are favorite candidates for this role, and in fact there is some highly interesting evidence to connect them with church architecture and with the simple layout of buildings to face the rising sun" (1975, 188).

John Michell also discusses church axis orientation in *The View Over Atlantis*:

> Most churches point in varying degrees north or south of East. This is explained by an old popular belief that churches are oriented towards the sunrise on the day of the saint to which they are dedicated. All over the ancient world, as Sir Norman Lockyer demonstrated, the second stage in the erection of a temple after its site had been chosen was to secure the correct orientation by stretching a line along its axis towards the point where the sun, moon, or a particular star crossed the horizon on a certain day. This practice, which still survives among the builders of Masonic Lodges, was universally adopted by the early Christians. (1969, 39)

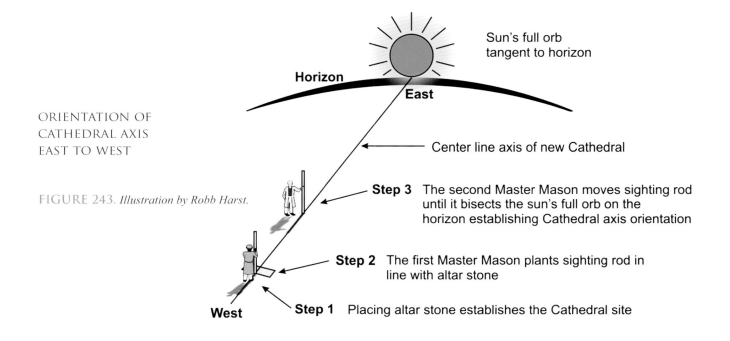

ORIENTATION OF
CATHEDRAL AXIS
EAST TO WEST

FIGURE 243. *Illustration by Robb Harst.*

Sun's full orb tangent to horizon

Horizon

East

Center line axis of new Cathedral

Step 3 The second Master Mason moves sighting rod until it bisects the sun's full orb on the horizon establishing Cathedral axis orientation

Step 2 The first Master Mason plants sighting rod in line with altar stone

West

Step 1 Placing altar stone establishes the Cathedral site

CATHEDRAL FLOOR PLAN LAYOUT USING THE PYTHAGOREAN THEOREM TRIANGLE 3-4-5

The operative masons used the 3-4-5 right angle triangle method to lay out square cathedral floor plans centuries before the use of modern surveying transits. The Pythagorean theorem states that in any right angle triangle, the longest side, or hypotenuse squared, equals the combined squares of the other two sides. See Figure 244.

To understand the 3-4-5 right angle floor plan layout method, see Figure 245. The layout process required Master Masons to tie three knots on a long rope: one thirty feet from the end, one forty feet from the first knot, and one fifty feet from the second knot, forming a large triangle when the ends are joined together. Three masons each held a knot in their hands and stepped backwards, pulling the rope tight, forming a giant ninety degree right-angled triangle.

The three masons then placed the rope triangle on top of the east-west axis previously established, with the thirty-foot length running along the east-west axis and the forty-foot length running what would become the west facade. Pegs were put into the ground where the knots marked the triangles' corners; the knot between the forty and fifty foot length would establish the first corner, at northwest, of the cathedral. They then turned the triangle over on the east-west axis and established the second corner of the cathedral at southwest. If they wanted the cathedral 300 feet long, they walked the triangle down the axis 300 feet and repeated the third and fourth corner steps with pegs. Applying the sacred triangle method four times automatically generated the four right-angle corners of the cathedral. Once the four corners were completed, the diagonal lengths were checked to make sure it was perfect. This tradition of the operative masons laying out a rectangular foundation floor plan was called "stretching the cord" and was passed down through the Middle Ages. See Figure 246.

PHYHAGORAS''S THEOREM: 47TH PROBLEM OF EUCLID

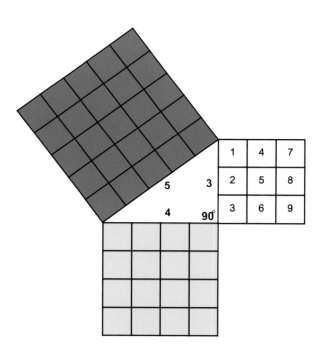

3-4-5 PYTHAGOREAN TRIANGLE
$$3^2 + 4^2 = 5^2$$
$$9 + 16 = 25$$

FIGURE 244. The 3-4-5 triangle and the 90-degree angle it forms inside the triangle. *Illustration by Robb Harst.*

CATHEDRAL FLOOR PLAN LAYOUT

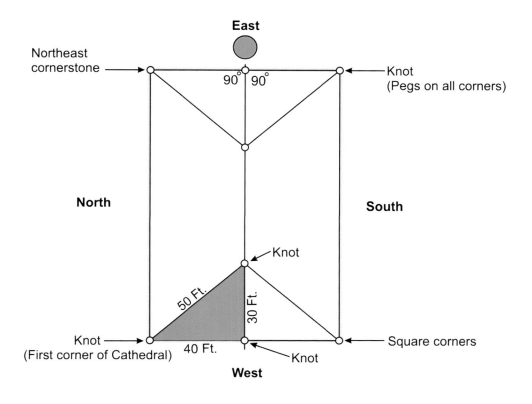

FIGURE 245. 3-4-5 right angle triangle method. *Illustration by Robb Harst.*

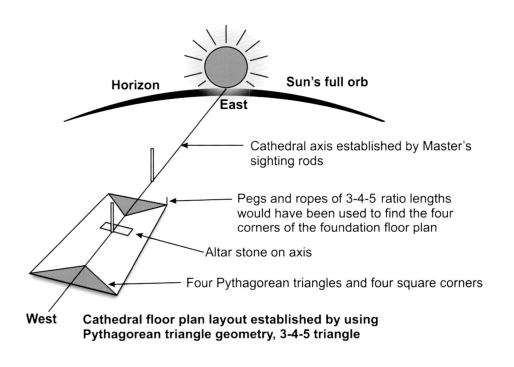

FIGURE 246. Drawing illustrating four right-angled triangles forming the rectangular floor plan axis east to west toward the rising sun. *Illustration by Robb Harst.*

INTENTIONAL BENT AXIS BETWEEN THE CHOIR AND NAVE INTERSECTION

There are several cathedrals that have intentionally bent axes at the intersection of the choir and nave. See Figure 247. The Master Builder aligned the cathedral axis east to west, which included the altar and choir sections of the sanctuary. The Master Masons then continued building westward on the axis until they reached the nave, at which point they intentionally changed the axis orientation angle a few degrees out of alignment.

INTENTIONAL BENT AXIS
ON SEVERAL CATHEDRALS BETWEEN
THE CHOIR AND NAVE

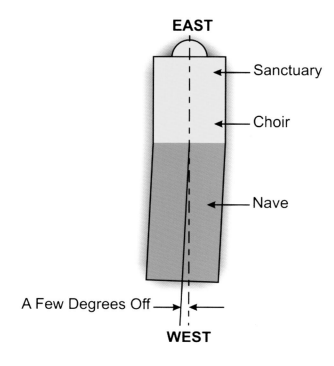

FIGURE 247. *Illustration by Robb Harst.*

The misalignment of the two axes is not noticeable to the average visitor. But when looked for specifically, it can easily be seen when standing at the west end and looking straight down the center nave aisle. Take Washington National Cathedral in Washington, DC, for example: Standing in the center of the west entrance and looking directly east to the choir wall, a carving of Christ in Majesty is seen, but He is not located in the center of the bay! One must step a few feet sideways to the right to make Christ's carving line up

exactly in the center. Likewise, when standing in the center of the eastern-most part of the choir and looking backward toward the western nave, the misalignment of the two axes will again be apparent. See Figures 248–251.

To my knowledge the only author that mentions this phenomenon is John James in *The Traveler's Key to Medieval France* (1986, 73).:"In more than half of all medieval churches there is a small deflection in the axis, the nave not being precisely in line with the choir." He mentions that the bent axis of Chartres Cathedral in France is off by one foot at the altar.

The bent axis phenomenon has puzzled and intrigued me for more than thirty years. Very few people, including a few cathedral administrators, are even aware of this phenomenon. The Master Builder established two distinct axes deliberately, separating the sanctuary from the nave. Why?

Though a few explanations have been put forward, I do not feel any of them are plausible. But I do have a theory myself. The Master Builder's role was to design, build, and replicate God's house or heaven on earth in his cathedral design. He wanted to please God in every small detail. Therefore, he demanded perfection in quality and craftsmanship from all of his men on the project. He wanted the cathedral to be perfect just like God. But more importantly he wanted God to know that he and his men were *not perfect*. Only God was perfect!

The Master Builder wanted to leave God some physical evidence in the cathedral design to illustrate the fact that he and his workers were not perfect builders, that they were sinners and had other imperfections. He wanted to acknowledge and show God his imperfections in his own subtle way, so he created an imperfection in the building alignment of the nave axis without it being easily noticeable by the public. By making this deliberate alignment mistake, he made it *right with God*, acknowledging that he and his craftsmen were not perfect.

There were two distinct parts of a medieval cathedral: the sanctuary for God's presence and the nave for the worshippers. Interestingly, the axis is perfectly aligned to the east through the altar, choir, and full sanctuary where all the services happen in God's presence. But the worshippers (sinners and common folk with imperfections) were prohibited from entering the sacred choir area. They were traditionally located in the nave with the misaligned axis.

The following are a few cathedrals with a slightly bent axis: Bristol, Chester, Ely, Exeter, Lichfield, Lincoln, Llandaff, St. Albans, Southwark, Canterbury, Chartres, Notre Dame Paris, Noyon, and Washington National Cathedral.

FIGURE 248. Washington National Cathedral, Washington, DC.
This view is from the center of the west entrance door. It showcases the
misalignment of Christ, who appears left of the three Gothic arches
because of the bent axis.

FIGURE 249. Washington National Cathedral, Washington, DC.
This view is from a few feet to the right of the view from Figure 248.
Christ now appears perfectly in the center of the three Gothic arches.

FIGURE 250. Washington National Cathedral, Washington, DC. This is a close-up of
Christ perfectly centered after the viewer moved a few feet to the right.

FIGURE 251. Washington National Cathedral, Washington, DC. This image was taken standing in front of
Christ looking backward toward the western nave entrance. The misalignment of the two axes is again apparent.
The three western Gothic arches do not line up with the three wooden arch columns in the choir.

Quarrying and Transporting the Stone to the Cathedral Site

The Romanesque and Gothic cathedrals were built out of stone, the most durable and longest lasting material in use at the time. Different types and grades of limestone were used to build the majority of the cathedrals; the Master Builder had to order stone from a reputable quarry or open up a new stone quarry himself. Extracting huge blocks of stone and getting them out of the quarry and ready for transport was an expensive and dangerous process.

Initially the Master Builder had to hire and arrange for all the different type of stone workers and their tools to be delivered to the quarry site. To reach a good solid bed of limestone, the masons had to first remove the top soil and rubble. Then, to extract the immense stone blocks, they would use a method called "plug and feathers" wherein several holes would be drilled in a straight line with star chisels and iron hammers. They would then drive small tapered metal wedges down into the holes, wedging and forcing the stone to split apart on a straight line. These aligned holes and wedges would be located vertically and horizontally to define the desired block size. The stones were then raised out of the quarry using hand-operated wooden derricks and placed onto wooden wagons and sleds for transport to the cathedral site.

The quarry would continually supply the correct stone type with regard to hardness, color, and quantity. But the cost of shipping the stone over land was very expensive, so if some could be shipped by river or sea, transportation costs could be dramatically reduced. Many of the English cathedrals used stone from France because of its good quality, but the shipping costs were then even higher than stone from an English quarry.

To help offset cost, in most cases the Master Builder in charge of the quarry operations set up a stonemason's lodge for the quarry masons. The masons would hew, dress, and ship the stones in specified block sizes to the cathedral site, as opposed to just shipping large uncut rough ashlars. Cutting stone to specified sizes meant only a minimum amount of scrap stone would need to be hauled to the cathedral site. Most of the scrap stone was left at the quarry, saving a considerable amount of money on freight and labor. Then the skilled banker masons at the cathedral site would dress the stones to the desired sizes and sculptural designs.

Digging the Foundation Trenches and Laying the Foundation Stones

The Master Builders directed the laborers to dig down to bedrock for a good foundation base. If no bedrock was found, the soil had to be dug deep enough and wide enough for the construction of a massive stone foundation that would support the enormous weight of the cathedral stones above ground. All of the foundation excavation trenches were dug by hand with primitive tools. Picks, bars, and shovels were used to excavate the ground, which was carried away in baskets and barrows. At some point, a wheel was attached to the barrow and it became a wheelbarrow, eliminating one man's labor! The foundation trenches were wider at the bottom and became narrower at the top or at grade level. The excavated trenches had to be level to form a good flat surface for the first layer of stones.

The stones brought from the quarries, dressed to size and shape by the banker masons, were lowered down below grade into the foundation trenches with hand-operated winches and cranes. The stonemason layers then mortared (cemented) the stones and laid up the foundation walls to ground level.

The foundation stones laid below ground were some of the most important stones in the entire cathedral. If a solid and level foundation was not provided, the cathedral would not last a thousand years. The foundation stones had to be strong enough, wide enough, and level enough to support the millions of pounds of stone, marble, plaster, mortar, lead, tile, glass, iron, and wood above them. If the foundation walls were not built plumb and level, the upper walls would shift or settle in time, collapsing the entire cathedral wall into rubble.

Additional foundation underpinning was provided below the giant clustered column supports at the crossing and under the flying buttress bases, because this is where most of the cathedral weight was concentrated. These specific areas had to have deeper and bigger foundation supports underneath. Only after the foundation walls were built up to ground level could the stone walls above ground be started.

STONE MASON MARKS AND POSITION SYSTEM MARKS

A mason's mark is a symbol, monogram, or initial incised on the surface of a carved stone identifying the stonemason who carved it. It was his personal signature. Mason marks have been chiseled upon dressed and carved stones for over a thousand years and are still readily found on Romanesque and Gothic cathedrals. Some of the mason marks are easily seen on cathedral stonewalls and others have been hidden forever on the inside of the walls or up in the bowels of the fabric. Some of the marks can still be identified and traced back to a particular stonemason's name by comparing them to a register of mason marks that had been developed. See Figure 89.

In the late 1980s on a visit to Wells Cathedral in England, I met Arthur Rice and his son David, both longtime cathedral employees. Rice gave me a booklet for my research: *Mason Marks on Wells Cathedral* by G.A.A. Wright and W. A. Wheeler (1980). The booklet illustrates 509 mason marks found, identified, and recorded at Wells Cathedral. Several marks were duplicates scattered throughout the fabric. I was also given a list of mason marks, including several unique-looking ones, on a visit to York Minster. The list was compiled by H. Stansfield, verger, 1890, along with a Mr. Green, architect, 1938, and T.P. Cooper.

Mason marks can also be found at Salisbury Cathedral in England. Salisbury and the surrounding grounds are enclosed inside a stone wall called a cathedral close. The close is laid up with stones that were once a part of the original walls of Old Sarum Cathedral about two miles away, which was torn down soon after the Salisbury Cathedral was constructed. Many of the old stones still show legible mason marks from the Old Sarum Cathedral in 1092.

Exeter Street in Salisbury runs parallel with a section of the cathedral close wall that still has dozens of mason marks visible on the stones. I stayed in the 600-year-old hotel on Exeter Street next to the wall and the following morning I photographed several of the mason marks. The wall also had a couple of carved human busts inserted into it. I do not know if the busts depict saints, the Master Builder of Old Sarum, or someone else, but I was delighted to find them. The carvings were completed more than 900 years ago, but their personal marks are still legible today.

Mason marks are also called banker marks. After the banker mason completed his stone carving, he inscribed his personal mark onto the stone. Many banker masons spent their entire lives carving intricate stone sculptures standing at their banker benches.

The mason marks were considered a signature of the mason's skill and craftsmanship as well. The overseer of the stonemasons would pass judgment on the quality of the carved stone and could easily identify the maker of the work by his mark. The mason would be paid his wages for good work, square work, and quality craftsmanship, but if the carved stone was not up to the proper standards, it would be rejected as inferior work and his wages would not be paid.

The personal incised mason marks are not to be confused with carved position marks. The position marks are used to position a particular carving or statue on a building in a predetermined location. On the west façade entrance of cathedrals it was typical to have dozens of carved stone statues mounted in rows as part of the exterior decorations. These statues were carved by the banker mason and taken to the front of the cathedral for mounting. A carved position mark was incised on the statue to determine its proper location on the wall.

Laying the Masonic Cornerstone

It has been an age-old Masonic tradition to lay the first stone of a cathedral or other public/private building in the northeast corner on June 21, summer solstice. It was called the Masonic **cornerstone** and was also referred to as the foundation stone or mark stone. Why place the first stone in the northeast corner? The answer to this question goes back to the original layout of the cathedral floor plan, when the sun's movements on the horizon were studied, understood, and then used in the cathedral's orientation layout. See Figure 245.

On June 21, summer solstice, the sun rises in the northeast direction and establishes the beginning of a new solar year with the annual swings of the sun along the horizon. The sun rises at different points on the horizon each day between the northeast and southeast quadrant during the annual swings back and forth. The masons studied astronomy and geometry for centuries, and they selected the summer solstice sunrise position in the northeast as part of their building tradition. Solstice means "stop" in Latin. The sun stopped moving along the horizon in the northeast position, then reversed itself to start a new year cycle again. I believe the stonemasons placed the first stone in the northeast corner of the cathedral because it was the beginning of the solar year and the beginning of their new cathedral project.

The stonemasons have always laid the Masonic cornerstone with impressive ceremonies and solemn rites in the northeast corner of the building. George Washington, first US President and Grand Master of Masons, laid the cornerstone of the US Capitol Building with grand ceremonies in Washington, DC, on September 18, 1793. See Figure 252.

George Washington Laying the Cornerstone of the United States Capitol, Sept. 18, 1793

FIGURE 252. Painting by John D. Melius depicting George Washington laying the cornerstone of the United States Capitol on Sept. 18, 1793. Note George Washington's gavel above the cornerstone, his Master's jewel, his Masonic apron, and the other Masons with their aprons in period dress. The three officers on the right are offering corn, wine, and oil during the ceremony. The Bible, plumb line, square and compass emblem, mortarboard with mortar, and trowel are all illustrated as well. Two brothers are lowering the cornerstone for placement and cementing. *Used with permission of the House of the Temple Historic Preservation Foundation, Inc. All Rights Reserved.*

How Did the Stonemasons Lift the Large Stones and Set Them into Place?

The stonemasons were faced with the daunting challenge of lifting heavy stones high into the air and then setting them into their proper place in the cathedral.

The Master Carpenter constructed an oversized wooden wheel about twelve feet in diameter and four feet wide with a large wooden axle mounted through the center. The axle was mounted on two outrigger bearings and had a rope wound around it. It was named a "windlass wheel" or "great wheel," and it looked like a large paddle wheel. The craftsmen mounted the wheel in the higher elevations of the cathedral and used it as a man-operated crane to lift the heavy stones. The end of the rope was attached to the stone below, and then one or two men literally walked inside the caged wheel, turning the axle and winding up the rope and stone to the desired elevation. As the building walls grew taller, the windlass wheel was moved higher on the framing until the cathedral was enclosed and completed at the top. See Figures 87 and 221.

One or two men could easily raise the heavy stones because of the leverage or mechanical advantage that occurred on the windlass wheel. With the windlass wheel some twelve feet in diameter and the rope axle only eighteen inches in diameter, a mechanical advantage occurred with a ratio of about eight to one. Two men weighing 150 pounds each (totaling 300 pounds) times an advantage of eight, equals a 2,400 pound load that could be raised. Wheel diameters ranged from about eight feet to sixteen feet. Years ago, I saw two double windlass wheels mounted on a building in a fourteenth century Bible painting. This example would have afforded a lot of lifting power.

In September of 2010, I visited Canterbury Cathedral and asked an elderly priest if there was a windlass wheel in the cathedral. He told me that as a young boy about nine years old he saw a windlass wheel up above the transept area. He said it was about twelve feet in diameter and had two men to operate it with one brakeman, though he could not remember what the brake system looked like. This is the only windlass wheel that I am aware of that had a braking system for stopping in any emergency. I have always wondered about brakes, not seeing any on those I visited.

I find it quite strange that I haven't observed any safety devices on the wheels to stop them at desired levels or to prevent them from unintentionally backing up and dropping the stone. There were clock pawls designed in those days, allowing rotary motion in only one direction, which would have prevented the wheel and stone from backing down. Why weren't they used?

There is also a windlass wheel at Salisbury Cathedral which is very unique. In addition to having two men walk inside the wheel for winding power, it also has two sets of round wooden dowels mounted on the outside so that two more men could help power the wheel, totaling four men. This windlass wheel is what is called a four horsepower wheel!

Most of the great wheels have disappeared over the years, but a few still exist in the cathedral towers. Several are still used today to haul up material for maintenance repairs. It is amazing that a medieval crane some 700 years old can still be used today for its original purpose. The following is a list of cathedrals that still have windlass wheels in place: Canterbury, Beverley, Peterborough, Salisbury, Wells, York, Exeter, Beauvais, Tewksbury, Freiburg, Mont-Saint-Michel, and Ulm. But I am sure there are many more that have not seen the light of day for centuries.

The stonemasons also used other hand-crank operated hoists called windlass cranes. There were dozens of different designs and arrangements for the various applications, but they were all operated by hands and legs. These types of hoists were used for the lighter loads, such as smaller stones, mortar, wood, etc.

The last method the stonemasons used to lift and move materials was done by hand or brute force. The men who completed this part of the work were generally known as the laborers. Though their jobs were considered unskilled, it must be remembered the work done by them was also necessary to the completion of the cathedral.

Building the Sanctuary (Altar, Choir, and Apse) East to West

The Master Builder traditionally started construction of the cathedral on the east end first and sequentially worked toward the west. Therefore, the sanctuary on the east end was completed before the formal entrance on the west end. The sanctuary, comprising the altar, choir, and apse, was the heart of the cathedral. It was completed first to allow the clergy to conduct religious services immediately after enclosing the roof. The people did not want to wait until the entire cathedral was finished, which could take many additional years, to begin services

The Master Masons began building the sanctuary by constructing large **compound piers** to support most of the vault and roof weight. These massive, thick, column support piers generally consisted of several shaft columns clustered together. They were built with thousands of dressed stones cemented together. The piers were placed in two parallel lines that spanned the full length of the cathedral and were spaced apart, forming the nave walls and bays.

At the same time the support column piers were being constructed, the masons also built and connected the arcade walls between the piers, forming the nave walls. The interior nave arcade walls at ground level were built by constructing pointed arch openings between each of the large column piers. These open arches allowed people to move freely between the nave and the side aisles. The walls in the upper triforium and clerestory levels were constructed with both solid stone walls and open stone tracery frames to hold the stained-glass windows in place, allowing more sunlight to enter the interior.

As the stone setter continued building and raising the walls between the support piers, the materials of stone, mortar, and wood had to be hoisted up to the new levels. Laborers carried the materials up by hand, along with the help of hand-operated winches and cranes. The crane hoisting rope was attached to the large stones with an ingenious three-piece metal device called a lewis. The lewis mechanism was placed inside a cavity slot chiseled in the top of the stone to help balance it while it was being lifted and set in place. See Figure 193.

An iron scissor lifting device was also used to move the smaller stones into place on the walls. As the walls grew higher, the heavier stones were hoisted up by the windlass wheel.

After the support piers and walls of the three levels were completed in the sanctuary, the round apse end of the cathedral had to be enclosed. It was constructed with similar support piers and walls placed in a radiating pattern that enclosed it.

Building the Crossing, Transepts, and Nave

Once the walls in the sanctuary part of the cathedral were completed, the work moved west to the next construction phases of the crossing, transepts, and nave. The square crossing was formed by the intersection of the nave and transepts. Many times a tower was mounted above the crossing, requiring much bigger foundation and support column piers at the four corners of the crossing.

The north and south transept additions were built in the same way as the sanctuary, but at right angles to the axis of the cathedral, forming the Christian cross. The transepts, like the sanctuary, had flying buttresses built outside of the walls.

The long nave was built westward from the transept crossing with the same pier spacing and wall width as the sanctuary. The west façade entrance usually had decorations and several statues mounted on the wall to impress visitors as they approached. The west entrance also had oversized doors to allow visitors easy access in and out. Again, flying buttresses were located outside the nave walls to prevent the upper walls from spreading.

ERECTING THE FLYING BUTTRESSES TO THE EXTERIOR WALLS

The sanctuary, crossing, transepts, and nave support piers and walls were now ready for the heavy vaulted ceiling and roof structure to be installed. But before the masons could begin construction, they needed to erect flying buttresses to the outer walls to prevent them from pushing outward from the vertical and lateral weight. See Figure 4.

Constructing these mammoth stone arches some eighty feet in the air was a difficult and dangerous job. Each one of the large **voussoir** (wedge-shaped) stones in the arch had to be perfectly cut and dressed by the banker mason to the exact same angle to form the desired radius arch. But how would he hold the stones up to cement and set them in place? To do this, the Master Carpenter constructed half-moon-shaped wooden frames to bridge across the outer wall piers down to the huge vertical buttresses. These temporary wooden bridges were called **centerings,** and they held the arch stones in place. The masons cemented the wedge-shaped stones

and placed them on top of the wooden centering, forming the arches. After the mortar dried, the stone arches became self-supporting. The masons were then able to remove the large temporary wooden centerings. The centering frame was then moved to the next bay and the same process was repeated until all the flying buttresses surrounded the cathedral like a birdcage.

These giant flying buttresses provided enough backup or counterweight support to prevent the inner walls from pushing outward when the roof weight was applied. The masons cut grooved gutters on top of the flying buttress arches to channel roof water down to the ground. The flying buttress ribs served as the structural support to hold the entire cathedral together, just like the strong rib cage does in a human. After the flying buttresses were in place, the stone vaulting and roof weight could then be placed on the piers.

STONE VAULTED CEILINGS TO COVER THE NAVE

The Gothic cathedrals were built with stone vaulted arched ceilings spanning the entire width of the sanctuary, transepts, and nave. This was a new element in Gothic design that used the pointed arches and cross rib vaults as arch supports spanning the openings. The masons used wooden centerings as a temporary support mechanism to hold the stones up in a vaulted arch position, similar to the flying buttress centerings. They placed two arched centerings end-to-end with a keystone

in between. The wedge-shaped vousiour stones were then cemented and set in place to dry. The mortar dried slowly in this process and could slow the stone vaulting operation. It had to dry completely before the temporary centerings could be removed and placed in the next bay. The masons would crisscross the ribs to get extra strength in each bay. The vaulted ceiling ribs were set on top of the vertical column piers built along both sides of the nave.

ERECTING A STEEP, GABLED ROOF TO ENCLOSE THE CATHEDRAL

Steep, gabled roofs were constructed across the pier support walls enclosing the sanctuary, transepts, and nave to make the fabric weatherproof. The carpenters built steep, gabled wooden frames for the roof, constructing and assembling the triangular **trusses** on the ground with mortise and tenon joints and then pinning them together with wooden dowels called treenails. The carpenter inscribed Roman numerals on the ends of the timbers to identify them for reassembly. The roof framing was then disassembled and

hoisted up to the roof line with small hand cranes and the windlass wheel to be reassembled. Upon completion of the roof framing and sheeting, the top roofing material was installed to seal it.

Generally, the roofing material used was lead sheets fastened together by crimping the edges to seal them. The cathedral was rainproof for a hundred years. Some of the cathedrals were also covered with slate or tiles, depending upon the materials available in the area.

Making and Meaning of the Rose Stained-Glass Windows

The rose and stained-glass windows surrounding the cathedral are the frosting on the cake! The great, round rose window is the focal point of the cathedral, showcasing a variety of brilliantly colored stained-glass petals. Some of the colossal rose windows crafted by the glaziers are around fifty feet in diameter. The masons designed very elaborate geometrical shapes in the stone tracery of the rose windows, and they are sometimes called the crown jewels of the cathedral. See Figures 253 and 254.

The rose windows represent three basic things: God's eyes looking in, God's light shining in, and the beautiful rose flower. God's eyes watch every thought, word, and deed of the bishop and parishioners through the rose window. The glory of God's light also shines in the rose window, enlightening the interior with God's Sun (Son) whose presence is with them during the worship service. The rose window is also shaped like a giant wheel with spokes divided into pie-shaped sections of colored glass representing the petals of a rose flower. Many of the round rose windows were designed and constructed exactly like a wagon wheel, with hub, spokes, felloes, and a rim.

Originally called cathedral wheels, rose windows probably came down to us from the ancient Beltane fire festivals celebrated in England. In pre-Christian days, fire ring wheels were rolled down the hill in the evening, symbolizing the sun rolling down from the sky. The sun represented death as it disappeared below the horizon at dusk and life as it rose again at dawn. The fire wheels were generally rolled on festival days such as the summer and winter solstices, the longest and shortest days of the year.

Many ancient Masonic lodges celebrated their summer festivals on St. John the Baptist's Day (summer solstice) and their winter festivals on St. John the Evangelist's Day (winter solstice). Bernard Jones discusses the wheel symbol associated with the two Masonic festival days:

> There seems good ground for assuming that the two saints' days were originally days of heathen rejoicing, being the summer and the winter solstices, cleverly appropriated by the Early Christian Fathers and by them fastened on the two Saints Johns. We find that the emblem of the wheel is common to both of the festivals, although chiefly associated with that of winter. A wheel used to be rolled about to signify the sun, which at the June festival occupies the highest place in the Zodiac. In some festivals it was taken to the top of the hill, straw was tied around it and set on fire, and the wheel was then set rolling down to the valley, it appearing "at a distance as if the sun had fallen from the sky…. The people imagine that all their ill-luck rolls away from them together with this wheel." (1975, 339)

Jones further addresses the fire wheel symbol adopted by the early Christian Church:

> The (Gothic) letter, the very symbol of the sun, is plainly the shape of a wheel, and is believed to be related to the Gothic word 'HVIL,' the same as the Anglo-Saxon 'HWEOL,' from which is derived the English word 'wheel'. The sun was likened to a wheel of fire, and the "element blazing out of him" was represented in the shape of a wheel. In the twelfth and thirteenth centuries, in France and other countries, there were religious rites at midsummer in which fires were lighted and blazing wheels, representing the sun, were rolled about. This pagan wheel-symbol appears to have been adopted by the Christian Church, as evidence of which we may note that a foundation-stone of an altar in a French church of 1171 carries five of these wheel devises engraven upon its top face. (1975, 407–408)

It is reasonable to assume that placing the rose windows in the old Romanesque cathedrals came from the custom of rolling the fire wheels down the hills, replicating the sun coming down out of heaven. I believe it symbolized the cycle of the seasons, life and death of Christ, crops and vegetation. The fire wheel or rose windows were assembled with colored glass to represent God's Sun (Son), who cast light through the rose windows.

The rose flower also has a connection with Christ and the cross. "The rose is the symbol of Christ, and the Cross, the symbol of his death —the two united, the rose suspended on the cross—signify his death on the cross, whereby the secret of immortality was taught to the world. In a word, the rose on the cross is Christ crucified" (Mackey 1924, 635). Henry Coil corroborates this connection: "The rose is dedicated to Venus and is also a symbol of secrecy, hence the term, sub rosa. In some way, the rose came to represent regeneration or regenerative energy and, hence immortality, and in that way, it became a symbol of Christ. Accordingly, the symbol of the rose on the cross means Christ on the cross or Crucifixion" (1961, 575). As a tribute to its significance, the rose window was mounted in the cathedral as a centerpiece.

In my opinion, the rose wheel flower was originally selected to represent the life, death, and immortality of Christ. The rose flower is beautiful and full of life in the summer, then withers away and dies in the winter. It is regenerated again in the spring with buds that begin to bloom during the summer. The rose windows were placed in the old Romanesque cathedrals to symbolize and replicate the cycle of Christ's life and hopefully the people's own life cycle.

FIGURE 253. A beautiful rose flower.

FIGURE 254. Colorful cathedral wheel rose window that replicates the natural beauty
of the rose. This rose window is in the south transept of Chartres Cathedral.

LANCET STAINED-GLASS WINDOWS

The tall, vertical stained-glass windows with sharp points at the top mounted around the walls in the nave are called lancet windows, getting their name from a pointed lance. These large bays of beautifully decorated stained glass allowed the light to shine in while also illustrating biblical and daily life scenes involving medieval man. They served as Bibles in glass for the people of the day.

In some of the darker cathedrals, the glaziers installed a plain or lighter colored green/gray glass called **grisaille**, which allowed additional light to enter.

The colored stained-glass windows were made by heating silica sand, beech wood ash, lime, and metallic oxides, for color, such as cobalt, gold, copper, iron, and manganese.

After heating the mixture white hot, the glass became pliable for shaping with the blow pipe. The glass blower gathered a small glob of molten glass on the end of a hollow blow pipe about four feet long and then blew air into the hot glass, expanding it into a balloon shape. He then collapsed and flattened the glass balloon and let it cool to harden.

These large pieces of colored glass were then cut into different sizes and shapes for the window pattern or design. The glazier mounted these hundreds of different pieces of glass into lead frames, forming a beautiful and sparkling painting. The large sections of glass windows were then mounted into magnificently carved stone tracery window frames.

ERECTING THE TALL TOWERS, STEEPLES, AND SPIRES

The towers, steeples, and spires were generally on the west entrance or above the central crossing of the cathedral or both. The question is, after some seventy-five years of constructing a cathedral at great expense and labor, why would the people want to spend more money and another twenty years of labor to construct a Gothic tower or spire? Church services do not require a tall steeple. And building a giant tower and attaching it to the fabric could create foundation and technical problems like leaky roofs.

I believe the Master Builders built these tall steeples to serve as physical beacons or conduit delivery systems to heaven, not just to be noticed from a great distance. I believe they were designed as an antenna for worshippers to send their prayers up to God and receive their answers back. The short towers mounted on top of the earliest Christian churches served the same purpose in my opinion. The Master Builders who built the soaring Gothic spires felt they were getting closer to God to deliver the peoples' prayers. It was their Jacob's ladder to heaven, as depicted on the front entrance façade of Bath Abbey in England. Angels are climbing up the ladder with their prayers to God on the right side, and bringing them back down on the left side. See Figure 80. It was their physical gateway to heaven.

The pilgrims walking across the countryside also used the high spires as landmarks to guide them to the cathedrals. These visuals served as symbols of civic pride for the citizens of the community and members of the congregation. Most of the tall steeples and spires were crowned with a large Christian cross.

The Germans built the tallest spires in the world, and I believe using the open, lacy spire design allowed them to do so. Cologne, Freiburg, Ulm, and Strasbourg all have these lacy spires. The German Master Builders experimented with spire designs and high wind loads, and their spires were created with an intentional open stone feature for several reasons: It gave them the required structural strength and spire height they were after; it allowed them to build the spires with considerable less stone, reducing some of the foundation requirements along with construction time, labor, and costs; and it allowed the high winds to whistle through the openings, thus reducing the high wind forces against the spire. The side wind loads were dramatically minimized and, as a result, the German Steinmetzen (stonemasons) were able to build the tallest spires to heaven.

The German Master Builders shared their new open lace spire design with other operative stonemason's lodges in the area, which would explain the similarity of the spires of Cologne, Freiburg, Ulm, and Strasbourg. If it were structurally possible, the German Steinmetzen would probably have built their spires a mile high, but the material weight of the stone and secure foundations prohibited them from doing so. I believe they built to the design limits of the materials.

Unlike the Germans, the English stonemasons generally designed enclosed spires, and over the centuries many of them were blown down and destroyed from high wind forces. Salisbury Cathedral, the tallest in England, is a fine example of an English spire still standing in majesty. See Figure 29. There are many other fantastic looking English spires still standing as well.

Like everything else about building a cathedral, constructing gigantic spires was a risky, time-consuming endeavor. The towers were a continuation of the cathedral walls taken up to higher levels and with a more substantial foundation. They were more of a challenge to build because of the scaffolding required and the effort of getting the stone and materials up to the work level.

The steeples were generally tapered like an upside down cone. To start the job, the masons built a scaffold inside the cone and then began to construct the exterior base of the cone. They continued building the scaffolding up on the inside while simultaneously constructing the cone upward. This process continued upward until there was no more room for the mason to physically maneuver inside the cone. At this elevation point, the craftsman moved outside the spire's cone and sat on a chair attached to ropes. He swung around the top of the spire and continued enclosing the cone with stone or wood until it was completed. Then a Christian cross was hoisted up with ropes and mounted on top of the spire.

It was dangerous to construct the spire, because there was no room to work and no place to put materials. These craftsmen worked hundreds of feet in the air, putting their lives at risk each day. I doubt they even took scheduled breaks, as it would take them too long to climb down and back up again.

Casting and Setting the Bells in the Bell Tower

Cathedral bells were usually installed in the crossing tower, so their peals could be easily heard all around town. The bells were rung at designated times to summon the worshippers to services. They had ropes attached to them for the bell ringers to pull, which swung the bell back and forth. The bell ringers had to be fully trained before they could properly ring the bells.

While most bells were cast iron, a few were cast in bronze, and they were fabricated by pouring hot liquid bell metal into clay molds contoured and shaped like a bell. After the molten metal solidified, the clay mold was broken apart, leaving the finished cast metal bell. The bells were cleaned, scraped, and then fine-tuned for the correct sound or pitch by removing small amounts of metal on strategic locations of the inside and outside surfaces. The highly trained craftsman who accomplished this precise task was a real specialist.

The finished bells were then rigged for lifting into the bell tower for placement. It was a challenge to hoist the heavy bells in a safe manner. Again, large windlass wheels, other hand-operated hoists, and cranes were used to lift the bells in place.

In later years it became a common practice to install additional bells in the bell tower. Many of these heavy cast bells swinging back and forth weighed several tons. In many cases the tower walls and foundations were not designed for this extra weight; when all the bells would swing back and forth in unison, the momentum and inertia would vibrate and literally shake the tower walls loose. In a few cathedrals, this problem was solved by constructing a separate and heavier bell tower building adjacent to the cathedral. A few other cathedrals stopped swinging and ringing the heavy bells before serious damage was done to the support structure. What a shame!

The Magnificent Cathedral Interior

The first-time visitor will be amazed at the excellent stone carvings displayed throughout a cathedral. The Saint's shrines and altars are impressive, especially considering the fact they were made with primitive hand tools. The stone screen separating the choir and the nave is also outstanding with its intricate details. See Figure 49. Many of the marble and stone pulpits are equally extraordinary, showcasing the artists' craftsmanship.

Inside the immense St. Lawrence Church in Nuremberg, Germany, there is an outstanding self-portrait stone carving executed by Adam Kraft, Master Mason. He carved himself kneeling, holding a chisel in one hand and a maul in the other. The detail in his hair and facial expression is remarkable. A little color was added to his cheeks, lips, and beard to enhance the realism. Behind the self-portrait is a tall Gothic tabernacle that Kraft also carved. See Figure 255.

There are hundreds of wonderful woodcarvings throughout the fabric as well. The choir holds impressive, detailed Gothic carvings on the seats, benches, misery cord seats, walls, cupboards, railings, etc. Most of the carvings are executed in oak and walnut.

FIGURE 255. Adam Kraft's self-portrait is a masterpiece of stone sculpture in St. Lawrence Church, Nuremberg, Germany.

Along with stone and wood carvings, the interior holds many types of adornments. Many professional oil paintings hang in the cathedrals, the details of which are strikingly realistic. There are hundreds of tapestries and needlepoint items hanging in many of the cathedrals as well. Other decorations included highly adorned silver and gold vessels used in the several services conducted each day. They were made and engraved by the best gold and silversmiths available and were used by the archbishops, bishops, and clergy.

One unique decorative figure found in many of the cathedrals and churches all over the British Isles and continent of Europe is called the Green Man. The green man carvings depict human faces or heads with green leaves (often acacia leaves) and vegetation sprouting out of their mouths, ears, eyes, and hair. Some have brown vegetation leaves. The faces of the green men portray different expressions and were carved in both wood and stone. The carvings are typically found inside, though a few are found outside of the churches. Many are high above in the ceiling areas, out of view from the average visitor, and others are near doors.

The original purpose and symbolism of the Green Man carvings were lost during the Middle Ages and have been a mystery ever since. There have been articles and a few books written on the Green Man, but to my knowledge no one has fully explained the symbolism and meaning.

Could the Green Man be a face-like evergreen symbol for the immortality of the soul? Could the brown leaves on the faces represent death and the spring green leaves represent rebirth again, evergreen and everlasting life? The green sprig of acacia is the evergreen and ever-living symbol of immortality and resurrection. Does the Green Man represent the death and resurrection of Christ and, hopefully, of man?

The medieval stonemasons always associated themselves with nature (humans, animals, and plants) by carving them as decorations in the cathedrals. I believe the Green Man was adopted by the early stonemasons as a symbol of immortality of the soul. Villard de Honnecourt sketched four different Green Men in his architectural design book. How interesting that he felt it was important enough to include them. See Figure 256.

Along with the Green Man, the visitor will see a variety of Christ crucifixes made of stone, wood, and iron placed around the cathedrals. My favorite is Christ on the cross, along with Mary and John on either side, hanging above the scissor crossing of Wells Cathedral. See Figure 56.

Many of the Romanesque and Gothic style cathedrals have outstanding painted walls and ceilings in contrasting colors. The hexagonal lantern with a painting of Christ in the center at the crossing of Ely Cathedral in England is a superb ceiling painting. See Figure 73.

The decorated ceilings of the transept crossings are also spectacular. My favorite is Canterbury Cathedral in England with the fan vaulting and color contrast details. See Figure 38.

And the nave ceilings replicating the heavens are beautifully decorated with paintings. Many of the ceilings have ornate fan vaulting and painted bosses.

The cathedral interiors were mammoth, and one wonders how they were heated during the cold winter months of the Middle Ages. Well, actually they were not heated! Imagine going to a service in the middle of January. It would be like sitting on the floor of a gigantic stone freezer. There were not even chairs or church benches in the cathedrals. The members would sometimes bring their own chairs or they would spread straw on the floor to sit. It has been reported that a few may have brought small charcoal burners along for heat. But what a fire hazard that would be. It would be difficult to calculate what the annual cost would be today to heat a cathedral with a million cubic feet of space.

Many years ago, I saw a reference about a bishop at Durham Cathedral in England who had a charcoal burner mechanism hooked up to a brass water circulating system to warm his hands during the service. The water heater had two columns with brass spheres on top. The warm water circulated from the natural heat rising in the system. During my two visits to Durham, I could never find anyone who knew anything about this hand warmer used by the bishop. But in Villard de Honnecourt's *Sketchbook* (1225–1250), he described how to make a brass hand warmer along with a sketch. "If you wish to make a hand warmer, you must first make a kind of brass apple with two fitting halves… A bishop may freely use this device at High Mass; his hands will not get cold as long as the fire lasts. That is all there is to it" (Bowie, 1959, 9). I would bet the members of the congregation could not wait for the bishop to finish his sermon, so they could all go home and warm their hands around their own fireplaces.

FIGURE 256. Villard de Honnecourt felt the Green Man was important enough to include in his sketchbook c. 1225–1250. *Reprinted with permission of Indiana University Press.*

Organs and Music Used in the Cathedrals

Music was an essential part of the early cathedral services, and organs played a vital role in the musical program. The first organs used in the early cathedrals were portable and small enough to be carried or hung around the neck with a strap. The organist played them in church processions and inside during the service. The player would use his right hand to play and the left hand to pump the bellows in the back of the instrument to generate the air for the pipes.

As time went on, more sophisticated organs were developed with stops and great keyboards that allowed players to control the air pressure to the various pipes. With these improvements, organs grew in size and weight. At this point, organs were permanently mounted inside the cathedrals, usually on the eastern end of the nave. In the later Middle Ages, the great organs became enormous in size and had sounds to match. Some of the organs had dozens of pipes, some twenty-five feet tall and fifteen inches in diameter, requiring several men to operate the bellows. Over the years, the older organs were replaced with magnificent newer ones that never cease to garner attention when they roar.

Choir singing was also a vital part of the services conducted in the cathedral during the Middle Ages, and predated the organ. Today, a variety of singing groups still perform in many cathedrals, especially at the Evensong services. The live performances offer a wonderful treat to many. One of the most famous singing groups is the Vienna Boys Choir, which I have heard twice. They are outstanding singers.

Acoustic Technology and Sound Wave Projection in the Cathedral

In the Middle Ages, the monumental cathedrals obviously did not have microphones or speaker sound systems to project the bishop's voice out to the congregation as we do today. In fact, the cathedrals were built some 600 years before electricity was even invented and harnessed for use.

The Master Builder understood acoustics inside the cathedral and designed the structure and furniture to improve the acoustics of sound projection. A few feet above the priest's pulpit, a round, wafer-shaped, horizontal, wooden board was mounted. It was called a **sounding board** and acted like a modern speaker, amplifying the priest's voice level to the audience. See Figure 34.

This fancy, decorated piece of furniture broadcast the reverberation and reflections of his voice to the parishioners. It functioned just like a sounding board inside of a fine violin, which amplifies the sound waves of energy to the audience. The masons experimented with and fine-tuned the boards until they received the maximum benefit from them. There were a few sounding boards that were adjustable up and down for better tuning effects.

I read an interesting article, "The Science of Sound," which described sound in concert halls, specifically the Symphony Hall in Birmingham, England. "Symphony Hall uses retractable sound-absorbing panels; controllable reverberation chambers; and, above the stage, an adjustable-height, sound-reflecting canopy" (*Compressed Air*, 1992). The Master Builders used these same adjustable sounding boards above the pulpits in the cathedrals to improve sound projection some 800 to 900 years ago.

The same article also stated, "Just as concert halls with a classic shoebox shape usually produce the best acoustics, a rectangular shape is often best for a home stereo room. As a rule of thumb for the home stereo room, length should be about fifty percent greater than the width" (*Compressed Air*, 1992). I believe the Master Builders were aware of acoustics in designing the barrel vaults and shoebox naves to the correct ratio of length to width in order to better enhance good sound transmission.

Sir Christopher Wren, Master Builder of St. Paul's Cathedral in London, designed a large elevated dome about 100 feet above the floor and 102 feet in diameter, called the Whispering Gallery. If one person faces the wall of the dome and talks against it, another person can put his ear near the wall on the opposite side and hear. The two can have a conversation! This is another case in point why the Master Builders were called Masters.

Dedication Ceremonies

After the carvings and decorations were finished in the interior and the cross was placed above the tall spire, it was time for a dedication of the new cathedral. The Master Builder and craftsmen could now sit back and admire the beautiful masterpiece they had envisioned.

The bishop and chapter members invited all the people in town and the surrounding area to attend the ceremonies. The word spread fast to neighboring countries and visitors came by carriage, horseback, and on foot from all points of the compass to join the celebration.

The bishop, archbishop, priests, chapter members, dignitaries, influential community members, pilgrims, and members of the congregation dressed up in their finest attire for the occasion. The portable organs played music and the folks sang their praises to God during the ceremonies. The masons, after many years of building, finally completed the cathedral and with community pride they dedicated and celebrated it.

CHAPTER 10

WITH MODERN TECHNOLOGY, COULD THE MASTER BUILDER HAVE DESIGNED AND BUILT A BETTER CATHEDRAL?

The building of the medieval cathedrals was such a monumental task that one has to wonder how it was even accomplished. Today, it is hard for people to imagine the commitment necessary to create a structure that would very well take longer than a lifetime to achieve. How does one design a cathedral that will last hundreds of years? And how does one even fathom the labor involved? Would modern technology have allowed the Master Builders to build a better cathedral? If they had gas, electric, and pneumatic-powered equipment during the Middle Ages, would the cathedrals have been built more sound or looked more magnificent than they do today? If they had hydraulic boom and tower cranes, modern scaffolding, diamond- tipped cutting blades, stainless-steel cables, laser transits, and computers for architectural and engineering calculations, would it have made any difference?

My answer is no! I do not think modern technology could have improved the design qualities of the fabric considering harmony, proportion, gracefulness, scale, and total majesty. The Master Builders *got it right* in their final refinements of the Gothic style of architecture. They removed and pared off all of the excess stone tonnage, leaving a stone skeleton framework that was still strong enough to support the beautiful stained-glass windows.

There is no question that men today could build the cathedrals much faster with modern tools and equipment and save a considerable amount of labor. They could also build them a little more secure physically, using modern high- strength steel here and there. But I do not think they could improve the quality and beauty the old hand-tooled craftsmanship left on the stone, marble, wood, and glass surfaces.

If the medieval stonemasons attempted to build a Gothic cathedral in America today, it would be impossible. First the federal, state, and local building codes and permit agencies would not know how to interpret the Master Builder's parchment drawings. Then, given today's countless inspection agencies, it could well take ten years for approval of the construction permits. If approval was eventually granted, the builders would need to change the parchment drawing specifications to include all the new regulations established in that ten-year waiting period. Assuming the permits are finally approved and the building process started, it would soon be stopped... I believe the scenario would unfold in this way:

> Before noon on the first day, a dozen Federal OSHA inspectors would arrive on the site accompanied by four Federal EPA inspectors and shut the building project down. The inspectors would cite the builders for seventy-four violations on the project out of the 1,457,679 regulations on the Fed's books. They would then fine them $23,987,423 for the alleged violations, order them to pay the fine, and then give them two months to correct all the violations. The fines would total more than the building was going to cost, and due to lack of commitment on the part of the parishioners, the builders would decide to cancel the cathedral project altogether. The parishioners would write the federal government a bounced check for $23,987,423, and that would be the end of it!

While the numbers may not be exact, the point is the same. I am glad the masons built the wonderful cathedrals during the Middle Ages, because we would never have had the opportunity to enjoy them today if they had waited.

CHAPTER 11

DAMAGE TO THE CATHEDRALS DURING WORLD WAR II, THE REFORMATION, AND CIVIL WARS

Hundreds of years after their construction, the presence of the magnificent cathedrals still inspire admiration and awe. But unfortunately, the passage of time has not allowed these houses of God to emerge unscathed. Severe damage has been done to the cathedrals from sheer negligence. Many cathedrals not being used for long periods of time were left to decay, subject to Mother Nature's elements of snow, wind, rain, freezing, thawing, and ice. Basic maintenance of the roofs and windows and other major repairs were not attended to. Centuries later, it has become almost prohibitively expensive to restore them to their original glory. It is also a challenge to find skilled craftsmen to do the work when money would became available. And while inattention has indeed been destructive to these beautiful structures, there have also been other forces equally or even more harmful.

World War II (c. 1939–1945)

During World War II, many of the cathedrals and churches sustained considerable collateral damage from the bombing raids throughout Europe. After thousands of tons of explosives and fire-bombs dropped on the cities, how did the cathedrals ever survive? Many cathedrals had men stationed on fire watches twenty-four hours a day, but they could not prevent all the damage inflicted. Were the pilots ever given any instructions to avoid bombing certain structures?

I have been intrigued by the fact that so many of the prominent cathedrals are still standing today in majesty. For years I questioned pilots, navigators, gunners, crewmen, military officers, National Museum of the US Air Force employees, the Pentagon, and military personnel at air shows. Many of those I questioned were of a younger generation, and no one had an answer as to how the cathedrals survived the bombs.

I also spoke with many people who had been directly involved in the war. I asked them two questions: "Were you or your crewmen ever given any verbal or written instructions *not to bomb the cathedrals* on your bombing missions? Did you ever see any instructions issued by the US government during World War II to avoid bombing the cathedrals?" I could never get any confirmation regarding instructions issued, though I did confirm that pilots used the cathedral steeples as set points for their location and orientation on their missions.

Was it a miracle that after several towns were blown into tons of rubble that the cathedrals survived the bombardments? Was it a case that the pilots and navigators made a decision on their own not to destroy the cathedrals during their bombing raids? Or was it divine guidance from God looking out for the well-being of the houses of worship?

Years later, I finally got an answer from a person who lived through the experience of participating in the bombing raids in Germany. His name is Milton Bennett, a great businessman and good Christian man from Perrysburg, Ohio. On April 10, 2010, my friend Tobe Riedel and I interviewed Bennett, who served in the Army Air Corps as a machine gunner on a B-24 bomber. He told us that General Dwight D. Eisenhower, Supreme Commander of the Allied Forces in Europe, gave the Air Corps instructions not to bomb the cathedrals. This was the first time I was told that there were specific instructions to avoid them.

On January 17, 1945, Bennett's plane was shot down while returning from a bombing run over Hamburg, Germany, and crash-landed in Sweden. Bennett gave me photos of the destroyed B-24 plane scattered in pieces. The other crewmen parachuted out after being hit by enemy planes while Bennett and the other waist gunner survived the crash, landing in four feet of snow. Bennett stayed in various houses in Sweden away from the enemy until the war was over.

I also found another veteran of the war who confirmed the reason for the cathedrals' survival. On November 10, 2011, my brother Jim Herner and I interviewed Robert Schild from Powell, Ohio. He joined the US Army Air Corps and was part of the 44th Bomb Group of the famous 8th Air Force. Schild was a turret tail gunner on the B-24 bomber, and he told us that his superiors in the Air Corps told them to avoid bombing any cathedrals or schools on their bombing missions in Europe.

Schild's B-24 plane was shot down by German fighters on his first mission flown from Norwich, England, to the French coast on January 24, 1944. Their assignment was to take out the large German guns along the French coast near LeHavre in preparation for the big invasion later. Schild pulled his chute just in time before the plane crash landed. He was captured by German ground troops and put into solitary confinement for ten days. During his capture, he was forced to march eighty-six days, some 500 miles, starting February 6, 1944. He was moved by boxcar and ship to different prison camps in Poland and Lithuania. He was a prisoner for sixteen months and lost sixty pounds until he was liberated on April 26, 1945, at camp Lucky Strike near LeHavre, France. General Eisenhower met the prisoners, shook their hands, and then fed them well. Schild returned from the war, raised a family, became a businessman, and was an active member in his community.

FIGURE 257. Cologne Cathedral, Germany. Cologne stood after hundreds of bombing missions by the Allied forces during World War II. While it survived, the city of Cologne was completely destroyed, as seen here. This image comes from a public display in front of the cathedral showing the destruction of the war.

Two years after Schild's interview, a third World War II survivor shared with me some additional information regarding the targeting of the cathedrals. On May 28, 2013, I interviewed 1st Lt. Michael Pohorilla from Canal Winchester at the Motts Military Museum in Groveport (Columbus), Ohio. Michael Pohorilla was a navigator on a B-17 bomber, *Sky Goddess*, and served in the 8th Air Force 385th Bomb Group. He joined the US Army Air Corps in 1942 at age 18 and was based out of Great Ashfield in England.

Pohorilla made an unbelievable thirty-five bombing missions over Germany from September 13, 1944, to February 1, 1945, against enemy firepower from the Luftwaffe fighters. On October 14 and 15, 1944, he made two bombing missions over Cologne, Germany, to target the railroad yards near Cologne Cathedral. He told me that after dropping the bombs on the railroad yards, he immediately turned right above the cathedral towers back to England.

When I asked Pohorilla if there were any specified instructions not to bomb the cathedrals, his reply was, "It was a given *not* to bomb the cathedrals." He told me their missions were specifically planned and the cathedrals were

never a target. Their task was to strategically bomb military factories, oil, gas, and chemical plants, railroad transportation systems, and bridges to destroy the German industrial system.

All three World War II survivors acknowledged directives to avoid the cathedrals. But to this day I have not been able to find any written documented instructions given by the US government on any bombing raids during World War II in Europe. I am absolutely convinced that the combination of Dwight Eisenhower's instructions to the Air Corp not to bomb the cathedrals, the pilots' and navigators' desire to avoid the cathedrals, and the divine intervention of God to protect them are the reasons that so many survived the war.

It is interesting to note that to further protect the cathedrals during World War II, many cathedral authorities from several countries on the continent of Europe and the British Isles decided to remove the stained-glass windows and bury them underground to spare them from destruction. Most of these priceless and irreplaceable windows were therefore saved, and after the war they were all releaded back into place. This was an enormous and expensive task, but worth every penny of the cost.

FIGURE 258. Coventry Cathedral, England. During World War II, Coventry Cathedral was destroyed by the German bombing raids. While the tower and spire were miraculously spared, the rest of the cathedral was completely flattened.

In September 2011, I visited Cologne (Koln) Cathedral in Germany to take more photos and gather additional data on the cathedrals. The city of Cologne was in the heart of much of the bombing during the war. While there, I purchased a German book, *Cologne Cathedral in World War II*, by Niklas Moring. From a German's viewpoint it describes the damage done from the raids and the steps taken during the war to protect Cologne Cathedral. A quote in the introduction ties right into my research on the cathedral's survival:

> Cologne was one of the Allies' principle bombing targets in World War II. In fact, 262 air raids were flown on the city during the conflict, razing virtually the entire city center to the ground. At the end of the war, over 40 percent of the buildings were destroyed and the city was covered in approximately 30,000,000 cubic meters of rubble. Then and now, many citizens of Cologne consider it something of a miracle that the cathedral survived the war relatively unscathed despite its immediate proximity to two strategically important targets, Cologne Central Station and the Hohenzollern Bridge over the River Rhine. Was this because the Allies intentionally avoided the cathedral during their bombing raids? To this day, many people are convinced that this was the case. (2011, 7)

A story taken from Moring's book also illustrates the utmost reverence and respect that the American soldiers had for Cologne, a church of God located on enemy soil. It took place in early 1945 as the war was winding down in Germany. Cologne had been damaged from collateral fire and had tons of debris around it. "On March 11, 1945, an American military chaplain celebrated mass in the Lady Chapel of the cathedral with 48 American soldiers." Accompanying the story was a picture of soldiers kneeling in the rubble (2011, 92). This story says it all. See Figures 257 and 258.

The Reformation (c. 1517–1685)

Four hundred years before World War II, a considerable amount of damage was intentionally inflicted on many cathedrals during the Reformation. In the year 1534, the Parliament declared King Henry VIII the supreme head of the English church. The monasteries were dissolved in 1536, and King Henry ordered the destruction of irreplaceable artifacts and relics within the Catholic cathedrals. In 1538, he ordered the saints' shrines to be dismantled. Relics, sculptured carvings, paintings, ornate decorations, and anything that may have been seen as ungodly idols to worship were destroyed or removed. Many decorative masterpieces crafted from wood and stone disappeared from the cathedrals, never to be seen again by future generations.

Lincoln Cathedral in England was one cathedral to have suffered this fate. "Between 1540 and 1548 the chantry chapels were dissolved, the body of St. Hugh was removed, the shrine was stripped of its jewels and the treasury of its contents and the complicated daily routine of services was vastly simplified… In Medieval times there would have been a **rood** on top of or near the screen, which is a representation of Christ on the cross, normally accompanied by his mother and St John. This was destroyed at the Reformation…" (Lincoln Cathedral 2006, 8 and 13).

English Civil Wars (1642–1651)

The English civil wars were major armed conflicts between two groups, the Royalists and the Parliamentarians, stemming from disagreements over politics and religion. Cathedrals were used as military fortresses against the enemy on both sides. They were used as barracks, prisons, stables, and storage for arms, gunpowder, and ammunition. The civil wars occurred in many parts of England, and dozens of English cathedrals, along with their contents, sustained considerable damage. Lead was even stripped from the cathedral roofs to supply additional munitions for the wars. In addition, Parliamentarians wanted to destroy the symbols and physical artifacts associated with Roman Catholicism such as statues, some stained-glass windows, screens, and organs. As a result, a great deal of medieval art was destroyed.

Lichfield Cathedral suffered severe damage to the central spire, stained-glass windows, and lead roofs during the wars. Other cathedrals that also suffered damage were Bristol, Canterbury, Chester, Exeter, Chichester, Gloucester, Lincoln, Worcester, Peterborough, Winchester, and Rochester.

PART II

CHAPTER 12

THE ORIGIN AND DEVELOPMENT OF FREEMASONRY

NOTE: This chapter may be more interesting to the Freemason than the non-Mason reader because of its in-depth exploration of Freemasonry's origins, but it also contains rich and interesting historical information cultivated from forty years of research.

What are the origins of Freemasonry? From where did it emerge? Who helped shape Freemasonry into its current form today? For years, scholars have wrestled with these questions, with no universal agreement. But I contend that Freemasonry descended directly from the ancient operative stonemasons who built the cathedrals and other stone structures during the Middle Ages.

As cathedral building declined in the late sixteenth century, the stonemasons began to accept nonoperative members into their lodges. The operative lodges that accepted these new nonmasons were later called speculative lodges. Freemasonry is rooted in the transition from operative stonemasonry (masons working with their hands and tools) to speculative Freemasonry (nonoperative masons pursuing the arts and sciences). The final product of this transition from operative masons and lodges into Freemasons and Masonic lodges is what we call today modern Freemasonry.

Initially, the transitional period moved slowly but picked up speed quickly in the formation of these new speculative lodges. While the origin of Freemasonry (in the form of the first laws, rules, and regulations that governed the craft) had its foundation written in England, the first phase actually emerged in Scotland around 1600. Once established in Scotland, Freemasonry later moved into England and from there it rapidly expanded around the world.

The Decline of the Masonry Trade

For centuries, the operative masons worked very hard constructing cathedrals until the stonemasonry trade dramatically slowed during the last half of the sixteenth century and nearly came to a halt in 1600. Stone structures were still being built, but at a substantially slower rate.

During this sluggish period, many of the masons suffered from a lack of work.

Just prior to 1600, the economic, social, and political climates of both the British Isles and the Continent were challenging. There was a certain amount of insecurity, divisiveness, and fear. Several historical events took place during this period that promoted this chaotic state of civil society and unrest in Britain. These events, in turn, affected the masonry trade. These events included:

The Inundation of Houses of Worship

One issue that affected the masonry trade was that England became saturated with places of worship. The British countryside was inundated with stone cathedrals, abbeys, minsters, parish churches, and other houses of God. The English scholar, John Michell, noted, "In England there are forty-four cathedrals and a greater number of ruined abbeys which are worth visiting, as well as some 15,000 parish churches and countless old chapels, shrines, hermitages, holy wells, and other types of religious sites or monuments" (1988, introduction). Henry Coil, a Masonic scholar, also documented that Gothic structures totaled 12,000 in England (1961, 69). This saturation certainly contributed to the slow-down of cathedral building.

The Black Death

The 1349 plague, known as the Black Death, swept throughout England and devastated the population. An estimated fifty percent of the people were killed, which included thousands of highly trained stonemason artists. It set the country back economically and from a labor reduction standpoint. This disastrous event left fewer trained masons available to keep the large cathedral projects going and their lodges functioning.

Mark Ormrod and Philip Lindley in *The Black Death in England* discuss the impact of the plague on the delay and development of the cathedrals in England.

At Ely and Exeter, then, the Black Death may really have been the unique cause of a decisive break in building and marked a watershed in these commissions; elsewhere, as at Winchester and York, the plague may have been an important contributory factor in delaying the architectural and sculptural enterprises of other churches. (1996, 143)

The 1349 plague was followed by another outbreak in 1361–2, and outbreaks continued intermittently throughout the fourteenth and fifteenth centuries and beyond. With approximately half the people wiped out, a serious economic climate was created for those remaining. They were desperate to find jobs and a means to feed and clothe their families. It is doubtful that there were extra resources available in their budgets to start a building fund for new cathedrals. It certainly slowed or stopped large building projects in the British Isles.

The Reformation

The Reformation in England in the mid sixteenth century transformed the traditional Catholic religion into the Church of England, thus forever changing the social and religious climate in the British Isles. The Monarchy declared that the English people had to renounce Catholicism and join the Church of England. When King Henry VIII ordered the destruction of the saints' shrines, relics, and decorations from the very cathedrals and churches the stonemasons' fathers and grandfathers might have worked on a generation or two earlier, it must have been devastating.

The various thoughts and positions on the Reformation no doubt created division among family members, neighbors, and close friends. The religious persecution and penalties were a serious matter to consider if one reacted the wrong way to the wrong people. With the Reformation change from Catholic to Protestant, along with all its religious uncertainties, who or what group of people would have a big appetite to propose and build a new cathedral? Bernard Jones believes the Reformation was responsible for putting an end to the Gothic style of building around 1600 (1975, 32).

The Collapse of Beauvais Cathedral

Another event that contributed to the decline of large stone construction projects was the collapse of the spire of Beauvais Cathedral in northern France. The tallest in Europe at the time, at 492 feet, the spire of Beauvais was completed in 1569. But just a few years later in 1573, the spire came crashing down, due to a faulty foundation the experts tell us. Bad news travels fast, and it is suspected that there was not much incentive for the Master Builders in England to build new Gothic cathedrals taller than Beauvais, which had just collapsed.

The English Civil War of 1642

For the people of England, the Civil War of 1642 was also a major upheaval. It divided the citizens and the families. Subsequently England was involved in other wars and skirmishes with Scotland and Ireland, which further divided the people and caused additional uncertainty and chaos. These wars went on for some twenty years creating fear, hatred, and turmoil in the British Isles. Consequently, they also further retarded the craft of operative masonry.

The Birth of Speculative Lodges

Major set-backs from the civil war and the Reformation, coupled with the thousands of lives lost from the plague and the rapid decline in building, all collectively created a near breakdown of civil society. The stonemasons and citizens formed deep-seated beliefs on the war, social issues, politics, and religion. They did not always know with whom they could discuss their views without causing trouble. Presumably there was no one in leadership in their communities to heal, mend, or consolidate society. Distrust and confusion ruled, with no thread of unity from anyone to stitch the people back together.

Strong leadership and organization was desperately needed to unite the people and form a more civil society. The church probably would have been an ideal candidate to accomplish this, but much division still persisted from the Reformation. Many would not have wanted to listen to a church leader who might be on the other side of the issues. An outside independent organization was needed that could reunite the people again.

At this critical juncture, from the early to mid-1600s, a group of stonemasons thought the core values or *Old Charges* of the stonemasons would be a good vehicle to help bring some segments of society back together and to ensure that the stonemason lodges survived and flourished. In considering the future solvency of their lodges, the answer seemed to lie in increasing their membership by accepting new members who were not affiliated with the stonemasonry craft. The establishment of an entirely new set of speculative lodges that were structurally different than the operative lodges seemed to be a good solution. Thus, the transition from operative stonemasonry to speculative stonemasonry first began.

The stonemasons felt their old organizational rules of conduct and harmony, which held their craft together for over 200 years, would be a good candidate to heal the deep-seated wounds of the divided masons. They felt if this set of rules of conduct, based on God and good moral values, was good enough to hold the masons together for centuries building the magnificent cathedrals, they certainly should be good enough to mend the wounds of good men during this chaotic religious, political, and social atmosphere as well. Professor David Stevenson from Scotland notes, "In the decades around 1600 secret societies thrived in Europe, many of them obsessed with the idea of finding some solution to the wars and religious disputes which seemed to be tearing

European civilizations apart" (1989, 5–6).

John Hamill, a Masonic scholar from London, in *Freemasonry, A Celebration of the Craft*, notes a theory on the transition put forth by the late Colin Dyer, a Masonic scholar from England, about the religious and political turmoil of the time:

> The context of Dyer's arguments is the religious and political turmoil of the seventeenth century. The period was one of growing intolerance in both politics and religion. No forum existed in which men of differing views could meet in harmony. Opinions became polarized and divisions over matters of belief were so acute that families, friendships, and eventually society itself were torn apart by the English Civil War in 1642… And so they founded a fraternal order that eschewed sectarianism in both religion and politics whilst continuing to root itself firmly in a belief in God and in an unwavering loyalty to the three great principles of Brotherly Love, Relief, and Truth. (Hamill 1992, 24).

The new lodges would be based on charity, religious principles (but not a new religion), a tolerance for one another's positions, and a desire for helping one another. And as men naturally enjoy the camaraderie of a group, the new lodges would also be a type of social club or fraternity where the members could openly discuss matters of the day.

It should be remembered that in the medieval days the operative masons met, worked, and talked in the old operative lodges on the construction site. They also took their breaks, naps, and meals there, and a few occasionally slept there. It served for some as their work place during the day and for others a place for discussions in the evening on a variety of matters. These young men (stonemasons) worked side by side for ten or twelve hours a day and were together continuously for years. They were like blood brothers, praying together, encouraging, advising, and providing charity for one another. They were very close! This closeness, along with the customs and practices of the masons in the old operative lodges are reflected in the tenets of modern Freemasonry lodges today. When many of the construction jobs slowed down and the transition of speculative Freemasonry started, it was easier for the masons to adapt to the new lodge system because many of the elements were familiar to them and had already been practiced. Many of the basic elements of modern speculative Freemasonry were developed in the early operative lodges.

The *Old Charges*

Over the centuries the English stonemasons developed a set of laws, rules, and regulations governing the conduct of their craft while working on the job and in their operative lodges. These old manuscripts also contained the ritual initiation ceremonies for the admission or reception of new masons into the lodges, including an oath of fidelity and silence. These old manuscript documents are called the *Old Charges* or *Gothic Constitutions*.

The *Old Charges* are essentially an English product and serve as a vital part of the operative masons' heritage. Starting with the oldest version, called the Regius Poem c. 1390, they have since grown into approximately 130 different updated versions. All of the *Old Charges* were copied, updated, and edited from the earliest originals to satisfy the changes and needs of the masons and lodges over the years. Continuous changes were made right up into the transitional period from operative to speculative Freemasonry and beyond. It is very fortunate for Freemasonry to have these *Old Charges* as a paper trail and a vital part of the historical records, bridging the gap and connecting the operative lodges to speculative lodges.

The core values of the *Old Charges* were a belief in God, tolerance and respect for one another's positions, good moral values, honesty, uprightness, and good character. Regius Poem c. 1390, Point No. 1 says, "He must love God well and the Holy Church always, And his master also, whom he is with, Wherever he goes, in field or wood; And love also thy fellows Because thy craft desires that thou do so" (Hunter, 1975, 106).

These core values of the English stonemasons' *Old Charges* became the pattern or foundation for the new speculative Freemasonry lodges that emerged in the first half of the seventeenth century in Scotland. The English stonemasons who wrote and developed this first system for governing the craftsmen are to be credited with developing the seed for modern Freemasonry. But while the English operative masons developed the seed for the first phase of modern Freemasonry, it was the Scottish masons who planted it.

Scottish Freemasonry

Who first stepped forward with a plan to change the operative stonemason lodges and reverse the loss of membership? William Schaw, an influential Scottish mason interested in architecture and building, along with his followers, came forward and established a new set of lodges in Scotland that brought in new members. They literally changed the operative lodges into speculative lodges.

The appointment of William Schaw by King James VI of Scotland to be Master of Works to the Crown of Scotland and General Warden of The Masons in 1584 put him in charge of the King's building projects and the masons. He had considerable authority and wielded much power. He wrote a new set of statutes or governing codes for the Scottish masons in 1598 and 1599, using a copy of the earlier English stonemasons' *Old Charges* as a blueprint. In essence, Schaw took the seed (*Old Charges*) previously developed in England and planted it around Scotland, accompanied by his new Schaw Statutes. He then watched it germinate, sprout, and grow into Freemasonry lodges. This was the origin of modern Freemasonry that emerged throughout Scotland. The Schaw Statutes were to govern the operative masons, as well as the new speculative masons. Schaw literally reorganized the lodges and their rituals with these new governing codes.

David Stevenson, professor of Scottish history and studies at the University of Aberdeen, made an extensive research study of the early masonic lodges in Scotland. He authored two books, *The Origins of Freemasonry* and *The First Freemasons,* and should be given much credit for his investigation into the Scottish origin phase of modern Freemasonry. This is what he had to say about the early development of Freemasonry in Scotland:

> In the years around 1600, the legacy of the Middle Ages was remodeled and combined with Renaissance themes and obsessions to create a new movement. Evolutionary development subsequently brought about many alterations and elaborations of this movement, yet what appeared in Scotland around 1600 contains the essentials of modern freemasonry. The man who more than anyone else deserves the title of creator of modern freemasonry was William Schaw (1989, 3).

William Schaw's Statutes of 1599 charged the lodge on December 28 of that same year to elect a scribe (secretary) to record the proceedings, initiation ceremonies of the two degrees, names, dates, and Master in charge (Carr, 1976, 56). The Schaw Statutes also required a Warden to be elected annually to preside over the lodges. In addition, they established an art of memory system for the masons to learn and to be tested upon in the degrees. To this day, there is some memory and ritual work involved in the degree rituals.

> Indeed, surviving minute books from Scottish operative lodges imply that some form of ritual work was carried on, in addition to the business of management and control of the trade. They also show the increasing admission of "Accepted Masons," to the extent that by the early eighteenth century the operative content of some of the lodges had become eroded and they were, to all intents and purposes, speculative lodges (Hamill 1992, 22).

Stevenson adds, "But these lodges were very different from the old type of building site lodges: they were clearly intended to contain all the masons in a burgh or district (not just those who happened to be working on a particular site), and to be permanent institutions with elected officials running them under the supervision of the general Warden" (1989, 3).

William Schaw and his followers, in developing the new speculative Freemason lodges, wanted the organization to be attractive to stonemasons and potential nonoperative members. They felt this new organization would serve as a vital tool in bringing influential members into the lodges, be a part of the renaissance revival of the craft, help provide a good liberal education to its members, and serve as a

vehicle to pull the citizens together. Thus, many of the new members brought into the lodges were not associated with the stonemasonry craft.

The lure of "masonic secrets" may also have been an attraction to potential members. Stevenson describes the possibility that "outsiders" would have an interest in being initiated for this reason: "Schaw organized Scottish masons into new-style permanent lodges, reinforcing older masonic lore with a heady mix of Renaissance ideas…But he may well have contemplated some outsiders with relevant interests being initiated into the secrets of the masons…Then, from the 1630s, outsiders begin to appear in the lodges, first in Edinburgh" (1989, 8).

Local businessmen, merchants, noblemen, high government officials, respectable leaders in the communities, scientists, and other tradesmen were all asked to join the new lodges to keep them prospering. These new nonoperative masons were called accepted masons. Many of the lodges at this point were initiating accepted masons from the higher social classes. This practice was probably done to legitimize the lodges and to show the people that the new Freemason lodges would be an acceptable organization to join. These higher social class men were called gentlemen masons. At the same time, other trade craftsmen, laborers, common folks, and merchants were joining the new speculative lodges as well, and these accepted masons were renamed speculative masons or modern Freemasons.

At this point the new lodges were attended by men from all different classes: the higher social classes, working masons, and nonoperative masons from other crafts. This may have been the first time that different classes of people were all meeting on the same level, crossing religious, political, and social status barriers and communicating in the lodges. Today the same tradition is still being practiced in Masonic lodges around the world, all social classes of brothers working together.

The Earliest Documentation of Operative and Speculative Masonry in Scotland

An examination of the records reveals that the earliest documentation of lodge minutes, as well as the initiations of both operative and nonoperative masons, occurred in Scotland at the end of the sixteenth century. Here are some key dates:

The earliest operative lodge minutes ever recorded occurred in Scotland, 1598.

> …the earliest lodge record in Scotland is the entry in the minute book of the lodge at Aitchison's-Haven for the "yeir of God 1598," the first five entries antedating the earliest preserved in the minutes of the lodge at Edinburgh for "Ultimo Julij 1599," which has the Warden's mark attached and relates to a meeting at which George Patoun was reprimanded for employing a cowan. (Coil 1961, 596)

Note: In Scotland, a cowan mason was a worker who built up a stone wall without mortar and was known as a dry-diker. A cowan mason did not go through the traditional rigorous and lengthy mason's apprenticeship program. He learned his trade in a manner regarded by the masons' fraternity as irregular. A cowan also could not be legally employed by the masons because he was not given the recognition word of the masons.

The earliest documented Entered Apprentice and Fellowcraft degrees were conferred on operative masons in Aitchison Haven Lodge, Edinburgh, Scotland, on January 9, 1598.

"Upon guhilk day Alexander Cubie was enterit prenteis to Gerge Aytone… Robert Widderspone was maid fellow of Craft in ye presens of Wilzam Aytone Elder" (Carr, 1976, 374).

In reading over the minute books of Aitchison Haven from 1598 onward, several Entered Apprentices and Fellows of the Craft were initiated between 1601 and 1630. These recorded documents confirm the existence of a two-degree system in operative masonry that was being practiced in an operative lodge in Scotland in 1598. The minutes also establish a paper trail of operative masons being initiated into a Scottish Lodge, which sets the stage for the transition into speculative lodges.

Note: Bernard Jones also comments on the importation of the Fellowcraft Degree from Scotland to England: "English masons might never have known the 'Fellow Craft' but for an importation from Scotland" (1975, 294).

The earliest recorded minutes of a nonoperative mason attending a speculative lodge occurred in Edinburgh, Scotland, 1600.

The first appearance of a nonoperative Freemason in a lodge shown by any of the preserved minutes occurs in the early records of Lodge of Edinburgh (June 8, 1600), where it is shown that John Boswell, Laird of Aucheinleck, was present at a meeting in which the Warden of the Lodge was fined for some breach of the regulations. (Coil 1961, 597)

These minutes also tie into the timing of the new lodge systems being set up by William Schaw in Scotland just two years earlier in 1598.

The earliest nonoperative Fellowcraft initiations into a speculative lodge were documented in Edinburgh, Scotland, in 1634.

Henry Coil explains the details of the first three Fellowcrafts initiated into a speculative lodge on the same day:

The first record of the initiation of a nonoperative in a lodge anywhere is contained in the minutes of Lodge of Edinburgh for July 3, 1634, when the Rt. Hon. Lord Alexander was admitted Fellowcraft and, on the same date, Anthony Alexander, Master of Work to the King, and Sir Alexander Strachan were admitted. Similar entries occur in 1635, 1637, 1638, 1640 and subsequent years, most of those so admitted being of the nobility or holding high government offices. (1961, 597)

There were also many other examples of nonoperative masons joining the lodges around Scotland continuing into the 1700s. William Schaw's new type of lodge was flourishing. In fact, Stevenson states that twenty-five Scottish lodges received nonoperative masons into their lodges before 1710 (1989, 5). Henry Coil also notes that by 1735 there were fully 100 lodges in Scotland (1961, 598). New lodges were sprouting up all over Scotland and membership grew.

These examples of initiating new nonoperative Freemasons into the Lodge of Edinburgh bridges the gap and links the operative masons to speculative Freemasonry. These documents also contribute to the paper trail from the operative lodges into the speculative lodges today.

English Freemasonry

Early on, the English masons brought the *Old Charges* to the party, outlining the laws, rules, regulations, charges, and initiation ritual ceremonies that served as the foundation of Freemasonry. But for centuries, the Masonic historians have noted the absence of any records indicating the development of Freemasonry and lodge activities in England. In less than a year after William Schaw's Statutes of 1599 ordered the appointment of a scribe in the lodges, lodge records began to appear all over Scotland, but not in England. There is no early documentation of Masonic activities, nor recordings of names, dates, places of meetings, initiations, or Masonic ritual ceremonies. What really went on in the English lodges prior to the transition, during the transition, and after the transition of operative to speculative masonry? There is silence and a vacuum of records! Why?

A key issue that has been indelibly attached to ancient craft masonry for centuries might explain the absence of the historical records. There may be good reason why no written records exist and masons themselves might not have grasped the importance of it. In the early medieval days every English candidate took an oath of fidelity and secrecy during his initiation into masonry, and he kept it. Today in speculative Freemasonry, it is called the member's Obligation. It was demanded of each candidate and repeated during each new initiate, so that every candidate and member would be reminded of this pledge. The oath goes back to the Regius Poem c. 1390 and is still part of Masonic ceremonies today. The oath stated that the mason would never make a mark or record upon anything movable or immovable whereby the secrets of Freemasonry may be unlawfully obtained. Simply put, the English masons took their oaths very seriously and would not violate them under any circumstances. Also, as mentioned before, the early English lodges did not have secretaries and therefore no records were kept. This might be a simple answer but there is great reason to believe it is a fact.

There is also some evidence that the absence of early English historical records of Freemasonry may be the result of some early documents being destroyed. James Anderson, author of *The Constitutions of 1723 and 1738,* reported that some valuable Masonic manuscripts and records were destroyed at the Premier Grand Lodge in London on its one-year Annual Festival (June 24, 1718) for fear that they would fall into the wrong hands. The then-new Grand Master, George Payne, "…desired any Brethren to bring to the Grand Lodge any old Writings and Records concerning Masons and Masonry in order the shew the Usages of antient Times; and this Year several old Copies of the Gothic Constitutions were produced and collated" (McLeod, 1991, 32).

But Wallace McLeod was not convinced that every Mason followed this dictate: "Even in those days there were reticent Masons who did not choose to risk disclosure" (1991, 32). Anderson also reported, "This Year, at some private Lodges, several very valuable Manuscripts … concerning the Fraternity, their Lodges, Regulations, Charges, Secrets, and Usages … were too hastily burnt by some scrupulous Brothers, that those Papers might not fall into strange Hands" (McLeod, 1991, 32). McLeod goes on to speculate, "Presumably these manuscripts so wantonly destroyed were copies of the old *Gothic Constitutions*" (1991, 33).

These comments on the intentional destruction of some early English Masonic documents should not be lightly dismissed. Even today some of the copies of the *Old Charges* that were once owned and documented have since been misplaced and lost.

The Earliest Documentation of Speculative Masonry in England

The first recorded initiation of an Englishman into a speculative lodge was Elias Ashmole in Warrington Lodge, England, on October 16, 1646. Ashmole would have been classified as a gentleman mason. He was also an antiquarian, mathematician, and interested in the sciences, arts, and the Renaissance movement. He notes in his diary, "I was made a Free Mason at Warrington in Lancashire, with Coll: Henry Mainwaring of Karnicham in Cheshire. The names of those that were then of the Lodge; Mr. Rich Penket Warden, Mr. James Collier, Mr. Rich: Sankey, Henry Littler, John Ellam, Rich: Ellam and Hugh Brewer" (Jones, 1975, 99). Bernard Jones explains, "The words 'Free Mason' in this extract constitute the first known use of the term carrying a speculative or symbolic meaning" (1975, 100). There were probably several other speculative masons also initiated into English lodges earlier than the date described above but not recognized

because of the English practice of not recording the lodge activities.

When this transition of new speculative Freemasonry started to evolve in England, there was an expansion of new speculative masons simply because of the total number of people. The population of England was close to six times greater than that of Scotland. The English stonemasons had constructed considerably more cathedrals, churches, and other stone structures than did the Scottish masons. Stevenson discusses this movement and expansion of Freemasonry into England: "But from the early eighteenth century the English began to innovate and adapt the movement, though Scottish influence remained strong, and at this point England took over the lead in the development of freemasonry from Scotland" (1988, 6).

Masonic scholar Harry Carr discusses the rapid changes of interest in the brethren soon after the transition from operative to speculative masonry. In the early speculative lodges, the stonemason trade conversations changed from the topic of building to new topics regarding social and charity issues.

> After a period of transition, which started apparently in the early 1600s, the character of the craft began to change very rapidly, and in the early years of the 1700s (say, from c.1700 to c.1740) the changes had so far accelerated that the lodges had lost all interest in the trade and trade-control, and become social and benevolent societies, still practicing the old ceremonies, but with a substantial membership of gentleman and tradesmen who did not belong to the Craft and had no interest in it. These were nonoperative lodges which later acquired the speculative teachings and principles which are the basis of modern Freemasonry. (1976, 64).

During this transitional period, both operative and nonoperative masons were attending lodges together, and while at first most of the members were operative masons, over a period of years the accepted masons outnumbered them. McLeod cites several places in Scotland and England where this occurred: "In due course there came to be lodges in which the number of nonoperatives outweighed the operatives. This was already the case at Ashmole's lodge at Warrington in 1646, at Chester about 1673, at Dublin in 1688, at Chichester in 1695, and at several locations in London and Yorkshire between 1693 and 1717" (1991, 24). It finally came to the point around the first quarter of the eighteenth century that most of the members in the new lodges were speculative masons with very few operative masons attending. At that point the transitional phase was literally completed, and modern Freemasonry was well on its way to maturity.

The new English speculative (gentlemen) masons met in public inns, ale-houses, coffee houses, and taverns for their meetings, as opposed to the Scotsmen who met primarily in the old lodges. Some of the English masons may have also met in the old lodges and initiated their candidates in them, but it was never recorded for the reasons described above. It may never be known how early nonoperative masons joined the English lodges.

Now how did the operative stonemasons feel when the first new accepted masons began joining the lodge? At the outset it probably upset a few to know that the man sitting beside them was calling himself a mason and had never worked a day in the craft. "He never held a trowel in his hand, hewed or set a stone in a wall, dressed a keystone, nor was required to do any geometry lay out work on a building; he never went through the long and vigorous apprenticeship program like we did, and he is now calling himself a mason?" These are a few thoughts that might have crossed their minds.

While initially there may have been some serious resentment issues against the so-called new brother masons who were being accepted into the lodges as equals, the working stonemasons realized that they needed new members in their lodges to keep them afloat. There must have been several debates in the new lodges concerning the status of the masons' craft, the economy, religion, and politics, and in all likelihood some of the debates probably got a bit lively and maybe a little out of hand. There were some growing pains in this transitional development of Freemasonry, as described by Stevenson: "There were a number of cases in the eighteenth century in which gentlemen nonoperatives gained dominant positions in old lodges, and the stonemason members reacted by leaving to form new operative lodges excluding the gentry" (1988, 197).

One example that showcases the tensions between the operative and nonoperative masons during this transitional period was the wearing of work aprons to lodge meetings. Both operative and nonoperative aprons were worn. Bernard Jones discusses a case of a mason being fined in a speculative lodge in England for wearing his work apron in the lodge. "In Scots lodges, say, the first half of the seventeenth century, speculatives were sitting side by side with operatives, who in their daily avocation wore a long leather apron; but, essentially, those operatives when they came to lodge were speculatives, too, and by adopting uniformly an apron of linen they demonstrated that their lodge apron was nothing more than a symbol. There is a case on record (1740–41) of a member of an English lodge being fined for wearing his working apron in lodge" (1975, 453). Apparently his old, torn, and dirty apron was not proper dress in the new speculative lodge.

When these disagreements occurred, I believe the old stonemasons remembered the core values of their *Old Charges* and acted accordingly. The core values then prevailed and took over the discussions of the divided brethren. These values of a belief in God, tolerance for one another's positions, honesty, having a good moral compass, having good character, and the practice of charity brought the brethren together and to some kind of common ground.

The Premier Grand Lodge in London, England, 1717

By the beginning of the eighteenth century there were several new speculative lodges established in the London area, all meeting independently. But apparently there was a desire and movement by some of the masons to join one another and have their lodges merge. A group of speculative masons from four well-established lodges, referred to as The Four Old Lodges, met in London at the Goose and Gridiron Alehouse in St. Paul's churchyard. They met on St. John the Baptist's Day, June 24, 1717, and formed the Premier Grand Lodge of London. It was the first grand lodge in the world and was later named The Moderns. The members of the newly formed grand lodge were essentially gentlemen masons in a fraternity club. After the formation of the new grand lodge, the membership continued to grow in London and around England. And subsequent meetings in London became known as The Annual Assembly and Feast.

Incidentally, there were no minutes taken at this historic event in the development of Freemasonry in London. The English masons continued their tradition of silence and secrecy in the recording of their lodge activities. In 1717, they still did not have a secretary appointed, not even at the formation of the Premier Grand Lodge of England. This notable event was not recorded until twenty-one years later when James Anderson included it in his work, *The Constitutions of 1738*, a compilation of the history of Freemasonry.

The Constitutions of 1723

The first written history on English Freemasonry was *The Constitutions of 1723*, by the Reverend James Anderson at the request of the new Premier Grand Lodge in London. He essentially took copies of the *Old Charges* along with other data available to him and then added his own interpretations of the history of English Freemasonry to form his work. He had guidance and council from Theophilus Desaguliers and George Payne, both prominent members of the Premier Grand Lodge.

John Theophilus Desaguliers was very influential in the development of Freemasonry in England. He was a minister, natural philosopher, physicist, and one of the most prominent members of the Grand Lodge, serving as its third Grand Master from 1719 to 1720. He was a fellow and curator of the Royal Society and brought other members of the Society into Freemasonry. Desaguliers even crossed the border into Scotland and was accepted into a Scottish lodge. This crossing was done occasionally during the sixteenth and seventeenth centuries, resulting in a very similar English and Scottish Masonic ceremony.

Albert Mackey in his *Encyclopedia of Freemasonry* says this about Desaguliers' contribution to the Constitutions of 1723: "…although attributed to Dr. Anderson, were undoubtedly compiled under the supervision of Desaguliers. Anderson, we suppose, did the work, while Desaguliers furnished much of the material and the thought" (1924, 207).

The Grand Lodge of England and Freemasonry would probably not have developed into its current structure had it not been for Desaguliers.

The Constitutions of 1723 became the first official set of laws, rules, regulations, charges, and initiation ceremonies written for governing the speculative masons in London. Much of it was similar to the *Old Charges* that governed the operative masons for centuries, and today it is the basis of the charges, regulations, and initiation ceremonies that are used in modern Freemasonry.

The charges in *The Constitutions of 1723* wanted to address the discord created by politics, religion, languages, and conflicts within all the nations involved. Therefore, the discussion of religion and politics, along with personal quarrels, was strictly prohibited in the new speculative lodges, as specified in Charge No. 6, item 2:

> Therefore no private Piques or Quarrels must be brought within the Door of the "Lodge," far less any Quarrels about Religion, or Nations, or State Policy, we being only, as Masons, of the Catholick Religion… we are also of all Nations, Tongues, Kindreds, Languages, and are resolv'd against all Politics, as what never yet conduc'd to the Welfare of the Lodge, nor ever will. This Charge has been always strictly enjoin'd and observ'd; but especially ever since the Reformation in BRITAIN, or the Dissent and Secession of these Nations from the Communion of Rome. (Knoop & Jones 1978, 179)

The new organization called Freemasonry became a forum where men could meet in harmony, as well as a fraternity of brothers, a social club, and an organization that practiced charity. These meetings were attractive to men who could find common ground without arguing over politics and religion. This prohibition is still being practiced today in the lodges almost 300 years later.

The Third Degree in Speculative Freemasonry

By 1700, speculative masonry had a two-degree system in place: Entered Apprentice and Fellow of the Craft/Master Mason degrees. (This was slightly different than the three-degree system of the operative masons: Apprentice, Entered Apprentice, and Fellow of the Craft/Master Mason degrees.) A third degree of Freemasonry, the Master Mason Degree, then emerged in Scotland in 1726.

> The earliest Lodge record of a third degree belongs to Scotland. Lodge Dumbarton Kilwinning (now No. 18 S.C.) was founded in 1726 and the minutes for January 1726 state that there were present the Grand Master (i.e., the W.M.), with seven Master Masons, six Fellow-crafts, and three Entered Apprentices. At the next meeting on 25 March 1726, Gabrael Porterfield, who appeared in the January meeting as a Fellow-Craft, was unanimously admitted and received a Master of the Fraternity and renewed his oath and gave in his entry money. (Carr 1976, 61)

In England, the third degree was adopted in 1730 (Carr 1976, 224). Bernard Jones also confirms that the third degree had been well established in several lodges in England by that date (1975, 243). Despite its name, the establishment of the third degree was not an additional degree added to the first two degrees. The original third degree in the operative lodges was called Fellow of the Craft/ Master Mason Degree. It was essentially split into two separate and distinct degrees, Fellowcraft and Master Mason. All three of the degrees were modified and expanded at the same time. Since that change, the three-degree system of Freemasonry has been Entered Apprentice, Fellowcraft, and Master Mason.

Also in 1730, Samuel Prichard wrote and published a booklet *Masonry Dissected*, that included the three distinct degrees of Entered Apprentice, Fellowcraft, and Master Mason. It served as an instructional booklet for the initiation ceremonies for the degrees in the lodges and may be the first documentation of them.

The English speculative Freemasons then expanded the initiation and ritual ceremonies by using the old mason working tools as symbols to teach the new masons the core principles and lessons of Brotherly Love, Relief, and Truth. The tools serve the same purpose today as they did some three hundred years ago, to teach the core principles and lessons of the ancient craft to the new candidates.

The United Grand Lodge of England, 1813

From about 1735 to 1750, the leadership of the Premier Grand Lodge of England had declined and many lodges in London fell by the wayside and closed. When the Premier Grand Lodge officials began to make changes to their ritual ceremonies, several members became disgruntled. The changes were contrary to the old traditions of masonry. About the same time a group of Irish masons were denied admission into the lodges in London, which caused much upset. The disgruntled group of English masons and the upset Irish masons joined forces in 1751 and formed a new rival grand lodge called the Antients. It was later named the Ancient Free and Accepted Masons (A.F. & A.M.). The original Premier Grand Lodge was called the Free and Accepted Masons (F. & A. M.) and later named the Moderns.

This new Ancients Grand Lodge of Masons grew rapidly and formed hundreds of new lodges in London and around England. It became a major rival to the original Premier Grand Lodge, the Moderns. These two competitive groups of Masons spread their new Freemasonry to other areas and countries over several years.

The Moderns and the Ancients had some quarrels over the rituals and traditions for years, but this competition made them both stronger. They went their own way for over sixty years until they realized it would be best for all to join one another. Therefore, in December of 1813, the two rivals patched up their differences forming the union called The United Grand Lodge of England. These lodges are still meeting in unity and harmony to this day under the same name.

The Growth of Speculative Masonic Meeting Places

Initially both the Scottish and English Masons held meetings, which they called "occasional" meetings, in a variety of places including churches (kirks), public buildings, public taverns, and coffee houses. But by the middle of the eighteenth century, when the transition was well under way and membership was growing, larger and more suitable quarters were needed to conduct business and to initiate new members in the fraternity. They eventually secured more permanent lodge quarters, which became known as Masonic Lodges and were built all over the world.

Masonic Ritual

In England, several different versions of the Masonic Ritual evolved over many years. In 1772, William Preston studied, categorized, and condensed the different versions of the ritual ceremonies into a booklet and published it for the Masonic lodges, taking the liberty of removing the esoteric or secret parts of the ritual. His booklet, *Illustrations of Masonry,* containing descriptions of the three-degree lectures, is essentially used today in most lodges around the world. Other Masons have since expanded the booklet with new versions of the ritual ceremonies and had them published. Regarding the date of ritual standardization, Harry Carr said, "Certain it is, that by the end of the 1820s the English Craft ritual had become standardized into a form so close to our present day workings that we may safely halt our study at that point" (1968, 154).

Harry Carr's *600 Years of Craft Ritual*

Harry Carr, noted Masonic scholar from London, provides additional evidence that Freemasonry descended directly from the operative stonemasons of the Middle Ages. He wrote an extensive twenty-seven page research paper, *600 Years of Craft Ritual,* and presented it to the premier Quatuor Coronati Masonic Research Lodge in London, providing much evidence connecting operative to speculative masonry. He is a past master of Quatuor Coronati Lodge in London, served as its secretary for twelve years, and was editor of the lodge publications for years.

Carr's research paper traces the chronological development of English Masonic ritual from 1356 to 1956. Carr states, "The 600 year span of recorded Masonic history in England represents the period during which we can trace the evolution, expansion and changes in Masonic ritual and practice" (1968,

154). Carr begins his timeline in 1356 in London and then follows the development of Masonic ritual in the *Old Charges* beginning with the Regius Poem c. 1390. He discusses two Scottish lodges, Mary's Chapel 1599 and Mother Kilwinning 1652, which have continuous lodge minutes unbroken to this date, creating a paper trail from operative to speculative Freemasonry:

> These were both operative lodges with a wealth of mason trade customs and history in their records and the whole course of the "Transition" can be traced through their minutes which provide clear and unimpeachable evidence of continuity. Nobody who has studied these in comparable records could doubt for a minute that our speculative Masonry is indeed directly descended from its operative ancestry. (1968, 201)

Carr continues the ritual paper trail to the formation of the Premier Grand Lodge of England in 1717 where he discusses the initiation ceremonies and wording given by the Masters and candidates in all the different ritual versions. He then discusses the United Grand Lodge of England in 1813 and describes the various Masonic ritual booklets printed over the years. He explains the good work done by William Preston in 1772 of consolidating the different rituals and lectures into a common booklet for the lodges. And finally he finishes by bringing the rituals up to modern times in 1956.

Harry Carr briefly summarized his paper to his lodge brethren with the following quote. "I do insist, however, that our present-day speculative Freemasonry is directly descended from the operative masonry whose beginnings we can trace to the earliest record of organization among masons in 1356" (1968, 200).

Several other Masonic and non-Masonic scholars share this same belief that modern Freemasonry had its origin in operative stonemasonry:

- Wallace McLeod is from Toronto, Canada, and is professor of classics at Victoria College at the University of Toronto. He is a full member of Quatuor Coronati Lodge No. 2076 in London, England and is a scholar on the *Old Charges.* In his book, *The Grand Design,* he states, "I take it as proven that our modern Freemasonry is descended in some sense from the operative stonemasons, the cathedral builders of England in the Middle Ages" (1991, 89).

- Douglas Knoop and G.P. Jones, two scholars of Masonic history at the University of Sheffield, England, are pioneers in the study of medieval stonemasonry building. Knoop served as master of Quatuar Coronati Research Lodge No. 2076 London, England in 1935. In one of their books, *An Introduction to Freemasonry*, they say the foundation of our current Masonic ritual has medieval roots. "Although much of our present ritual dates from the later seventeenth or early eighteenth century, the foundation on which the ceremonies are based is genuinely old and bears the stamp of its medieval origin" (1937, 68).

- David Stevenson, professor of Scottish history and studies at the University of Aberdeen, has done extensive research on the early masons and the minute books from several Scottish lodges. He believes that speculative Freemasonry, as we know it today, emerged in the Scottish lodges around 1600. In his book, *The First Freemasons*, he states, "Evolutionary developments subsequently brought about many alterations and elaborations of this movement, yet what appeared in Scotland around 1600 contains the essentials of modern freemasonry" (1989, 3).

In conclusion, I maintain that Freemasonry descended directly from the ancient operative stonemasons of the Middle Ages and was rooted in the transition from operative to speculative Freemasonry. Its foundation was based on the English *Old Charges*. Freemasonry then emerged in Scotland and later moved back into England. It then rapidly expanded around the world. This established a transitional path from operative to speculative Freemasonry, forming a paper trail from 1390 to the eighteenth century:

- The English Stonemasons wrote the *Old Charges,* which became the foundation of Freemasonry. The Regius Poem c. 1390 is the oldest copy of the 130 versions known.

- William Schaw, Master of The Works and General Warden of The Masons to the Crown of Scotland, wrote a new set of statutes in 1598 and 1599 using the *Old Charges* as a pattern. The statutes were to govern the operative lodge members and the new type of lodges he was developing.

- Harry Carr, a Masonic scholar, notes that the oldest recorded regulation for secretary originated in Scotland in the Schaw Statutes in 1599.

- The Schaw Statutes of 1599 required a Warden to be elected annually to preside over the lodges.

- The earliest known operative lodge minutes were recorded in Aitchison Haven Lodge, Scotland on January 9, 1598.

- The earliest known recorded Entered Apprentice and Fellowcraft degrees were conferred in Aitchison Haven Lodge, Edinburgh, Scotland, on January 9, 1598. This confirms the existence of a two- degree system of operative masonry being practiced in a Scottish lodge. It serves as the first paper trail of initiation ritual ceremonies in a lodge.

- The earliest known recorded minutes of a nonoperative mason attending a speculative lodge occurred in Edinburgh, Scotland, on June 8, 1600.
- The earliest known recorded nonoperative Fellowcrafts being initiated into a speculative lodge occurred in Edinburgh, Scotland, on July 3, 1634.

- Over a dozen Scottish lodges accepted and initiated nonoperative masons into their lodges before 1710. In 1735 there were 100 speculative lodges in Scotland.

- In England the earliest known recorded nonoperative mason to be initiated into a speculative lodge occurred in Warrington Lodge, Lancashire, England, on October 16, 1646.

- By the latter half of the seventeenth century nonoperative masons outnumbered operative masons in the lodges.

- The Premier Grand Lodge in London, England, was formed at the Goose and Gridiron Ale-House in St. Paul's Church Yard on St. John the Baptist's Day, June 24, 1717, by The Four Old Lodges.

- The first history of Freemasonry in England was written by James Anderson and named the Constitutions of 1723. The second edition was printed in 1738.

- The third degree of Freemasonry emerged in Scotland in 1726 and in England in 1730. The original third degree was Fellow of the Craft/Master Mason. It was then divided into two distinct degrees, namely the Fellowcraft and Master Mason degrees. The three degrees became Entered Apprentice, Fellowcraft, and Master Mason.

- In 1772, William Preston categorized and condensed several versions of the ritual ceremonies and wrote a booklet titled *Illustrations of Masonry* that became the accepted ritual ceremonies for the lodges for many years. He also arranged and wrote the three Masonic lectures in the booklet that most lodges still use today.

- The United Grand Lodge of England was formed in 1813, by which time most of the Masonic rituals were becoming common in the lodges.

- The new Masonic lodges used the old stonemason working tools as symbols to teach the new Masons the core principles and lessons of Brotherly Love, Relief, and Truth.

- The new speculative Masonic lodges expanded and spread literally all over the world during the eighteenth century.

CHAPTER 13

CONNECTIONS THAT LINK MODERN FREEMASONRY AND ANCIENT CRAFT STONEMASONRY

There is no shortage of documented evidence making the connection between ancient craft masonry and modern Freemasonry. One only needs to look at the parallels between the oldest masonic document, the Regius Poem c. 1390, and the Freemason's constitution, by-laws, and rituals of today. Some of the verbiage in both documents is almost identical over 600 years later.

To further illustrate the connection between operative masonry and Freemasonry, the following are more detailed descriptions of a few shared practices.

Old Charges

All of the early versions of the *Old Charges* were written by English masons to regulate the English operative stonemasons, but many of the later versions were edited to govern the speculative/modern Masons.

Deacons' Rods

Deacons' rods were also called surveying rods, sighting rods, staffs, staves, wands, or simply rods. In ancient craft masonry they were used to orient the cathedral axis by positioning straight lines between points. "… in the annals of the old Scotch lodges are found details of the use of a sighting rod under the direction of the Master Mason when the alignment of a church was fixed by sunrise on a specified day" (Alfred Watkins, 1977, 88).

In modern Freemasonry deacons' rods are a symbol of authority or a token of office. "His wand is an emblem of power, dignity, and significance deriving from ancient days" (Jones, 1975, 380). Masonic lodges today have officers called deacons and stewards who carry rods in the rituals and ceremonies of the different degrees. The senior deacon's rod has a sun symbol on top and the junior deacon's rod has a moon symbol, both of which are references to the operative masons aligning architectural structures to the sun and moon on specific days.

Pythagorean Theorem

Today some of the masters and past masters' officer jewels have the Pythagorean triangle engraved on them.

Laying the Cornerstone

Just as in the old days, modern Masonic lodges continue the tradition of conducting cornerstone laying ceremonies for private and public buildings, but not necessarily on June 21. Freemasons also place coins, valuables, and memorials inside the cornerstone cavity during the laying ceremonies as references for future generations to open. In addition, a new Entered Apprentice candidate is launched into the Masonic craft in the northeast corner of the lodge where he represents the cornerstone to build his moral and Masonic edifice upon.

The Green Man

A sprig of acacia or evergreen is used in Masonic funeral services today. The Masons attending the service place a small sprig of acacia in the casket of the departed brother as a symbol of the immortality of his soul.

The Rose Window

Scottish Rite Freemasons name their Eighteenth Degree for new candidates the "Rose Croix Degree," French for "rose cross." The rose is suspended from the cross in the ceremonial degree.

There are hundreds of other connections that link operative masonry to modern Freemasonry, but I am not at liberty to share them, since they would be direct quotations from the ritual ceremonies of the many Masonic degrees. Still, the connections listed here clearly show that Modern Freemasonry descended directly from the operative stonemasons of the Middle Ages.

OPERATIVE STONEMASONRY	MODERN FREEMASONRY
Regius Poem, c. 1390: "In that time, through good geometry, This honest craft of good masonry was established and made in this manner: By imitation of these teaches together; At prayers of these lords, they demonstrated geometry, And gave it the name of masonry, For the most honest craft of all. In this manner, through the good knowledge of geometry, Began first the craft of masonry."	Geometry is the most important of the seven liberal arts and sciences and the basis of Freemasonry today. Operative masonry depended upon the science of geometry in designing and building the cathedrals. Geometry and masonry were originally synonymous terms used in the Middle Ages, as seen in the Old Charges (Regius Poem, c. 1390)
Regius Poem, c. 1390: Includes the seven liberal arts and sciences (grammar, dialect, rhetoric, music, astronomy, arithmetic, and geometry). The seven are chiseled in stone on the entrance of Chartres Cathedral.	The seven liberal arts and sciences are still taught today in the Fellowcraft lecture of Freemasonry.
Regius Poem, c. 1390, Fifteen Articles and Fifteen Points: "The two sets of admonitions roughly correspond to what we now call constitutions and by-laws." (Frederick M. Hunter, 33rd degree mason)	The grand lodges and subordinate lodges are governed by constitutions and by-laws. The laws, rules, and regulations of the Old Charges are the basis of the Masonic code, ritual, and customs and practices.
Regius Poem, c. 1390: Required the operative masons to take an oath of fidelity and secrecy in the initiation ceremonies of the degrees.	Today, some 625 years later, the Freemasons take a similar oath of fidelity and secrecy called an "obligation" with a few words almost identical.
Regius Poem c. 1390, The First Article: "The first article of this geometry: The master mason must be fully and surely Steadefast, trusty and trewe."	Freemasonry's Open Installation to the public – Charge to the Master Article No.1: "You agree to be a good man and true, and strictly to obey the moral law, to work diligently, live creditably, and act honorably by all men!"
Regius Poem c. 1390: "The third article is, in truth, That the master shall take no apprentice Unless he has good assurance of dwelling Seven years with him, as I tell you, To learn his craft, which is profitable."	To this day, Masons are taught that the Master took responsibility for the apprentice like a father to his son. The seven-year apprenticeship program is still used today.
Regius Poem c. 1390: "The tenth article is to make known Among the craft, to high and low, That no master shall supplant another, But (all) shall be together as sister and brother."	Charge to the brethren today. "I therefore trust you will have but one aim -- to please each other, and unite in the grand design of being happy and communicating happiness. May kindness & brotherly love distinguish your conduct as men and as Masons."
Regius Poem c. 1390: "Seventh Point, That thou shalt not lie with thy master's wife, Nor by thy fellow's, in any manner, Lest the craft should despise thee; He must be punished."	This is essentially part of the Ritual today.

OPERATIVE STONEMASONRY	MODERN FREEMASONRY
Regius Poem c. 1390: "The fifteenth point is of very good teaching. Such ordinance was laid at the assembly, for, those who are disobedient, certainly, against the ordinance that there is of these articles, which were moved there, by the great lords and masons all together. And if they will not do so (i.e. forsake the craft) The sheriff shall come to them immediately."	Freemasons are to be quiet and peaceful citizens, true to their government and just to their country.
"In the operative system, c. 1400, when the lodge was a workshop…there was only one Warden. His duty was to…serve as a mediator in disputes and to see that 'every brother had his due.' We have documentary evidence of this in the Regius and Cooke MSS of c. 1390 and c. 1410." (Harry Carr)	The Masons still have a senior warden in the lodges today. One of his duties is to mediate all disputes among the brethren in the lodge. He does not let anyone go away dissatisfied and keeps harmony among the brethren, because it is the strength, support, and core value of Freemasonry.
Cathedral building was based on architecture and building.	The entire Fellowcraft Degree of modern Freemasonry is based on Architecture.
The operative lodges had Entered Apprentice Masons.	Modern Freemasonry has Entered Apprentice Masons.
The operative lodges had Fellow of The Craft Masons.	Modern Freemasonry has Fellowcraft Masons.
The operative lodges had Master Masons.	Modern Freemasonry has Master Masons.
The stonemasons conducted cornerstone and foundation stone laying ceremonies at the cathedrals for centuries.	Freemasons still conduct cornerstone laying ceremonies at Masonic and public buildings all over the world.
Operative masons aligned the cathedrals east to west.	Freemasons lodges today are aligned east to west.
Operative stonemasons quarried rough ashlar stones and then dressed them into "perfect ashlar: stones for the cathedral.	Today you will find in many lodges a "rough ashlar" and a "perfect ashlar" stone prominently displayed. They are included in the Masonic ritual.
The "trestle-board" was used by the Master Builder to draw his designs upon.	The "trestle-board" is still discussed and used in the Masonic degree ceremonies today.
Pythagorean 3-4-5 triangle was used by the operative masons to lay out a square foundation floor plan.	Pythagoras has been explained in Masonic rituals over the centuries and in the Master Mason Degree of modern Freemasonry.

OPERATIVE STONEMASONRY	MODERN FREEMASONRY
Operative masons used rods to measure and align the cathedral axis.	Freemasons use rods (called deacons' rods today) in the ceremonies of the degrees.
Operative stonemasons' tools were used in the Middle Ages to build cathedrals and other stone structures. The tools were used to hew, carve, and dress the stones, and to plumb, square, and level the cathedral.	Stonemasons' tools are used today in the Masonic Lodges as symbols to teach and demonstrate the moral lessons to the members. Many examples are illustrated in the lodge officer's installation ceremonies open to the public.
The "square" was used by the operative masons to square their work (to check that all the dressed stones had ninety degree corners).	The "square" teaches a mason to regulate his actions by rule and line and to harmonize his conduct by the principles of morality and virtue. The Master wears the "square."
The "level" was used by the operative masons to prove horizontals. The use of the level confirmed that the foundation and all stonewalls were kept level.	The "level" demonstrates that all are descended from the same stock. The senior warden wears the "level" around his neck as a badge of his office.
The "plumb" was used by the operative masons to try perpendiculars of walls. The plumb line confirmed to the mason the walls were built perfectly plumb.	The "plumb" admonishes Masons to walk uprightly in several stations, to hold the scales of justice in equal poise. The junior warden wears a "plumb" as his badge.
The "compass" was used by the Master Builder Mason to design and make layout drawings for the buildings. The masons used the compass to draw circles on stone, marble, wood, tile, glass, lead, and drawings.	The "compass" today teaches Masons to limit their desires in every station, that, rising to eminence by merit, they may live respected and die regretted. The compass plays an important role in Masonic ritual ceremonies.
The "twenty-four-inch gauge" was used by the operative masons to draw straight lines and to measure their work.	The "twenty-four-inch gauge" is used in modern Freemasonry as a moral lesson in Masonic ceremonies.
The "line" was used as a guide by the operative masons to lay the stone perfectly plumb and horizontally in a cathedral.	The "line" teaches the criterion of moral rectitude, to avoid dissimulation in conversation and action.
The "common gavel" was used by operative masons to rough dress the ashlar stones from the quarry to later be refined.	The Worshipful Master uses the "common gavel" as a tool of authority in controlling the affairs of the Lodge.
The "setting maul" was used by the stonemason to split stone. The maul was also used as a hammer to hit various sized chisels for stone carving and sculpturing.	The "setting maul" plays a very important role in one of the ceremonial degrees of Freemasonry today.
The "square" and "compass" were two primary tools used by the Master Builder and the operative masons.	The "square" and "compasses" form the Masonic emblem of Freemasonry known around the world.

OPERATIVE STONEMASONRY	MODERN FREEMASONRY
Mason marks were chiseled on the cathedral stone surfaces to identify the mason's name.	Mason marks are part of the ritual in one of the advanced degrees and masons still have personal marks today.
The stonemasons wore leather aprons to protect their clothing from stone abrasion.	Freemasons wear white lambskin or linen aprons in lodge as a badge of a Mason.
The stonemasons wore leather gloves to protect their hands from abrasion.	Freemasons wear white gloves for certain degrees at regular and formal meetings.
Operative stonemason lodges practiced charity in a big way.	Charity is a core value of Freemasonry. Freemasons give away hundreds of millions of dollars to charity each year.
Harry Carr recorded 600 years of continual craft ritual from 1356 to 1956 from the *Old Charges* and lodge minutes. A paper trail of craft ritual was created through the transition to modern Freemasonry.	This paper trail further links operative masonry to modern Freemasonry through the common evolution of the rituals to this day.
James Anderson in 1723 wrote *the Constitutions (Charges)* of the speculative Freemasons using the operative masons *Old Charges* as a pattern.	Anderson's new *Constitutions of 1723* really bridged the gap between operative and speculative Freemasonry today.
Constitutions of 1723, Charge VI #2: "Therefore no private Piques or Quarrels must be brought within the Door of the Lodge, far less any Quarrels about Religion, or Nations, or State Policy."	Freemasonry's open installation to the public – Charge to the Master No. IV: "You agree to avoid private piques and quarrels, and to guard against intemperance and excess." Religion and politics are prohibited as well.
The "Masons word" was used in Scottish operative masonry early in the seventeenth century.	The "Masons word" is still used today in Freemasonry.

CHAPTER 14

DESCRIPTION OF FREEMASONRY AND MASONIC LODGES TODAY

Freemasonry certainly cannot be described adequately in a short chapter when scholars have written hundreds of volumes on the subject without covering it completely. Joseph Fort Newton, a Masonic scholar, speaks of the depth, complexity, and age of Freemasonry in *Short Talks on Masonry*: "Neither author, nor date, nor locality is attached to it. It is a Monument, not of an individual, but of a mighty and mysterious past—like a cathedral the names of whose builders are lost. The genius that produced it has been forgotten in the service rendered. Today we sit in a lodge listening to a ritual, not knowing when, where, or by whom it was written" (1969, 142).

The Grand Lodge of Ohio states, "Freemasonry is kindness in the home, honesty in business, courtesy in society, fairness in work, pity and concern for the unfortunate, resistance toward evil, help for the weak, forgiveness for the penitent, love for one another, and above all, reverence and love for God. Freemasonry is many things, but most of all: 'Freemasonry is A Way of Life.'"

If ten Masonic scholars were asked to define Freemasonry, there would be ten different answers. The answers would reflect what Freemasonry meant to them individually. For the benefit of the non-Mason, I will attempt to briefly describe it.

First, Freemasonry is not a secret organization, but rather an organization of a few secrets. A secret organization is one that meets underground, with no one knowing who the members are or when, where, or for what purpose they are meeting. Conversely, Freemasonry publishes its meeting times and dates, and a membership list is printed with those members belonging to the craft openly acknowledging it to the public. The members proudly identify themselves as Masons by wearing lapel pins and rings, and by other visible means.

Members of the fraternity come from essentially every profession and social class. There are farmers, factory workers, school teachers, builders, craftsmen, laborers, technicians, religious and military leaders, doctors, scientists, and average citizens alike. Fourteen presidents were Freemasons, along with several signers of the Declaration of Independence, US senators, congressmen, chief justices, state governors, and businessmen. Paul Revere, Red Skelton, John Wayne, John Hancock, Benjamin Franklin, Wolfgang Amadeus Mozart, Norman Vincent Peal, and the US's first president, George Washington, were all Freemasons.

In the old operative stonemason days, the lodge was a temporary work shed in which the stonemasons designed cathedrals and dressed stones for them. Today Masons meet in Masonic lodges. These local lodges are governed by the laws, rules, and regulations set down by the grand lodge in their state, province, or jurisdictional area. The grand lodges are the administrative bodies in charge of the local lodges, and they meet annually with representatives from each lodge in the state to vote on any new legislative proposals made by the members.

The local lodge receives petitions from candidates for membership. Each petitioner for Freemasonry must believe in the existence of a supreme being and be of good moral character. Freemasonry typically has an officer structure in the symbolic lodge consisting of: Worshipful Master, Senior Warden, Junior Warden, Treasurer, Secretary, Chaplain, Senior Deacon, Junior Deacon, Senior Steward, Junior Steward, and Tyler. The number of officers and names in a lodge vary slightly in different jurisdictions around the world.

The membership of Freemasonry is based on a system of degrees that the candidates must go through in the symbolic lodge. The first three degrees are called Entered Apprentice, Fellowcraft, and Master Mason. After completing these three degrees, a candidate is considered a full Master Mason and can visit lodges in other states and countries with proper identification.

In American Freemasonry there are additional degrees and ceremonies that a candidate can earn on his journey through the craft. These added degrees shed more light on ancient craft masonry, but they are not any more important than the first three degrees of becoming a Master Mason. A candidate can receive the degrees in the Scottish Rite or the York Rite. In the Scottish Rite, a candidate can earn up to thirty-two degrees. A 33rd degree may also be awarded, but it is strictly an honorary degree and is conferred by the Supreme Council. The York Rite has a different set of degrees.

There are many other Masonic organizations that members are free to join. Among them are the Shrine Masons, Grotto, Tall Cedars of Lebanon, High Twelve International, and Eastern Stars for members and ladies. There are also youth groups for the Masons' children: Rainbow Girls, Jobs Daughters International for the girls and DeMolay International for the boys.

Since its inception, charity has been one of the core values of Freemasonry and has been practiced around the world for centuries, helping those inside and outside the fraternity. The stonemasons first practiced charity in their operative lodges during the Middle Ages by setting up charity boxes and funds to help those in need. Today, there are several Masonic philanthropies, foundations, and programs that do a great deal to support mankind. The Shriners operate a network of hospitals providing specialized care for children with orthopedic conditions, burns, spinal cord injuries, and cleft lip and palates, regardless of the families' ability to pay. The Scottish Rite sponsors speech and language disorder clinics, and Knights Templar sponsors an eye foundation, to name a few. The Freemasons also provide retirement homes for the elderly in Masonic centers scattered around the country. Moreover, Freemasons are involved in their communities, providing friendship, transportation, meals, help with household projects, and other forms of care for the elderly and needy.

To give an idea of the emphasis Freemasonry places on charity, more than $750 million dollars (over $2 million dollars per day) was donated in North America in 1995. Over half the contributions went to the general American public (Morris, 1997, p. 18). Also, in 2003, The Grand Lodge of Ohio did a study on the charitable contributions of the Freemasons in Ohio and it totaled more than $15 million dollars annually. In addition, for both the September 11, 2001, terrorist attacks and the 2005 Hurricane Katrina disaster, the Masonic Service Association of North America collected and distributed more than $3 million in disaster relief funds to the grand lodges in those areas (Braatz, 2013, 6). The Freemasons have been contributing to these types of disasters for more than ninety years. They quietly give enormous sums of money each year without fanfare or publicity.

Freemasonry teaches faith, hope, and charity. The core values, tenets, and principles of Freemasonry taught in the degrees are Brotherly Love, Relief and Truth, Fatherhood of God, Brotherhood of Man, and Immortality of the Soul. Freemasonry teaches tolerance for one another's opinions and not to dictate to others one's beliefs in business, politics, or religion in a lodge. Simply put the sole mission of Freemasonry is to "make good men better."

In summary, Freemasonry...

- is the oldest and largest fraternal organization in the world;

- is an international organization of men;

- has several million members in the craft;

- is universally known by its trademark of the Masonic Square and Compasses, a symbol of character, charity, brotherly love, and truth;

- is recognized by another trademark, the white leather stonemason's apron;

- has always been known as a fraternity of builders;

- is a brotherhood of men that believe fraternalism is the real working tool of a mason's life;

- has roots in cathedral building by the stonemasons;

- is a remnant of the ancient operative building lodges and guilds;

- is a system of morality based on Sacred Law;

- was founded by and on Christian principles, but has over the years included many other faiths in the fraternity;

- believes in the Fatherhood of God, but is not a religion;

- requires a belief in a Supreme Being for membership affiliation;

- does not discriminate against any religion or social class;

- prohibits the discussion of religion and politics within the Masonic lodge;

- practices Brotherly Love, Relief, and Truth;

- requires an oath to act by moral and ethical standards towards Masonic brothers and the world;

- has been teaching moral lessons based on symbols to its members for centuries;

- uses a system of degrees;

- has initiation and degree work that entails a certain amount of ritual;

- is an educational organization that prepares officers to confer the degrees in the lodge;

- stresses architecture and geometry in its lessons;

- teaches the Seven Liberal Arts and Sciences;

- has members meet in buildings called lodges;

- promotes honesty and square dealings in business relationships;

- supports families, schools, our troops, and government;

- practices a great deal of charity work within and outside the membership;

- has charitable foundations for grants to individuals in need;

- has a family organization called the Shriners that operates children's hospitals;

- provides Masonic homes for the elderly, burn hospitals, eye foundations, etc.;

- aids medical research;

- provides visitation programs to hospitals for its members;

- provides scholarships to its members, as well as students outside of the fraternity;

- operates schools that serve children with learning disabilities and has student assistant programs for dyslexic students;

- is involved in programs for teaching teachers how to detect students on drugs;

- provides Adopt-a-Highway programs for trash pick-up on state highways;

- improves leadership skills;

- improves public speaking abilities, especially when going through the officer line;

- greatly expands one's circle of good friends;

- is a character-building fraternity;

- expects members to lend helping hands to family members, friends, neighbors, acquaintances, and strangers as part of the ritual teachings;

- has always been about being builders and doers in communities;

- has a National Heritage Museum in Massachusetts;

- requires a person to ask a Mason to become a Mason.

If I were asked to squeeze a definition of Freemasonry into one short sentence, my reply would be: "**Freemasonry is an international Brotherhood of Men, commenced in the furthest corners of remote antiquity, which brings men to light using operative mason trade tools to symbolically illustrate its wonderful lessons.**"

Freemasonry resembles several old English and Scottish plaid patterns, a photographic record of a centuries-old family history with hundreds of designs, colors, fabrics, and bands woven into the cloth created by thousands of different people contributing to the final product. I am very proud to be a Freemason and member of the oldest and largest fraternal organization in the world. See Figure 259.

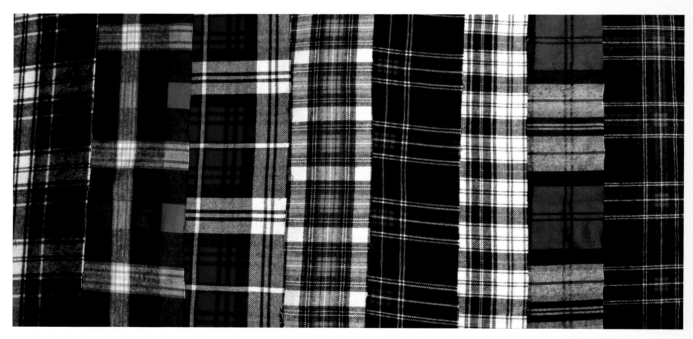

FIGURE 259. This collage of Scottish and English plaid patterns paints a physical picture of Freemasonry, capturing its age, history, art, diversity, tolerance, and range of colors, all woven with geometry and harmony.

APPENDIX

MASTER BUILDERS, MASTER MASONS, AND WORKING STONEMASONS

This is a partial list of active stonemason craftsmen who built stone structures in Europe and the British Isles during the Middle Ages.

ENGLISH MASONS

Adam Lock
Alan Walsingham
Christopher Wren
Henry of Reyns
Henry Yeveley
John Aylmer
John of Glouscester
John Harry
John Lewyn
John the Mason VII
John Ramsey
John Wastell
Michael of Canterbury
Nicholas of Ely
Richard Beke
Richard Farleigh
Richard de Farnham
Richard Wolveston
Robert of Beverley
Robert Spillesby
Stephen Lote
Thomas of Canterbury
Thomas Mapilton
Thomas Stanley
Walter of Canterbury
Walter of Herford
Walter Coorland
Walter of Coventry
William Atwood
William Colchester
William the Englishman
William Hurley
William Joy
William Orchard
William Ramsey
William of Wykeham
William Wynford

GERMAN MASONS

Erwin Von Steinbach
Gerard of Cologne
Gerlach of Cologne
Hans of Cologne
Hans Parler
Hans Schmuttermayer
Hartmann of Ulm
Heinrich Parler
Johann Hultz
Johann Parler
Konrad Roritzer
Mathaus Boblinger
Mathes Roritzer
Mathieud de Arras
Michael of Cologne
Michael of Freiburg
Michael Parler
Peter Parler
Robert Luzarches
Rudolf of Strasburg
Simon of Cologne
Ulrich Von Ensingen
Wenzel Parler
Wenzel Roritzer

FRENCH MASONS

Adam of Pointiers
Bernard de Soissons
Berthaut of Chartres
Hugh Libergiers
Jean de Soissons
Niciel of Bourges
Nicolas de Soissons
Pierre de Montreuil
Ricardus of Paris
Robert de Luzarches
Rogerus of Chartres
Teudho of Chartres
Villard de Honnecourt
William of Sens

GLOSSARY

CATHEDRAL BUILDING TERMS

Abutment: A solid wall of stone to counter the side thrust of an arch or vault.

Aisle: Parallel sections of a cathedral, adjacent to both sides of the nave.

Ambulatory: Walkway or circular aisle surrounding the eastern choir and apse part of a cathedral.

Apse: A semicircular extension on the eastern end of the main body of the cathedral.

Arcade: A series of arches mounted on columns or piers separating the main nave and side aisles.

Arch: Round, curved, or pointed group of wedge-shaped stones joined together and held together by their own weight downward. Arches support masonry weight above them.

Ashlar: Stone blocks of varying sizes that have been cut, hewn, sawn, and dressed to size for use in a wall.

Ashlar Rough: A block of stone from the quarry not cut, hewn, or dressed.

Axis: The centerline of a cathedral; the building parts are built symmetrically around it.

Barrel Vault: A semi-cylindrical, tunnel-shaped vaulted roof form; basically, a long round Roman arch roof.

Belfry: The upper part of a cathedral tower that contains the cathedral bells.

Boss: A carved ornamental ball between the ends of the vaulted ribs to conceal them. Usually they are carved figures and painted.

Buttress: Stone projections on the outside of the walls used to counter and absorb the side thrusts from vaults, arches, and ribs.

Capital: Richly carved capstone that serves as the transition stone between the column or pier top and the arch it supports.

Cathedra: A Latin word for the bishop's chair or throne. The cathedra was literally a stone chair in the sanctuary.

Centering: A temporary wooden framework that supports the arch stones as they are being cemented into place. After the mortar is dry, the wooden centering is removed and the arch stands alone.

Choir: The section of the cathedral that is east of the transepts and west of the apse where the choir sings during the service.

Clerestory: The uppermost story of the nave and choir; its windows light up the interior of the cathedral. It is above the triforium level.

Column: A round, structural member mounted vertically to support arches, vaults, and roof loads in compression.

Compound pier: Is a group of vertical columns clustered together to support arches, vaults, and roof loads in compression.

Cornerstone: The Masonic Cornerstone was the first stone placed in a new cathedral or building. It was placed in the northeast corner on June 21, summer solstice, the longest day of the year.

Cowan: A mason who worked with stone but was not considered a legitimate mason because he did not go through the apprenticeship training program. He was also called a dry-diker, one who built stone walls without mortar. He was a mason without the 'mason's word' and was never allowed to join the lodge.

Crossing: Square area formed at the intersection of the nave and transepts of a cruciform-shaped cathedral.

Cruciform: A cathedral floor plan in the shape of a Latin cross where the nave and transepts cross at right angles.

Crypt: Vault, chamber, or rooms generally below the east end of a cathedral.

Dome: A masonry hemispherical structure with the walls curving upwards to the center point. Visualize a hollow ball cut in half, forming two round domes.

Drum column: Stone cylindrical blocks or donuts stacked on top of one another, forming a vertical support column.

Fabric: The traditional description of the cathedral building itself.

Façade: Exterior surface of a building or cathedral, generally the decorated west entrance or street side.

Fan Vaulting: A Gothic style of vaulted ceiling designs resembling conical horns and fan-shaped ribs. They are large, highly decorated horns hanging from the ceiling.

Flèche: A slender spire generally mounted above the intersection of the nave and transepts of a church or cathedral.

Flying buttress: A stone arch attached at one end to the upper outside wall of a cathedral and at the other end to the vertical buttress. It carries weight and absorbs the side thrust of the vault down to the buttress.

Freestone: A fine grained limestone or sandstone that highly detailed stone carvings could be made from by the most skilled and trained stonemasons.

Gable: A triangular-shaped structure mounted at the end and above the main body of the building.

Galilee: Name given to the porch area at the west entrance to a cathedral.

Gargoyle: Sculpted forms that collected roof water and distributed it out and away from the cathedral walls in a waterspout; grotesque-looking animals with round pipes inside them to transport the water outward.

Gothic cathedral architecture: Style that used the flying buttress, pointed arch, stone ribbed cross vaulted ceilings, high vaulting, clustered columns, and lots of stained-glass windows.

Grisaille: A grayish white colored glass that allows more light to enter the cathedral than the typical colored stained glass.

High Altar: East of and adjacent to the choir where the mass and services were held.

Hurdles: A portable platform or scaffold made of woven branches used by the masons to work on.

Keystone: The center topmost locking voussoir stone in a round or pointed arch, which ties or keys the arch stones together into one strong arch.

Lady Chapel: A chapel dedicated to the Virgin, generally on the east end of the church or cathedral. It is the most elaborately decorated chapel in the cathedral.

Lancet Window: Tall narrow windows pointed at the top like a sharp lancet. They are generally grouped in three or five pane widths making up gigantic stained-glass window bays.

Lantern Tower: A tower generally at the crossing with clear windows to allow light to penetrate the cathedral.

Minster: A large church that is or was attached to a monastery.

Misericord: A bracket underneath the wooden hinged half seat in the choir; intricately carved wooden seats the monks could lean on.

Narthex: An enclosed vestibule on the west entrance of a church or cathedral.

Nave: The central main part of the cathedral between the side aisles and on the western end. It is where the congregation was housed during the services.

Pier: Vertical support structures comprised of round, octagonal, or clusters of columns tied together. They were located down through the cathedral on either side of the nave as supports.

Pillar: A vertical support member usually round in cross section to support vertical loads in compression.

Pinnacle: Tall slender upright stone members highly decorated that come to a sharp point at the top. They are placed at the extreme top of roofs, gables, and towers. They were placed on top of buttresses for additional weight to counter side thrusts.

Prayer Chapels: Built around the outside parameter walls of the transepts and eastern ambulatory aisles. They were varied in design and location for each cathedral.

Putlog Hole: A square or round hole drilled into the stone wall to hold temporary scaffolding.

Radiating chapels: Chapels that were built on the east end of the cathedral in a radial or round formation.

Rafter: One of the sloping wood timbers of a roof structure.

Ribs: Parts of the stone arch forming the vaulted ceilings into bays.

Romanesque cathedral architecture: Style that used round Roman arches, thick walls, round column pillars, and very small windows.

Rood screen: A carved stone or wood screen dividing the choir from the nave.

Rose window: A round window with decorated stone tracery and colored stained glass in the tracery.

Sanctuary: Section of the cathedral east of the crossing including the altar.

Scaffolding: Temporary platforms set up to support the workers and materials during the construction phase.

Sounding board: A wafer-shaped horizontal wooden board mounted above the Bishop's pulpit that amplified his voice to the congregation. They were highly decorated.

Template: A full-size wooden pattern designed and prepared by the Master for the stonemasons to cut and dress stones to match it.

Tracery: The structural stonework pattern inside of a rose or lancet window that holds the stained-glass windows.

Transept: The north and south lateral arms of the cathedral at the crossing of a cruciform church.

Transverse arch: A vaulted ceiling arch that is set at right angles to the axis and divides the vaulting into bays.

Triforium: The middle story between the lower arcade aisles and upper clerestory level. It has a passageway and gallery in it.

Truss: A triangular rigid framework consisting of wooden beams and timber members to support rafters in a roofing system.

Tympanum: Space above a doorway between the top gable arch and horizontal lintel. Many times a carving of Christ is sitting inside a vesica placed in this area.

Vesica: A pointed oval shape created by the intersection of two circles of equal diameter.

Voussoirs: Different size stone blocks cut into wedge shapes forming an arch when assembled.

Windlass wheel: A man-operated hoisting machine. It consisted of a large wooden wheel mounted on a shaft with bearings and was turned by men walking inside it. A rope was wound around the axle and as the men would walk, it raised the stones up into the cathedral during construction.

REFERENCES

Anderson, W. 1988. *The Rise of the Gothic.* New York: Dorset Press.

Borst, L. 1975. *Megalithic Software, Part 1, England.* Williamsville, New York: Twin Bridge Press.

Bowie, T. 1959. *The Sketchbook of Villard de Honnecourt.* Bloomington, Indiana: Indiana University Press.

Braatz, G.O. 2013, *The Short Talk Bulletin, Volume 91, no.1: New Milestones for MSA.* [Brochure]. Silver Spring, Maryland: The Masonic Service Association of North America.

Carr, H. 1968. *600 Years of Craft Ritual.* London: Quatuor Coronati Masonic Research Lodge No. 2076.

Carr, H. 1976. *The Freemason at Work.* London: Burgess & Son.

Charpentier, L. 1972. *The Mysteries of Chartres Cathedral.* New York, New York: Avon Publishers.

Coil, H. 1961. *Coil's Masonic Encyclopedia.* New York: Macoy Publishing & Masonic Supply Company.

Gamble, J.D. 1986. *Broad Axes.* Los Altos, California: Tanro Company.

Gruber, R. 2011. *St. Stephen's Cathedral in Vienna.* Vienna: Church Office of St. Stephen's Cathedral.

Hadingham, E. 1975. *Circles and Standing Stones.* Garden City, New York: Anchor Press-Doubleday.

Hamill, J. 1992. *Freemasonry, A Celebration of the Craft.* St. Albans, United Kingdom: Mackenzie Publishing.

Harvey, J. 1988. *Cathedrals of England and Wales.* London: B.T. Batsford Ltd.

Harvey, J. 1969. *The Gothic World.* New York & Evanston: Harper & Row Publishers.

Harvey, J. 1971. *The Master Builders.* New York: McGraw-Hill Book Co.

Hunter, F. M. 1975. *The Regius Manuscript Masonic Poem.* Portland, Oregon: Research Lodge of Oregon, No. 198 A.F. & A. M.

James, J. 1986. *The Traveler's Key to Medieval France.* New York: Alfred Knopf.

Jones, B. E. 1975. *Freemasons' Guide and Compendium.* London, England: George G. Harrap & Co. LTD.

Knoop, D. and G. P. Jones. 1937. *An Introduction to Freemasonry.* Manchester, England: Manchester University Press.

Knoop, D. and G. P. Jones. 1947. *The Genesis of Freemasonry.* London: Quatuor Coronati Lodge No. 2076.

Knoop, D. and G. P. Jones, 1978. *The Genesis of Freemasonry.* London: Quatuor Coronati Research Masonic Lodge No. 2076.

Lincoln Minster. 2006. *Lincoln Cathedral, The Story So Far* [Brochure]. Lincoln Minster Shops Limited.

Mackey, A.G. *Encyclopedia of Freemasonry, Volume II.* Chicago, New York, London: The Masonic History Company. date?

McLeod, W. 1991. *The Grand Design.* Highland Springs, Virginia: Anchor Communications.

McLeod, W. *The Old Gothic Constitutions.* Bloomington, Illinois: The Masonic Book Club.

Michell, J. 1988. *The Traveler's Key to Sacred England.* New York: Alfred A. Knopf.

Michell, J. 1969. *The View Over Atlantis.* Great Britain: Sago Press.

Miller, M. 2010. *Chartres Cathedral.* Andover Hampshire, UK: Pitkin Publishing.

Moring, N. 2011. *Cologne Cathedral in World War II.* Koln, Germany: Verlag Kolner Dom

Morris, S.B. 1997. *Masonic Philanthropies: A Tradition of Caring.* Lexington, Massachusetts, and Washington, DC: The Supreme Councils, 33°, N.M.J. and S.J.

Newton, J. F. 1969. *Short Talks on Masonry.* Richmond, Virginia: Macoy Publishing & Masonic Supply Company, Inc.

Ormrod, M., and Lindley, P. G. 1996. *The Black Death in England.* Stamford, England: Paul Watkins Publishing.

Reinthaler, G. 2003. *Hammered Symbols.* East Sussex, England: Frogmore Associates.

Saliger, A. 1990. *Cathedral and Metropolitan Church: St. Stephen's in Vienna.* Munich and Zurich: Verlagschnell &Steiner GMBH.

The Science of Sound. 1992. Compressed Air Magazine.

Shelby, L.R. 1977. *Gothic Design Techniques.* Carbondale and Edwardsville: Southern Illinois University Press.

Simson, O. 1974. *The Gothic Cathedral.* Princeton, New Jersey: Princeton University Press.

Stevenson, D. 1989. *The First Freemasons.* Great Britain: Aberdeen University Press.

Stevenson, D. 1988. *The Origins of Freemasonry.* Cambridge, Great Britain: Cambridge University Press.

Sugar. (c. 1144–48). *The Book of Sugar, Abbot of St. Denis on what was Done Under his Administration: Chapters XXIV, XXV, XXVIII, XXXIII.*

Waite, A.E. 1970. *A New Encyclopedia of Freemasonry.* New York: Weathervane Books.

Watkins, A. 1977. *The Old Straight Track.* London: Abacus Publishing.

A Way of Life, Freemasonry. Ohio: The Grand Lodge of Ohio.

Wright, G.A.A., and Wheeler, W.A. 1980. *Mason Marks on Wells Cathedral Church.* [Brochure]. Wells, England: The Friends of Wells Cathedral.